LONG INNINGS

SIR PELHAM WARNER IN 1950

Photo Elliott and Fry

Long Innings

The Autobiography of

Sir Pelham Warner

George G. Harrap and Company Ltd
London   Sydney   Toronto   Bombay

First published 1951
by George G. Harrap & Co. Ltd
182 High Holborn, London, W.C.1

Dewey Decimal classification: 796.358

*Composed in Bembo type and printed by Western Printing Services Ltd,
Bristol.   Made in Great Britain*

PREFACE

WHEN Messrs Harrap asked me to write my autobiography I pondered long and deeply. I was doubtful of my mental processes and of my physical energy, and above all I was fearful of the personal pronoun. Much persuasion, however, was brought to bear on me, and it was pointed out that many people had written their autobiographies without being accused of having too much ego in their cosmos. And thus it happens that I now strew the memories of a long life about to the public.

In writing about them I have made use of parts of my earlier books, and I tender my grateful thanks especially to Messrs Chatto and Windus and Messrs Sporting Handbooks, Ltd, for permission to quote here and there from *Cricket between Two Wars*, and to Messrs Hodder and Stoughton, Ltd, for similar permission concerning *My Cricketing Life*. I am also indebted to the Editor of *The Spectator* for leave to quote in two or three instances from the pages of that journal, to the Oxford University Press for a quotation from Canon Iremonger's *William Temple: Archbishop of Canterbury*, and to the Editors of *The Times*, the *Sunday Times*, the *News Chronicle*, and the *Western Daily Press and Bristol Mirror* for short quotations from these newspapers.

P.F.W.

CONTENTS

ILLUSTRATIONS

In the Text

I

EARLY LIFE IN THE WEST INDIES
1873–87

My Father and Mother—The Hall and Brunswick Square, Port of Spain—Queen's Royal College—Harrison College—School Cricket—My Grandparents—The "Essex Ring"

I WAS born at the Hall, Port of Spain, Trinidad, on October 2, 1873. My father, Charles William Warner, C.B., for many years Attorney-General of Trinidad, married twice, and I was the youngest of his eighteen children. By his first wife (*née* Carmichael) he had six children, and twelve by my mother. He was born on October 19, 1805, two days before Trafalgar, so at the time of my arrival he was nearly sixty-eight years of age. Two of my sisters and one brother died in infancy, and one brother, Francis Charles William, died as a Naval Cadet at Dartmouth on June 30, 1868, when he was within two months of his fifteenth birthday.

His death was a shattering blow, and my mother, who was in Trinidad at the time, never got over it. It seems that he contracted sunstroke while playing cricket, and, I fear, was not too well looked after: Dartmouth was a pretty rough place in those days. He died five years and more before I was born, but, curiously, I have an extraordinary affinity with him. Over and over again I dream of him, and I feel very near to him. His miniature shows that he was a charming-looking boy, and to the end of her long life—she died in London on May 7, 1913, at the age of eighty-three—I more than once found my mother crying over letters and mementoes of his, and I used to try to comfort her. Perhaps that is why I feel so often that he is near me.

My father was born at sea between England and Barbados, and was educated at Eton: he was there under Keate, famous, and perhaps infamous, for his consistent belief in the birch, but I do not remember my father's saying that he had suffered at his hands. My father was one of the best-looking men I have ever seen, with great charm of manner. A scholar, he also kept in touch with affairs in England, and every mail brought parcels of books, *The Times*, and weekly papers like the *Spectator* and the *Illustrated London News*. In the *History of Trinidad* Mr Lionel Fraser wrote: "The Master Mind . . . like Warwick or Wolsey or Richelieu, nominally the adviser, really the ruler. For five-and-twenty years he held absolute sway."[1] And J. A. Froude, the historian and author of *The English in the West Indies*, said of him: "To have seen and spoken with such a man was worth a voyage round the globe."[2] I can but say that, though I was only thirteen when he died, in February 1887, he exercised a rare influence over us all.

My mother was a Miss Cadiz—a daughter of John Joseph Garcia Cadiz, a Spaniard. He was born in Trinidad—the Spaniards were in possession of the island until 1797—and was partially educated in England. He married a Miss Galwey, an Irish girl, so that I have English, Irish, and Spanish blood in my veins. My grandfather was a barrister who became a magistrate in Trinidad, and was a descendant of those Spaniards who were stranded on the shores of the west coast of Ireland after the defeat of the Armada. I believe that there are several people in Ireland to this day, among them Cadiz's, whose forbears served in Philip of Spain's Navy. I know of one at least—Sir Francis Joseph, Bart.,[3] whose original name was José, which was Anglicized to Joseph, an outstanding figure in the industrial world. My grandfather was a Roman Catholic, and my grandmother was not, but he changed his religion for hers.

I was devoted to my mother, and she did a great deal for me, sending me to Rugby and to Oxford, and there was not a great deal of money with which to do that. A few weeks after my father's death we came to England, and she brought with her a letter from Sir Stephen Gatty, then Attorney-General of Trinidad, and an old Wykehamist, addressed to the Headmaster of that famous school, asking him to find a place for me, if possible, and commending me as "a nice little boy, who, I am told, shows considerable promise as a cricketer." What happened I will relate in another chapter. The portrait of my mother shows a very

---

[1] Lionel Mordaunt Fraser, *History of Trinidad* (1896), vol. ii, p. 359.
[2] J. A. Froude, *The English in the West Indies* (1888), p. 85.
[3] Sir Francis died in February 1951.

charming old lady, and she must have been very pretty in her youth. No more unselfish woman ever lived.

My father had built a charming house with a lovely garden containing a swimming-bath in which I learned to swim, and a pond, in which I sailed my boats, and my young life was all happiness. The garden was a delight, and we had lots of pets, including a huge goat with a swaggering gait and very sharp horns, on whom I wrote an ode:

> Hail, Ram Goat, with the flaming beard!
> When on thee I gaze I am afraid
> Lest thy great horns and hoofs should rend
> My body and my life-blood spend.
> And yet, methinks, I thee could slay,
> And turn thy vile body into clay;
> For in mine eyes I hold the spell
> That could send thy carcass down to Hell!

This shocked my mother: "My dear little Pelham, what have you been reading?" I told her that Milton had been read to us, and that my masterpiece (!) was based on some of his verses.

We had, too, a deer, "Sos Sos," who used to walk into the dining-room, and I can hear the patter of his hoofs on the wooden floor to this day. Also a monkey, "Sally," a most affectionate beast, who, however, once bit a niece of mine on a part of her anatomy which I dare not mention. At one time I was called Sally, as I was said to be like her!

There was one affair which I do not forget. Two most desperate criminals escaped from the French penal settlement at Cayenne, in French Guiana, to Trinidad, and proceeded to rob us. They went through every room, and as they did so scattered a powder which, thank goodness, made us all sleep very soundly. They were arrested a few days later, and were given heavy sentences, for they were armed with villainous-looking knives, and said that if anyone had interfered with them they would have had no hesitation in killing them. They were a cut-throat-looking pair. It is easy to imagine the fear they put into us, and it was a long time before we forgot the "Cayenne Men," as we called them. After that we had a couple of dogs, to whom the gardener told us he used occasionally to give rum mixed with 'Jack Spaniards'—the name for a local wasp—to make them savage! In the warm climate, with doors and windows open, houses were very easy to break into, and more than once we were robbed, but not by such desperate ruffians as the "Cayenne Men."

I rode a snow-white donkey, "Jack," and many an hour did I spend in the stables grooming him and blacking his hoofs, and the smell of saddle and bridle remains with me.

I cannot remember when I was not keen on cricket, and I used to practise often before breakfast in my night-shirt on a marble gallery which made a perfect wicket, bowled to by one Killebree (the patois for 'humming-bird'), a native boy who did all sorts of jobs about the house and garden, and who assured my father that I should be a good bat when I grew big. Even in those early days I devoured *The Field* and *Wisden*, and I knew the names of all the great English and Australian cricketers, and acquired a knowledge of their doings which rests with me to this day. My brothers Aucher and Raymond, who returned from Oxford at the end of 1882, gave me much encouragement, and when the North American and West Indian Fleet and the Training Squadron arrived, as they did each year, there was, of course, a cricket-match in the beautiful Savannah, and I watched every ball. We kept open house, and many famous sailors were our guests, among them Prince Louis of Battenberg, and Captain Commerell, V.C., while some of the midshipmen even slept in the galleries—by no means an unpleasant experience in a hot climate. Thus began my interest in the Navy, which led me to read in later years many a book on naval history.

We sold the Hall a year before my father's death, and took a house in Brunswick Square, which later became the City Hall, and it was in this house, and actually in the room in which my father died, that in February 1948 I was, so to speak, given the "freedom of the city" before a large gathering, among which were present the M.C.C. team under the captaincy of G. O. Allen. There were speeches, followed by champagne, and altogether it was a notable day in my life. The building in which this ceremony took place has since been completely destroyed by fire.

I began lessons with a governess, and when I was nine went for a year to the Queen's Royal College, in the little Savannah, a hundred or so yards beyond the low stone wall which surrounded the garden—a day school, under the Headmastership of Mr Miles. My brothers had been there many years before me, and Aucher

MY FATHER, ABOUT 1886

MY MOTHER IN 1908

had won a scholarship at Oxford—he went to Oriel, where I was subsequently to follow him—which was worth £150 a year for four years.

Early in 1884 I was sent to Harrison College, Barbados, under the Headmastership of Mr H. Deighton, an old Cantab, a man of most imposing, and rather frightening, presence, with fine eyes and a long beard—a very keen cricketer, who, like Keate, believed in the rod, but to a limited extent as compared to Eton's Head. His instrument of correction was a bamboo cane, which was most unpleasant I was told by those who suffered at his hands, but which, heaven alone knows why, I was fortunate enough to escape. Mr Deighton made Harrison College, and it remains to this day a famous school. Cricket was indeed the only game, though I remember a boy, Johnson, producing a Rugby football, and most of us taking part in a huge "punt about," as it is called at Rugby, the originators of the great game. There was a lawn-tennis court—but cricket was *the* game. I got into the Third Eleven—there were about two hundred boys in the school—at a very early age, and we used to play the Second Eleven of The Lodge, at the other end of the island. E. L. Challenor, afterwards Brigadier-General Challenor, D.S.O., who played later for Leicestershire, and was a distinguished soldier,[1] and myself were the Grimmett and O'Reilly (!) of our side, and I used to make a few runs.

When I was thirteen I was in the First Eleven, and here again The Lodge were our chief opponents, though we played other matches, of course, including that against the Garrison, both at the school and on the Garrison ground, when we were given a sumptuous lunch and entertained most charmingly.

We played on pretty good wickets, and I do not recall being coached in any special way. One developed one's natural style, and I think the marble gallery at the Hall helped considerably in my acquiring a fairly straight bat.

Both Harrison College and The Lodge have produced a large number of good cricketers, and I doubt very much whether any school of its size has turned out so many in so short a time as Harrison. They made us work hard, too, and behind our thirst for knowledge was the spectre of that bamboo cane!

[1] E. L. Challenor, a brother of George Challenor, the first of the famous West Indian batsmen, was also a first-class hockey-player. He first played for Leicestershire in 1906, and died in 1935.

On my visit to Barbados in 1948 I was welcomed at an 'At Home' in the College Hall by the Old Harrisonian Society, and among the large number who attended was the Governor of Barbados, Sir Hilary Blood. There were speeches, and a band, and Mr Haskell, the Headmaster, and Mr Robert Challenor, President of the Old Harrisonian Society, another brother of George Challenor and no mean batsman himself, said nice things about me, and, of course, I had to reply. As I stood on a platform in the College Hall memories came chasing back across the long years, from the day I arrived in a sailor-suit to the day on which, early in 1887, at the age of thirteen, I made 31 against the Garrison, and was for a short while something of a small hero, and there was a lump in my throat when I spoke.

I owe much to Harrison College, for it was there that the foundations of any skill I may have acquired at cricket were built, and where many friendships began which continue to this day. Well indeed do I recall the Challenors, the Piles, the Howells, the Skeetes, the Spencers, the Sealys, the Evelyns, George Hickson, who gave me my First Eleven colours, and others. They were all very good and kind to me, and occasionally I was allowed to spend a week-end at one or other of their comfortable country houses. Harrison was almost entirely a day school, but there were some twelve or fourteen whole-term boarders, boys, like myself, who came from other islands, and some weekly boarders who went home for the week-ends. I, like the other island boys, went home for the holidays. I confess to having been often homesick, but that was only natural in one who loved his home as much as I did, and who, as the youngest of a large family, was, perhaps, petted too much.

Before leaving my boyhood days in the West Indies I may perhaps add that I come of a very long-lived family. My father, as I have said, was born in 1805—he remembered the battle of Waterloo—and his father, Colonel Edward Warner, was born in 1780, and joined the Army in 1798. He was a friend of the Prince of Wales, and, "after serving in the Mediterranean, at the express desire of the Prince of Wales received a Lieutenancy in the 10th Hussars."[1] He is more than once mentioned in *The Creevey Papers* as being a guest of the Prince at Brighton. He

---

[1] *United Services Magazine*, vol. iii (1849), p. 477. Quoted in *Sir Thomas Warner*, by Aucher Warner (1933).

MY BROTHER FRANCIS

THE HALL, TRINIDAD, ABOUT 1870

SOME OF THE CLASSROOMS AT HARRISON COLLEGE

Thus fret not at their Convents narrow Room
and students are contented with them selves.

MY STUDY AT RUGBY

saw much service, and gained a military medal and clasp for his gallantry at the capture of Martinique and Guadeloupe. The Heralds' College tell me that there are few people living to-day who can claim a grandfather who was born over a hundred and seventy years ago. He died in London on August 22, 1849.

He married Katharine Jane, the eldest daughter of Major-General Sir Charles Shipley, R.E., who was in command of the Royal Engineers when the Spaniards surrendered Trinidad on February 17, 1797, and whose portrait is in the Mess at Chatham. He received the thanks of both Houses of Parliament in 1809, and in 1813 was Governor of Grenada, where he died, in 1815.

Every one has heard of the "Essex Ring," which Queen Elizabeth gave to the Earl of Essex with a promise that should he ever be in extreme peril and should send her the ring, she would protect him, and how Essex, under sentence of death in the Tower, sent the ring to the Queen, but it fell into the hands of the Countess of Nottingham, who kept it. The Queen, when told, was so enraged that she shook the dying Countess, saying, "God may forgive you, but I never can."

There are two rings, the "Thynne Ring" and the "Warner Ring," in respect of which it is claimed that it is the identical ring which the Queen gave to Essex. The "Warner Ring" was given by Charles I to Sir Thomas Warner in 1629 on the occasion of his being knighted at Hampton Court "for his energetic activities in extending His Majesty's dominions." From here it went from father to son as an heirloom, until it came into the possession of my father, from whose house in Trinidad it was stolen in the year 1863. I have before me as I write my father's letter, dated October 25, 1863, to my mother, who was at the time in England.

TRINIDAD
October 25, 1863

I have something to tell you which distresses me very much, and I think more because I fancy how it will distress you. The Essex Ring has been taken, stolen, I fear. You don't know with what shame I write this. I kept it in the drawer of your escritoire. I was in the habit of going to the drawer from time to time to verify some date in my life. I seldom, very seldom, opened the case. On Saturday, yesterday week, I asked G— if she had ever seen the ring, and went for it. It was gone! When I had last seen it I cannot tell, and

I reproach myself for want of care. In the middle I keep your letters and my papers. In the lower part is kept what of silver I use daily now. In the upper part are the little memorials of our children, some locks of hair, my medal of the Bath. Only the ring is gone. I cannot explain it. The loss has hurt me more than I can describe, or could have imagined. I feel as if I had brought dishonour on the family and my name. Don't blame me for it. I blame myself. What value is the ring to anyone here? I have sent round to all the jewellers and pawn-brokers.

In the early eighteen-nineties there was a considerable correspondence in some of the London newspapers as to which was the genuine "Essex Ring." The antiquarians differ, but even if ours was not the genuine "Essex Ring" it is a matter of considerable pride in our family that a ring was given by the sovereign to our ancestor.

2

RUGBY

1887–92

IT HAD always been intended that I should be sent home, as we always called England, to a public school, and a couple of months after my father's death my mother, my brother Raymond, two sisters, Dorothy and Audrey, and I left Trinidad. We arrived at Plymouth in the middle of May 1887, and a few days later I was taken to Lord's by Mr A. Bowen, an old friend of the family, and, in Eton jacket and top-hat, sat on the seats in front of the old tennis-court, where the Mound Stand now is. I was thrilled by the cricket—M.C.C. were playing Sussex—and I felt the history, tradition, and atmosphere of the famous ground all about me. It caught my youthful imagination, and from that day I have loved every stick and stone of Lord's, and as the years pass I love it more and more. Even now, after so many years, I feel something of a thrill as I walk down St John's Wood Road, and my heart, maybe, beats a shade faster as I enter the ground.

During the luncheon interval I passed near the great W. G. Little did I dream then that I should ever play with that colossal figure, and go in first with him in M.C.C. and Gentlemen *v.* Players and North *v.* South matches.

But there were other things to do besides going to Lord's, and within ten days of my arrival in London I was at a preparatory school, under the mastership of Mr Turner, at 10 Collingham Road, S.W., working for a scholarship to Winchester.

I was a weekly boarder. There was only one other—a French boy, and a very nice one—and we slept in the same room. There must have been some forty day boys. We used to play cricket at Lillie Bridge, and I made the first century of my life (123, not out), for boys who hoped to go to Oxford against those whose ambition was the other place, and I also took a lot of wickets. And then came the scholarship examination at Winchester, but how Mr Turner ever thought I was anywhere near scholarship form, especially a Winchester scholarship, I cannot imagine. He must have been a supreme optimist. I knew some things fairly well, but of many others I was very ignorant.

The Winchester examiners found many holes in my defence, and I lasted only one day. My number was 32, and to this day I can see the blank opposite that number in the list at Wells's, the famous booksellers at Winchester. There is, however, quite a happy sequel to my failure, for many years later I was playing for Middlesex *v*. Hampshire at Southampton, and at the luncheon interval was not out some 70-odd runs, and as I was walking back to the pavilion J. A. Fort, who had been Captain of Lord's, as the Captain of the Winchester Eleven is called to this day,[1] and subsequently a master at Winchester, and a great personality, came up to me and said, "Well played, Warner, well played! What idiots we were at Winchester! We should have tested you at the nets, and not with a Latin prose, and then we should have had you!"

I remember well those two days at Winchester, and it may, perhaps, be of interest to Wykehamists to recall that the wickets on New Field were pitched in the opposite direction to that in which they are pitched to-day. The Hon. F. J. N. Thesiger (later Lord Chelmsford) was Captain of Lord's that summer. He was afterwards Captain of Oxford, Governor of Queensland and of New South Wales, and, later, Viceroy of India and First Lord of the Admiralty. In 1922 he was President of the M.C.C., and one of the best and most charming Presidents the Club has ever had. I saw a good deal of him during my visit to Australia in 1911–12, and I shall never forget his and Lady Chelmsford's kindness to me during my serious illness on that tour.

Mr Turner was not to be gainsaid, and a few weeks after the Winchester debacle I tackled the scholarship examination at Rugby, with the same result, but a vacancy was found for me, and in September I went to Rugby, to Mr Robert Whitelaw's house.

A friend of the family, Mr Herbert Bowen, a relation of the

---

[1] At one time there was a triangular contest between Eton, Harrow, and Winchester at Lord's, which ceased after 1854.

Bowen who had taken me to Lord's, and a great educationist, had written to my mother, saying, "Rugby under Percival ought now to be good." John Percival (afterwards Bishop of Hereford) went to Rugby in May 1887, at a time when the school was not doing too well. He had been Headmaster of Clifton College, and later was President of Trinity College, Oxford, but the governing body of Rugby persuaded him to descend from the dignity, ease, and environment of a famous college to undertake the care of Rugby, and in a very few years he had restored the school to its old position. He was a reformer, and, of course, was criticized, but he was a great Headmaster, and Rugby owes him an immense debt of gratitude. He was a fine-looking and dignified man, with beautiful features, and one of his great merits in my eyes was that he was very fond of cricket, and gave it every encouragement. In one of my reports, under "Head-master's Remarks," he wrote: "I like to see a boy who plays cricket so well working so hard," but I fear that on this occasion he was guilty of "a terminological inexactitude," as Mr Churchill would put it. As I grew older I was occasionally asked to dine at the School House, and Dr Percival used to talk cricket, and surprised me when he spoke of Arthur Shrewsbury and William Gunn, the two great England and Nottinghamshire batsmen of those days. Two of his sons—Launcelot, Prebendary L. J. Percival, Chaplain to the King, and Arthur, a Lieutenant-Colonel and a D.S.O., killed in the First World War—were famous football-players. Lance was at Clifton, and later in the Oxford and England Fifteens, and Arthur was in the Rugby and Sand-hurst Fifteens.

Robert Whitelaw, my housemaster, was one of the best friends I ever had. I arrived a rather forlorn boy, and he immediately took me under his wing and helped me enormously. I felt the English winter, with its cold and sunless days, and was inclined to be delicate and was not allowed to play football. But he was careful to see that I was amused on half-holidays, and I remember Mrs Whitelaw taking me for walks and pointing out to me the different trees and the beauties of the countryside and questioning me about the West Indies and its people.

Whitelaw was a renowned scholar with a European reputation, and was the master of the famous XX, the form below the Sixth, where were gathered together the ablest boys in the school.

No boy was allowed to be in the Sixth until he was fifteen and a half, and many a brilliant boy spent a year or more in Whitelaw's form. He was a great teacher, but a bit of a 'slave-driver,' and sometimes kept boys in school beyond the regulation time for the end of a lesson, with the result that they arrived in their houses late for breakfast—and a cold one too! If he got going on some Greek passage which appealed to him clocks did not exist. Nothing would stop him. I never was in the XX—the Fifth was as far as I got—and when Mr J. Collins, the master of the Fifth form, asked me, "How would you like to be in your friend Mr Whitelaw's form next term?" I replied, "It would probably kill me dead, sir, and, in any case, I should not get a run." He smiled, and I stayed where I was.

However, I was 'up to' Mr Whitelaw for what was called 'Tutor,' and he inspired me with such zeal that I won a prize open to the Lower Fifth. I was carried away by his enthusiasm, and used to delight in the way in which he literally sang Homer to us. When the Headmaster read out my name in Old Big School the whole school shouted with laughter, but, as a matter of fact, I knew that particular book of Homer pretty thoroughly. It was the only prize I won at Rugby.

I can to this day picture the scene in the room in our house where Whitelaw took 'Tutor,' and especially one particular occasion. A boy, Russell Roberts, who afterwards won a D.S.O. and lost a leg in the South African War, was called on to construe, and there was no reply.

R.W.: "Roberts, Roberts, Roberts!"—very fiercely.

"Benny" Forwood, the boy next to Roberts: "He's asleep, sir"—whereupon Whitelaw seized a Liddell and Scott, no light weight, and hurled it with all his might at Roberts. This, naturally, caused Roberts to stir himself!

R.W.: "So you are awake, sir, are you? I am disgusted with you! I shall have nothing to do with you!"

R.W. was no cricketer, but he picked up and hurled that Liddell and Scott after the manner of one of Jack Hobbs's fastest returns from cover-point. Luckily it only just brushed "Monkey," as we used to call Roberts, and we often speculated as to what would have happened to him had it caught him fair and square in the face. "Benny" always maintained that he was certain he would have died!

But "Bobby," as we always called him, trusted and believed in his boys, with the result that we in our turn liked and admired him, and tried to live up to his opinion of us. Ours was a happy house, and a famous one. Did not the *Westminster Gazette* say in its obituary notice of "Bobby" that "to have been in White-law's House was a distinction in itself"? In Canon Iremonger's *William Temple, Archbishop of Canterbury, His Life and Letters*[1] we read R. G. Collingwood's summing-up:

> A first-rate teacher, a man who touched nothing that he did not adorn . . . whose obviously sincere assumption that you knew as much as he did stimulated his pupils to incredible feats. . . . "White-law says so"; that was enough.

Later Russell Roberts was concerned in another incident. He used to walk in his sleep, and one night indulged in an acrobatic performance which shook to the core the dormitory in which he slept. There were sixteen boys in the dormitory, two boys being in a compartment, open to the rest of the room, with basins, jugs full of water, towels, etc., on a large washing-stand, and above these compartments were the windows of the dormitory. Well, one night in June 1890 Roberts, in his sleep, got on the washing-stand and thence climbed on to the window-sill. After a few minutes he thought that he would descend from his perch, so put his foot on the towel-rail, and naturally came a tremendous cropper. Rails, basins, jugs, etc., fell broken into pieces, and H. L. Behrens, his stable companion, received most of the flying fragments, plus the contents of the two jugs of cold water. There was a fearful crash, punctuated by shriek after shriek from Behrens, who thought that his last hour had come. Roberts was found squatting on the floor in the middle of the dormitory, and every one cursed him freely. My bed was opposite to his, and I can hear his yells now. I laughed in my sleep for the rest of that night, and I am laughing now as I write this. You never heard such a row—the crash of china, the roaring of the waters, and Behrens's shrieks of horror! Next morning he was suffering from nervous prostration, and no wonder!

Whitelaw asked me, "What can we do about this annoying fellow Roberts?" I replied, "Tie him to his bed, sir." "Good idea! Good idea!" And so "Monkey" was tied to the bed. We gave him plenty of rope, but unfortunately did not make the

[1] Oxford University Press, 1948, p. 19.

knot round his waist secure. A night or two later he had a terrible dream, for he dreamt that he was tied to the metals, and that an express train was approaching! He struggled hard, but the more he struggled the tighter the rope grew, and when he was rescued, after dragging his bed almost into the middle of the room, his waist was the size of a wasp's.

After that he was exiled to a private part of the house, and Behrens slept in peace, and the rest of us also!

I never heard of, or saw, a single case of bullying in the five years I was in Whitelaw's. There was a good deal of fagging, conveniently arranged, a system in which I am a great believer, for it teaches one to obey and, later, to rule. I hated the winter term. We had to be in chapel at 7 A.M.,[1] and I particularly remember one morning when Humphreys, the butler, and a great character, came into the dormitory saying, "Half-past six, gentlemen; snowing hard; coldest day we have had this winter" —to which we replied, "Go to h—l, Humphreys," by way of contrast to the weather!

At last the summer term of 1888 arrived, and with what delight I looked forward to it! I made o in the first game I played, but on June 9 I won my house tie, and on June 18 I was given my Twenty-two by A. W. Dixon, Captain of the Eleven:

New members of the XXII: P. F. Warner, C. J. Sitwell, F. C. Earle, R. Bond.

(Signed) A. W. DIXON

I was only fourteen and eight months, wore Eton collars, and was a fag. I was in the Second Eleven of the School against the old Rugbeians, scored 19 and 6, and took nine wickets. Early in July I made my first appearance on New Bigside, scored 20 on a sticky wicket against Barratt, the old Surrey left-hander, and clean bowled one of the best batsmen in the Eleven with a ball which pitched outside the off stump and hit the top of the middle and leg stump. But I was thought too small to be in the Eleven, though odds were laid by my friends in Whitelaw's, and in Upper Middle Two—W. P. Brooke's form, the father of Rupert Brooke. I was accused by one of the masters of "dreaming of cricket," and I could not deny the charge.

In September I went into stick-up collars, but R. W. called

---

[1] This rule no longer exists, and I believe Eton is the only school to-day which has school before breakfast.

me up after prayers one evening and, putting his hand affectionately on my shoulder, said to me in the most charming manner, "I like you better in an Eton collar," so back into Etons I went. I was still a fag, but was made head of toast fags, and, later, head of fags.

And how was I getting on in school? I was 'up to' Mr W. G. Michell in Upper Middle One, and I cannot believe that there was ever a man who understood boys better. He was a fine teacher, and had a way with him. He was strict, however, and stood no nonsense. Not that any of us would have attempted to take any sort of liberty with him: we liked him too much for that. He inculcated into us a love of Shakespeare, and used to make us take parts: "Young Warner, you shall be Mark Antony; Slater—Julius Cæsar." To this day I can quote many lines from *Julius Cæsar, Henry V*, etc. He also taught us Virgil, and I think all of us, even the idlest, enjoyed it. That winter I was allowed to play football, and began in Two Belows,[1] in which I figured as a three-quarter, generally at centre, and got a good many tries, but I was too light to be of any real use. There were House Twenties, and everybody, except the School Fifteen or a 'cap,' played in long white-flannel trousers. Next year the Twenties were reduced to Fifteens, and 'shorts' were introduced.

On June 18, 1889, I was given my Eleven Colours, and it is curious what a lucky day June 18 was for me, for on that date I got both my Twenty-two and my Eleven. On July 31 I made my first appearance at Lord's, scoring only 3 and 16,[2] but I can still feel on the bat the first four I ever made at Lord's—past extra-cover, when batting at the Nursery end.

I give the score of the match in full. Marlborough were captained by J. B. Wood, afterwards in the Oxford Eleven of 1892 and 1893, later Sir John Wood, a prominent figure in the Indian Civil Service, and Rugby by A. W. Dixon, a stockily built and very charming boy, who played for Yorkshire while still at Rugby. We collapsed in our first innings on a good wicket, but made a fight, Dixon, fast right, from the Pavilion end, bowling very well. Marlborough were one of the strongest school elevens of the year, and were clearly the better side.

[1] The lowest grade of football at Rugby.
[2] I did, however, manage to get H. R. Blore caught by F. J. Nicholls. This was, of course, my first wicket at Lord's. Blore, later, had a very distinguished military career in the South African War and in the First World War, in which he gained the D.S.O.

RUGBY *v.* MARLBOROUGH

Played at Lord's, July 31 and August 1, 1889
Result: Marlborough won by six wickets

RUGBY

First Innings		Second Innings	
L. F. Cotton, b. Hill	11	b. Shorland	2
A. M. Benham, run out	1	c. Wood, b. Hill	10
F. J. Nicholls, b. Etlinger	0	b. Etlinger	8
E. F. Rutter, b. Hill	3	l.b.w., b. Collins	28
P. F. Warner, st. Moir, b. Etlinger	3	c. and b. Hill	16
A. W. Dixon (Capt.), b. Shorland	9	run out	41
E. J. Whitting, c. Etlinger, b. Collins	15	b. Shorland	51
J. A. Paul, c. Moir, b. Shorland	8	c. Moir, b. Hill	7
H. D. Rendall, not out	4	b. Hill	0
F. W. Menzies, c. and b. Etlinger	4	not out	1
C. Headlam, b. Etlinger	0	b. Shorland	0
Byes 6, leg-byes 2	8	Byes 3, leg-byes 5	8
Total	66	Total	172

MARLBOROUGH

J. B. Wood (Capt.), b. Dixon	22	c. Whitting, b. Nicholls	41
A. E. Cheales, b. Dixon	23	b. Nicholls	11
L. G. A. Collins, b. Cotton	48	b. Paul	39
C. G. Moir, b. Dixon	0	run out	4
A. J. L. Hill, b. Paul	0		
O. H. Stone, b. Dixon	0	not out	5
C. G. Chambers, b. Menzies	4		
H. R. Blore, c. Nicholls, b. Warner	12		
T. E. Etlinger, not out	5	not out	1
H. M. Rogers, b. Dixon	2		
E. T. Shorland, b. Dixon	1		
Byes 6, leg-byes 2	8	Byes 8, leg-byes 5	13
Total	125	Total (4 wkts.)	114

BOWLING ANALYSIS

First Innings				Second Innings			
MARLBOROUGH							
	O.	M.	R.	W.	O.	M.	R.	W.
Hill	15	10	7	2
Etlinger	15.1	3	26	4
Collins	9	4	15	1
Shorland	10	4	10	2

	O.	M.	R.	W.
Hill	24	5	59	4
Etlinger	22	7	44	1
Collins	10	3	19	1
Shorland	12.4	5	22	3
Wood	3	0	10	0
Stone	1	0	1	0
Rogers	1	0	9	0

RUGBY

	O.	M.	R.	W.
Dixon	24.2	8	37	6
Menzies	15	7	24	1
Paul	13	5	20	1
Warner	5	2	8	1
Nicholls	11	5	23	0
Cotton	6	3	5	1

	O.	M.	R.	W.
Dixon	12	3	18	0
Menzies	4	2	5	0
Paul	11	4	23	1
Warner	4	1	6	0
Nicholls	12.1	4	22	2
Cotton	20	9	23	0
Benham	3	2	4	0

Umpires: J. West and T. Mycroft

After this match we played Harrow Past and Present at Althorpe Park, Lord Spencer's, the "Red Earl"—he had a reddish beard and hair—who was a Governor of both Harrow and Rugby, and we spent two delightful days. And it was there that I first met Dr Welldon, Headmaster of Harrow, Sir Stanley Jackson, Captain of Harrow that summer, and A. C. MacLaren.

The year 1889 was Tom Emmett's first at Rugby. He was a character, if ever there was one, with a prominent nose, slightly tinged with colour, merry eyes, an attractive laugh, and very upright in his walk. A renowned Yorkshire and Players cricketer, he had also visited Australia. He was a good coach, who liked us to hit the ball, and he did not indulge in over-refinements of batting. He allowed us to develop on natural lines, with no rigid or mechanical style. He had four rules, and four only, so far as I remember—(i) the correct way to play forward and back, moving the left leg to the ball when playing forward and bringing the right leg up to the bat when playing back; (ii) no facing of the bowler; (iii) "Smell her, sir, smell her!" and (iv), in jumping out to drive, "If you come to her, come. You may as well be stumped by two feet as by one inch."

I have heard of coaches who forget that no two batsmen bat alike, and who worry bowlers because they do not conform to theory, but they lose sight of the fact that a natural method of delivery is not to be ignored—we are all built differently—and many great bowlers I could name did not come up to accepted theory. Theory can be overdone. Individuality should be encouraged, though, of course, a glaring fault should be corrected.

In the winter term of 1889 I got into the House Fifteen as a forward—and a very bad one too—and I played a fair amount of rackets. Joseph Gray, the professional champion for many years, was the coach, and he gave me an hour a week, conceding me 10 aces, and always beating me with ease, for he could have given me 14 and won.

With Tom Emmett keeping a close eye on me, my batting improved greatly during the summer of 1890, and against the Free Foresters I made 177, not out, in a total of 303. I was 20, not out, at the close of the first day's play, and that evening the old Colours in the Eleven were allowed to dine with the Free Foresters at the George Hotel. The dinner and the pleasant company evidently did me good, and how can I forget the applause at the end of my innings when I came back to the pavilion amid a long lane of cheering boys? I was 99, not out, at lunch. One of the masters, the Rev. F. B. Westcott (later a Canon of Norwich), insisted on carrying my cricket-bag across the Close to the old pavilion on Old Bigside, where we kept our cricket-bags, and spoke words to me which I have always tried to follow: "Young Warner, you play with a very straight bat. Keep a straight bat and a modest mind, and you will go far." In the Free Foresters' side was F. C. Cobden, one of the heroes of the Varsity Match of 1870, when he performed the hat-trick, Cambridge winning by 2 runs. He was now forty years of age, and I remember liking his bowling!

Tuesday, June 17, 1890, was one of the great days in my cricketing life. We were beaten by Marlborough at Lord's, but I made 38 and 85, and the *Morning Post* had some nice things to say. I was carried into the pavilion, and Mr Perkins, the Secretary of the M.C.C., presented me with the ball off which I had made my runs in the second innings, and more than one bat was given to me.

I played a good deal during the holidays, and took part in a delightful week at Lord Goschen's place, Seacox Heath, Hawkhurst. Lord Goschen and his brother, Sir Edward Goschen, were both Rugbeians, as were George, his eldest son, and William, who was at Rugby with me. Lord Goschen was a keen follower of cricket, and in a speech at the Annual Dinner of the M.C.C. in 1887 remarked that even in times of political excitement he always looked first at the cricket scores in the morning newspapers. During the week W. H. Patterson, the Kent Captain, asked me to play for Kent against Warwickshire at Birmingham, but I had no sort of qualification, as I lived in London; I was not then seventeen years of age.

Then there were another ten days in Devonshire and Somerset with the Ishmaelites, a side sponsored to a large extent by W. G. Michell and F. D. Gaddum, an old Rugbeian, and a Cambridge Blue. I was their guest, and was not allowed to pay one single penny of my hotel bills. We played at Exmouth, Sidmouth, Seaton, and Taunton, where we met a strong side, including H. T. Hewett, the Somerset Captain, and a sort of left-handed Jessop, L. C. H. Palairet, W. N. Roe, and S. M. J. Woods, and when I drove Woods past extra-cover for four, a "Well played, well

played, little fellow!" came from him. The next ball my bails
flew different ways. All this cricket was, of course, a great help
in my development.

Just before I returned to Rugby for the winter term of 1890
my brother Raymond suggested that as I looked like being a
decent cricketer, could I not get off football, as I might be
injured? I answered, "You can't be at Rugby and not play football." But often since then have I wished that it had been possible to have followed his advice, for half-way through the term
I was rather badly hurt, a boy barging into me as—after, I
thought!—I was 'making a mark,' and I went off to London
for an operation, and did not return until the following term.
That accident set my cricket back, as I was always more or less
strained, and was not allowed to bowl, on one occasion Whitelaw coming on to the ground and ordering me 'off'—and at a
moment when I had just dismissed two opening batsmen in a
house match!

I was strapped up in the most uncomfortable manner in the
Rugby v. Marlborough match,[1] but was able to play in W. G.
Michell's 'Week' at Rugby immediately after Lord's. We played
strong elevens of Old Wykehamists, Old Carthusians, and Old
Reptonians, and Michell put up both his own and the visiting
sides, and dispensed lavish hospitality. We slept in various rooms
or in the dormitories, and breakfasted and dined in hall. The
occasions on which I played in his 'Weeks' are among the happiest of my memories, and it was, of course, a high compliment
to a boy to be asked to form one of his side. Michell was a great
athlete. A Wellington boy, he was in the Cambridge crew and
Fifteen, a capital rackets-player, and a fine shot. A useful batsman
and bowler, he also kept wicket, and was an admirable captain,
who once wrote out the batting order in Greek, and I was
ὁ παῖς, 'the boy.' He had scores of friends, as became so
charming a man. He possessed two lovely Russian borzois, who
followed him about and were the pets of all.

The M.C.C. played Cheltenham at Lord's in those days, but
there were no other inter-school matches besides Eton v. Harrow
and Rugby v. Marlborough. Clifton and Tonbridge, Cheltenham and Haileybury, Beaumont and Oratory, had not yet

---

[1] The match was ruined by rain. Rugby made 71 for three wickets, myself 36. C. A.
Alington, afterwards Headmaster of Eton, was in the Marlborough Eleven.

arrived, and there were no representative school matches such as take place to-day.

There had just started, however, at Richmond, a match between a Public School Eleven and the Gentlemen of Surrey, and I took part in it. I made 8 in the first innings, and then ran myself out. In the second innings I was very fortunate indeed to score 101, not out, for before I had made a run I was palpably caught at the wicket off C. Wigram (now Lord Wigram), the Winchester Captain. The umpire, however, turned down a loud appeal, and to this day Wigram and I talk and laugh about it. Among the School Eleven were two boys destined to win fame —C. B. Fry and J. R. Mason.

When I returned to Rugby I was given 'Sixth Power,' which was confined to the house itself, though as Captain of the Eleven I could commandeer a boy to take a note or message to another house. I played no football, and only a very occasional game of rackets, but managed to amuse myself, and was very seldom bored. I read some history, being allowed to transfer from "Latin Verses"—I was no rhymster!—to what was called "Verse Equivalent," and Marlborough's campaigns captured my imagination. I learned, too, some Latin prose, and Mr R. A. Wilson (now Canon Wilson), who for a time was a master at the school, wrote: "He wasn't in the Sixth, but he was a very fair performer in school. I can recall prose of his that was Latin, and he couldn't have learned that from *Wisden* and *Lillywhite*." Canon Wilson and I still meet every year at the Rugby *v.* Marlborough match. A brother of C. E. M. and E. R. Wilson, he was a very good medium-paced right-handed bowler, whose residence at Cambridge coincided with that of Woods, Jackson, Streatfeild, and Wells, and he missed his Blue.

On March 15, 1892, I was elected a member of the M.C.C. I had been down less than a couple of years, but it was far easier to get into the M.C.C. in those days. The arrival of this letter from the Secretary of the M.C.C., Mr Perkins, was such a pleasant shock that it coincided with my going to the sanatorium with influenza, which was raging at the time, and I remained there for three weeks! It left me weak, and much of my ill-health in later years could be traced to it. Curiously enough, I was nominated President of the M.C.C. fifty-eight years later in a letter dated March 15, 1950, written from H.M.S. *Chequers*, off

Tripoli, by H.R.H. the Duke of Edinburgh, so March 15 has been one of my lucky days.

Rugby had a poor Eleven in 1892, and Marlborough beat us by an innings, P. R. Creed scoring 211. I failed completely, 1 and 0, but made the photographer—and others—laugh when I begged him: "Hurry up, please, and take this duck-and-one captain!" In the holidays I played in Michell's 'Week,' and made runs, and captained the Public School Eleven v. the Gentlemen of Surrey, with Bailey, a young Surrey professional, at Richmond, where we won a most exciting match on a soft wicket by two wickets. I made some runs, and was 'in at the death.'

During my time at Rugby the cricket was at a low ebb. Tom Emmett worked with unabated zest, as did Michell, R. A. Wilson, H. C. Bradby, A. K. Watson, and E. A. St Hill, of the masters, but the material simply was not there. Wickets too were far from good, certainly nothing like what they are in these days, and there were a lot of stupid regulations as regards spikes in our boots or shoes, etc. Proper batting practice in the nets was almost impossible among the smaller boys. However, all this nonsense was done away with early in my time, and a year or two after I left Rugby began to produce good elevens. For all these most desirable improvements the Old Rugbeian Society were largely responsible and gave generously. It was owing to their beneficence that Emmett came to Rugby.

The Eleven, however, were very lucky in their fixtures. We played four Oxford colleges—Balliol, New College, Oriel, and Trinity—and two-day matches against Rugby Town, Free Foresters, Butterflies, Old Rugbeians, and the M.C.C., who invariably included two, and often three, professionals, nearly always county cricketers. So we were well tested, for meeting professional bowlers at an early age is an excellent experience and produces good results. The Eleven were excused quite a few lessons, and the "foreign" matches, as they were called, were keenly looked forward to. We had to pay for our lunches in the pavilion, as had our visitors! But in my year of captaincy I approached Dr Percival on the subject, and he was quite shocked, especially in regard to the visiting teams, and at once decreed that all lunches in future should be paid for by the school. John Percival was so fond of cricket that when I had to go to London

to see a surgeon about my strain he suggested the first day of the
Varsity Match. "That's the University Match, isn't it? You
might go and have a look at it too, mightn't you?" So, armed
with my M.C.C. membership card, I was at Lord's by 12.15,
and saw M. R. Jardine and V. T. Hill make centuries, and C. B.
Fry score 44, and Jackson, Wells, Streatfeild, and Bromley-Davenport bowl.

Rugby has, of course, changed considerably since I left, and
there is no greater school to-day. But let the Archbishop,
William Temple, speak. I quote some passages from a letter to
his wife, dated July 21, 1916, from Fulham Palace, again from
Canon Iremonger's book:[1]

> Winchester is the oldest, and in some sense the pattern School.
> Being small, it has kept itself intellectually select. Its intellectual
> standard through the School as a whole is far and away the highest;
> and as regards its top forms Rugby and, at times, Eton—no others
> —may equal it. Eton has the most distinct individuality. . . . It has
> a splendidly scholarly staff, so that a boy who wants to work prob-
> ably gets better teaching than anywhere else. . . . No boy is so
> pleasant as the good sort of Etonian. . . . For brilliance of achieve-
> ment in scholarship or public life, no School ever comes near it.
> But there, as elsewhere, the brilliant are few; and for 'the rest'
> Eton does not supply the needed stimulus. . . .
>
> Rugby is the exact opposite. . . . It makes everyone work. Prob-
> ably it is the most strenuous of Schools. . . . The great glory of
> Rugby is not the brilliancy of its results—it has few Cabinet Ministers
> and so on—but the incomparably high level of usefulness reached by
> its average products. Eton will produce, say, 2 or 3 Viceroys:
> Rugby will produce 20 or 30 first-class provincial administrators.
> But before all comes its influence on other Schools. Here it far
> surpasses any . . . well: that's all. . . . Oh yes: It was the first School
> (of the Public School type) to have a Rifle Corps (now the O.T.C.),
> or to teach science. Also of course it is the only one whose game
> has become a national sport.

[1] Pp. 13–15. Quoted by kind permission of the Oxford University Press.

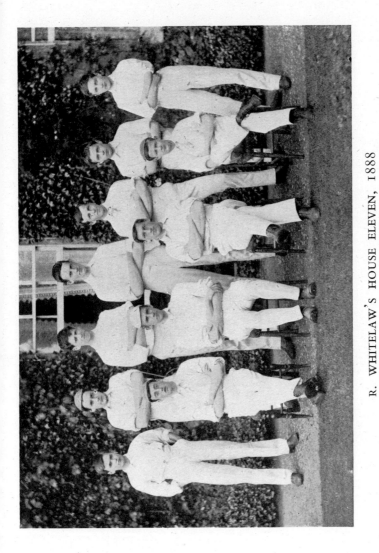

R. WHITELAW'S HOUSE ELEVEN, 1888

Left to right—Back row: H. G. Gregson, H. D. Rendall, H. C. Wrigley, S. H. Rendall, V. O. C. Dawson, A. Whitelaw, H. J. Mappin. *Front row*: C. Headlam, V. H. Rendall, W. E. Oakeshott (Capt.), P.F.W.

THE RUGBY MASTERS IN 1891

Left to right—Back row: C. G. Steel, W. W. English, W. N. Wilson, W. P. Brooke, Rev. F. B. Westcott, G. Stallard, H.T. Rhodes, H. P. Highton. *Middle row:* J. Collins, Rev. W. F. Stokes, Rev. W. H. Payne-Smith, A. E. Donkin, W. G. Michell, L. Cumming, J. L. Paton, Mons. Vecqueray, W. Dewar, G. F. Bradby, B. B. Dickinson. *Front row:* S. Barnard, Rev. C. Elsee, W. Sargent, G. Nutt, Rev. P. Bowden-Smith, the Doctor, E. A. Scott, Rev. F. D. Morice, R. Whitelaw.

3

OXFORD
1893–96

I WENT up to Oxford in January 1893, and I spent the previous autumn in preparing for Matriculation at Oriel, and Responsions—'Smalls,' as it is called. A tutor polished me up for a couple of hours three days a week, and I defeated the examiners. In my time there were only seventy or eighty men at Oriel, and everybody knew everybody else. It was a very happy college, especially renowned for its prowess at cricket and Association football—and, as L.., of Modern Oxford reminds us:

> There was a young fellow of Oriel,
> Who climbed up the Martyrs' Memorial,
> Where he stood on his head
> And indignantly said,
> "Who states we're not active at Oriel?"

In recent years Oriel has also won fame on the river, but in my day cricket and football took pride of place. I lived out of college during my first term, and caught the usual 'Freshman's cold,' which, my landlady assured me, would quickly pass if I would follow her advice and tie the socks which I had been wearing during the day round my neck at night. This sounds somewhat unpleasant, but she was right.

My tutor was the Rev. A. G. Butler, the hero of "Butler's Leap" at Rugby, and a keen follower of cricket. He was a little man, with a charming and gentle manner, who was liked and respected by all. He taught me Herodotus, which, curiously enough, was one of the subjects for Law Preliminary, and I satisfied the examiners in due course. However, I failed the first

C

time in 'Diviners,' but as the legend went that Gladstone had met with the same fate I was not unduly depressed.

The clothes we wore would astonish the modern under-graduate. On Sundays we clad ourselves in a cut-away coat and a bowler, and carried a stick, and on week-days we wore a round coat and a cloth cap during the winter and a straw hat in summer. The soft collar was only just appearing, and few, if anyone, went about bare-headed. Sixty years ago the bicycle was rarely seen, and the motor-car had hardly been dreamt of. Life was very pleasant indeed, and the cost of living incredibly low compared with these days. Dinner, and a very good one, at Vincent's Club, was only 2s. 6d., a bottle of champagne 9s. 6d. to 12s. 6d., and we were allowed twelve penny stamps a day free—plus a glass of beer during the morning! If one did not hunt, and was not particularly extravagant, one could live on £200 a year, vacations included. The pound was worth a pound, and railway travelling, clothes, shoes, etc., were 150 per cent. cheaper than to-day, while taxation had not, of course, reached anything like its present most burdensome figure.

As regards cricket, we dressed much the same as we do to-day, except that we nearly all wore stiff-fronted shirts, and our caps had much smaller peaks, while the moustache was very much in vogue, but never in my case. Pads were smaller, but were protected inside, with no huge flapping tops such as seem almost universal to-day, and militate, to my mind, against quickness of foot, while batting-gloves were less flimsy and afforded excellent protection. To-day when a batsman is hit on the gloves there is often a badly bruised or broken finger. In those days there were many really fast bowlers about, but it was seldom indeed that we heard of anyone sustaining a broken finger after receiving a rap on the gloves. The manufacturers of batting-gloves might well give their attention to this question.

My first summer at Oxford was one of almost continual sunshine, but another attack of influenza, to which I seemed an easy prey, in the Easter vacation laid me low, and I was in poor shape when the season began, and got few runs for some time. At the end of term I was fairly successful for Oriel, and in the vacation made several big scores for the Free Foresters, Butterflies, Oxford Authentics, etc., and took part in some cricket weeks at country houses—delightful in every way, but, alas, things of the past in these strenuous days. They are memories which none who were fortunate enough to take part in them can forget, and invitations were eagerly looked forward to.

During the winter I read law, and became something of an authority (!) on the law of contract, and enjoyed the lectures, and especially those of Sir William Anson, author of the standard work on contracts, and a Fellow of All Souls, whither I was bidden to lunch on one or two occasions, and enjoyed, and profited by, the good talk and the port! I also attended lectures on Lex Aquilia by Duff, of All Souls, a great character, who had a most amusing way of stressing points of law, which stuck, or should have stuck, in my brain.

In the spring of 1894 I stayed with the Palairets at Cattistock Lodge, Maiden Newton, and enjoyed some splendid practice against Martin and Walter Hearne, the Kent professionals. I did a little fishing—both the Palairets, L. C. H. and R. C. N., and their father were keen fishermen—but I cannot say that I caused any apprehension among the fish.

I had got into good form, but just before I went up to Oxford influenza attacked me once again in the most virulent manner, and I was very far from well. I suffered a great deal of pain, which, curiously, always came on at 11.30 A.M. and 4.30 P.M., punctually to the minute, and sometimes at night. I saw more than one doctor, and must have swallowed enough bismuth to float the whole of the British Navy. My trouble was a duodenal ulcer. Few, if any, seemed to know anything about such things those days, and eventually it led to two operations, before which I nearly died in Sydney in 1911, which F. A. Iredale, the Australian cricketer, used chaffingly to regret: "We should have given you a wonderful funeral, Plum!" But enough of my duodenum, beyond saying that I do not think any cricketer has ever met with so many slings and arrows of outrageous fortune in his health and yet played so much cricket and lived so long! As a famous Yorkshire professional once remarked to me, "If you had had a stomach like me or — you would have had all the bowlers begging for mercy. As it was, you didn't do too bad"—a nice compliment indeed, of which I am very proud.

After scoring 163 and 70, not out, for Middlesex Second Eleven against Kent Second Eleven at Lord's on July 27 and 28, my first connexion with Middlesex cricket, I was asked to play for

Middlesex against Somerset at Taunton on August 6, 7, and 8, and this was my first appearance for the county with which I was destined to have such a long and happy association. We won a thrilling match by 19 runs, but I had little to do with the result, for I made only 6 and 4. There were no fewer than seventeen amateurs in the two sides, nine Somerset and eight Middlesex.

The next match, at Clifton, against Gloucestershire, ended in a draw greatly in our favour, and it was a memorable occasion for me, for it was the first time I played with W. G. I scored 14, not out, and 29, not out, and in my second innings was missed by E. M. Grace at point, and there was a chorus of comment, headed by W. G.'s "You ought to have caught it, Ted." I recollect vividly his arrival on the ground, clad in white flannel trousers and a black hat—half topper, half bowler—and his cheery cry: "Eight o'clock to-night, Webbe; don't forget. It's down the well"—'it' being the champagne.

And what a delightful evening it was! W. G. and his wife were perfect hosts, and the Old Man was full of fun and good humour, and roaring with laughter. His daughter, Bessie, a very nice-looking girl with grey-green eyes, was there, but, alas, she died young, as also did W. G., junior, who, if not anything like the cricketer his father was, played for Gloucestershire and Cambridge, and was a fine fieldsman and a useful bowler. He was a Wrangler and an Instructor at Dartmouth. Another son became an admiral, and at one time there were no fewer than seven Graces, all relations of W. G., in the *Navy List*.

In the Easter term of 1895 Cecil Rhodes, who was an old Oriel man, and who in his will left a large sum of money to the college, and Dr Jameson spent a week-end with the Provost, Dr David Binning Monro, and I was one of the half-dozen or so undergraduates bidden to meet him at breakfast, when I was fortunate enough to sit next to him. I have a good memory for some things—cricket scores and incidents, and conversations which interest me—and, though it is fifty-six years ago, the following is an almost word-for-word record of part of that conversation:

C.J.R.: What are you going to do when you go down?

P.F.W.: I am going to the Bar, and am "eating dinners" at the Inner Temple.

C.J.R.: Do you ever meet any coloured men there?

P.F.W.: Yes, a few.

C.J.R.: Do you ever sit near them?

P.F.W.: Yes, we are often placed in messes of four.

C.J.R.: Do you talk to them?

P.F.W.: Yes.

C.J.R.: Do you like them?

P.F.W.: Yes, I do.

C.J.R.: Well, I don't. I suppose it is the instinct of self-preservation. In South Africa we have perhaps a million or two whites, and many millions more of black people.

Those, I maintain, are practically the *ipsissima verba*. And to-day the colour question is one of the great problems of the world, and nowhere more so than in South Africa. I must say that I was surprised that this great man and great Empire-maker felt like this, but it only shows how far he was looking ahead.

Rhodes had the head of a Roman Emperor, with rather untidy blond hair. The Matabele called him "Lamula M'Kunsi"—"The Separator of the Fighting Bulls"—and "The Great White Chief." Jameson was a slightly built man, with a large forehead and a great deal of magnetism; and both of them radiated charm. Rhodes especially seemed to fill the room. He was devoted to Jameson, and when Groote Schuur (the "Big House") was burned down, and they brought him the news, he said, "My God, I thought something had happened to Dr Jim!"[1]

The summer of 1895 was a glorious time for me. I got my Blue, and revelled in the pleasant life which is the good fortune of a member of the Varsity Eleven. Oxford to me was paradise, and how can I forget the moment when G. J. Mordaunt, the Captain, came up to me—we were in the field at the time, playing the M.C.C.—and said, "Plum, I think you would look very nice in a dark-blue cap"? Cricket has bestowed on me many favours, but I cannot forget that moment.

We started favourites for the Varsity Match, but Cambridge, splendidly captained by W. G. Druce, beat us by 134 runs. We did not bowl too well, but what really 'did us in' was the atrocious light on the first evening, for the umpires, Phillips and W. A. J. West, were deaf to our constant appeals. Never have I played in such a bad light. H. K. Foster's 121 in Oxford's second innings stands out as one of the finest innings played in these matches.

[1] Stuart Cloete, *African Portraits* (Collins, 1946).

I spent some weeks of the vacation at Dinard, and the day I
arrived there played for Dinard *v.* the 1st Battalion of the
Northamptonshire Regiment, who insisted on taking my brother
Aucher and myself to Jersey, where they were stationed, and
there we had a week's cricket against a good "Moonlighters"
side, brought over by Nichols, the Somerset professional. We
were the guests of Captain C. E. Higginbotham, an old Rugbeian. Later, as subaltern in the 4th Royal West Kent Regiment,
I was attached to this battalion, famous for its musketry and
marching, for manœuvres, and we seemed to me to march all
over England. It was a wonderful experience.

Returning from Dinard, I began working for my Schools,
and in October shared rooms with G. R. Bardswell at 15 Oriel
Street. It was here that I first met Cosmo Gordon Lang, afterwards Archbishop of Canterbury. He was at the time Vicar of
St Mary's, and his sermons used to draw many undergraduates,
including most of my cricketing friends. He dined with us on at
least one occasion, and his delightful conversation, uncommon
good looks, and charm of manner radiated a wonderful and happy
atmosphere. Many years later I was to meet him again at a big
night at the Inner Temple, where I was summoned to his presence
by Lord Simon, whose guest I was—"Plum, the Archbishop
desires converse with you"—and he recalled his Oxford days
and the many undergraduates he knew—the Leveson Gowers,
Crawley, the father of Aidan, now a prominent M.P., and others.
His "mental processes," as Mr Churchill would put it, were
remarkable.

It was about this period that I began to take a keen interest in
naval and military history, and read several books, including
Archibald Forbes's *Memories and Studies of War and Peace*,[1] which
I delight in reading to this day. I struggled, too, with the works
of Justinian, of Lodge, and of Anson, attended lectures on Real
Property by Dr Prankerd, of Brasenose, and was generally
guided by my Tutor in Oriel, Mr Montagu. Time passed
quickly, and not by any means unpleasantly, for we were comfortable in our rooms, and there were occasional dinners at 15
Oriel Street, at Vincent's and in other rooms and colleges, and
at the various Wine Clubs. I was President of the Ran Dan
Wine Club of Oriel, when, after dining in Hall, we repaired to

[1] Cassell, 1895.

a room and drank good wine, but never too much, as it was the tradition of the club that no one should overstep the mark. On one occasion Malcolm Seton, a Reptonian, and afterwards Sir Malcolm, a big, scholarly, and very nice man, brought Hilaire Belloc, then President of the Union, as his guest, and for a while I was under the impression that he had little use for a mere cricketer, but I knew that he had served as a conscript in the French Army, and after I had mentioned Forbes's book, in which the great battles of the Franco-Prussian War are most graphically described, we got on like a house on fire.

H. D. G. Leveson Gower was Captain of the Varsity Eleven in the following summer, and he led us with great ability and a sense of humour, which kept us all happy and got the best out of us. We won six out of nine matches, including the Varsity Match, and made a good fight for two days against H. Trott's fine Australian side, and I remember particularly H. K. Foster's second innings of 40 for two amazing strokes which he made off E. Jones, who was "quite fast," as W. G. put it. Foster hit two good-length balls in succession far over cover-point's head first bounce into the ring, the second nearly clearing the ropes on the Christ Church ground. After the second stroke Jones took off his cap, scratched his head, and, turning round to me, who was in at the other end, asked, "Does this cove make a habit of strokes like this?"

The Varsity Match of that year is historic, Oxford winning by four wickets after we had been set 330 runs to win. At lunch-time Mordaunt, Foster, and myself were out for only 60 runs, and the odds looked 50–1 against us, but G. O. Smith made 132, Leveson Gower 41, C. C. Pilkington 44, and Bardswell 33, not out. It was the occasion of the famous incident of the no-balls and wides which F. Mitchell, the Cambridge Captain, instructed E. B. Shine to bowl in order to prevent Oxford from following on. The follow-on was then compulsory, and not optional, as it became a year or two later. Cantab was divided against Cantab, and brother against brother, and The Times was very annoyed with Mitchell. The Cambridge Eleven were hooted, and never before, or since, has there been such turmoil and so many angry words in the pavilion itself. Mitchell was right in his action—F. S. Jackson had done the same thing in 1893 —and it was surprising that after the first incident the M.C.C. had not acted at once. The law as it then stood penalized the side which had gained a strong initial advantage, and Cambridge had had a sad experience of this against the Australians at Fenner's in 1893, and had not forgotten it. In these days, I think I may say, the M.C.C. would have acted immediately after such an incident as occurred in 1893.

I did only fairly well during the term. I was more or less consistent, but never really got into proper form. The shadow of the Schools was over me, and poring over one's notebooks in the pavilion during the intervals of a match is not the best preparation for cricket. I had a bad four days before the Varsity Match, as I was 'viva-ed' for three-quarters of an hour, and then was run out in each innings. I was placed in the Third Class, and my coach, Cousins,[1] said I must have been in love, as he had regarded me as a certain Second! The examination was something like a Test Match. I did well for three days, and got several Seconds (one a B+), but the weather was hot, and I failed physically and mentally on the last two days.

I had had four wonderful years, and what I owe to Oxford I can never express or repay. To this day, as I approach it in the train, I never fail to look out of the window and take off my hat to the glorious city of spires.

[1] Cousins occupied a unique position in Oxford. Although he was somewhat frowned upon by the Dons as a 'crammer,' generation after generation of law students from my day right down to the recent War sought his services, and his vivacity, enthusiasm, and wit can never be forgotten by his pupils. He was an inspiring teacher, and had an uncanny knack of spotting the likely questions in the year's Schools.

4

FIRST TOURS ABROAD
1897–98

The Bar Final—In the West Indies under Lord Hawke—"The Baron"—First Hundred at Lord's—In the U.S.A.—Alfred Lyttelton—Work as a Law Pupil— In Oporto, the U.S.A., and Canada—The Season of 1898

THE HONOURS School of Jurisprudence at Oxford excused one from many of the papers in the Bar Final Examination, and I spent the autumn of 1896 reading Torts and Criminal Law, being coached by Mostyn Pigott, founder of *Isis*, a barrister, an able man, with a shock of red hair, who wrote verses for *Truth* which attracted a great deal of attention, and especially so in their Christmas Annual.

I satisfied the examiners early in December, and on January 13, 1897, sailed for the West Indies, the first of the many cricket tours I was destined to make. It was a great distinction to be asked to go on tour with Lord Hawke, and one could not possibly have begun under better auspices, for he was the ideal leader on such expeditions. He was called the Odysseus of cricket, for he had already taken sides to Australia, South Africa, India, the United States, and Canada. A man of fine presence and very like his great ancestor—Hawke of Quiberon Bay, the first Baron Hawke—he was blessed with charm of manner. We all loved "The Baron." He was always very good and kind to me, and, I fancy, early on picked me out as a possible leader of teams abroad, for at a later date, in South Africa, he deputed me to captain the side on the few occasions on which he did not play, and when, at the last moment, he was unable to go to New Zealand because of the illness of his mother he entrusted me with the captaincy. I have a feeling that he was largely responsible for my being appointed Captain of the first team the M.C.C. ever sent abroad, in September 1903.

Lord Hawke's influence on cricket affairs was great. He made Yorkshire cricket, and at Lord's he was an important figure on the Committee, and was subsequently both President and Treasurer of the M.C.C. He and Lord Harris were the 'big' men at Lord's. I often wish we had them still. Lord Hawke commanded respect and affection, and his leadership was of the kind which resulted in this sort of attitude: "No, we must not do that. Martin would not like it." And what finer tribute could a captain have paid him? It was said of him that in selecting his teams the two qualifications he demanded were good manners and good temper. In later years, when he was often in London, many a delightful dinner did we have at his house in Belgrave Square, and he often included me in his theatre parties. He was a great letter-writer, and never forgot anyone who had entertained him abroad. I consider myself very lucky indeed to have been 'brought up' by him. Many a time on tour I used to say to myself, "What would the Baron have done here?"

As a batsman he was a bad starter, but once he began to see the ball he was a powerful driver and a really beautiful late cutter. He was not what one would call a good fielder, but he was a fast runner—did he not win the hundred yards at Eton?—and many a hard hit found a safe resting-place in his big hands. I have heard it said of him that he was a bad loser, but I do not agree with this. Under his leadership Yorkshire won match after match in succession for many years, and maybe he was surprised when he was beaten, which was, perhaps, not unnatural, but all I know is that when Middlesex, me duce, beat Yorkshire at Lord's in 1903 no one could have been nicer or more genuine in his congratulations than he.

And what a tremendous amount he did for the professional cricketer! He took over the captaincy of Yorkshire at a very difficult period, but he insisted on strict discipline and parade polish, and no Yorkshire Eleven ever took the field in his day which was not smartly turned out. And he looked after them in the winter. It was he who first initiated winter pay, managed their finances, and took a personal interest in every individual and his family. It was said of him that he was a bit of a dictator at the Yorkshire committees—he was President for years—but I imagine that he was a benevolent one. Years later he ran into a bit of trouble by saying in a speech, "Pray Heaven a professional will never captain England!" but what he really meant was that he hoped English amateur cricket would never reach so low an ebb that an amateur could not be found to lead England; and in this a very large number of people will agree with him. Maybe he sometimes spoke on the spur of the moment and without thinking what might be the reaction, but, whether this be so or not, it is certain that no man ever did more for the professional cricketer than he.

Just before we sailed from Southampton for the West Indies H. V. L. Stanton ("Wanderer" of *The Sportsman*) asked our captain whether he could arrange for one of the team to send home fortnightly descriptions of the cricket, and Lord Hawke, turning to me, said, "Plummy, you're last from school. Why shouldn't you do it?" And that is how I began to write cricket for public consumption. As it happened, I made a lot of runs, which was embarrassing, as may be imagined, but I made an arrangement with Leveson Gower, and whenever I was successful he wrote about me, and whenever he was I wrote about him; and things turned out all right, and we did not make the mistake of undue flattery! On the contrary, we were very careful in this respect. Some years later *The Sportsman* passed out, to the great regret of many people, for their accounts of cricket were excellent.

I naturally looked forward to a visit to the scenes of my childhood, and when, on landing in Trinidad, a cab nearly ran over me the driver was rated soundly: "Good God, man, what you do? Nearly run over Mr Pelham. Can't you see it's Mr Pelham grown big? Take your d— jackass away!" In the opening match of the tour in Trinidad I made 119, and several men broke on to the Queen's Park ground, shouting out, "I taught you, Mr Pelham. You play well, sir. I am proud of you," while one said, "This is a great day for me, sir. I see my little boy make a hundred. I go home and tell my wife, sir, and she die of joy, sir." And my old nurse, Kitsey, embraced me in front of the hotel, to the huge delight and amusement of the rest of the team: "Oh, Puggie darling, I am glad to see you! Let me look at you well. You not so pretty as you were—you pretty little boy. Still, you not bad." Kitsey lived to a great age, and when I was in Australia in 1903–4 she wrote me a most affectionate letter in which she said, "I hear my little boy become a big cricketer."

What a delightful tour that was, and what an experience and an education! I was particularly anxious to see St Kitts, where a direct ancestor of mine, Sir Thomas Warner, Kt, ruled as the first

Governor-General, as it was then called, of the West Indies. I was taken to see his tomb, and he was clearly a man of distinction, judging by the eulogies on it: "His Courage Bold," "Great in Acts of Fame," etc. He died on March 10, 1648, and his name is to be found in any history of the West Indies. I fancy the Warners of those days were inclined to be extravagant, and another kinsman of mine once owned property where Maddox Street now is, but he got into financial difficulties with Empson and Dudley, Henry VII's tax-gatherers, and sold his equity of redemption. I have always regretted this!

We played fourteen matches during the tour, winning nine, drawing three, and losing two, both to Trinidad, who were captained by my brother, Aucher. It was clear that the West Indies would one day be formidable opponents, for they were natural cricketers, and were inspired by intense enthusiasm and love of the game. They took rather longer than I thought they would to reach Test Match status, but they have come with a rush during the last fifteen years. Lord Hawke's team was made up as follows: Lord Hawke (Capt.), A. E. Leatham, H. R. Bromley-Davenport, C. Heseltine, H. D. G. Leveson Gower, G. R. Bardswell, A. D. Whatman, R. W. Wickham, R. Berens, W. H. Wakefield, J. M. Dawson, and myself.

And so the tour ended, and on the voyage home A. E. Leatham remarked to me, "The worst of these tours is that one always hankers after another." It was to prove only too true in my case. Three years later, in 1900, William Heinemann published my first book, *Cricket in Many Climes*, in which this tour is described.

I returned to England very fit, and on May 12 made my first hundred at Lord's—108, not out, for the M.C.C. *v.* Yorkshire—which *Wisden* described as "splendid batting." It was a perfect wicket, on which one could force even the good-length bowling of the Yorkshiremen. I took part in every match that season for Middlesex, under the captaincy of A. J. Webbe, who became one of my best and most valued friends, and had the honour of going in first with W. G. in the Gentlemen *v.* Players match at the Oval. I played quite a lot of country-house cricket: there were far fewer county matches in those days, Middlesex playing only sixteen matches.

In September I took a side to the United States. It consisted of the following: P. F. Warner (Capt.), G. L. Jessop, H. D. G.

Leveson Gower, H. B. Chinnery, H. H. Marriott, F. W. Stocks, F. G. Bull, J. N. Tonge, R. A. Bennett, W. M. Hemingway, J. R. Head, and A. D. Whatman. We played our chief matches in Philadelphia against the Gentlemen of Philadelphia, who were then, and in some subsequent years, a very good side. Did they not twice beat the Australians? And in J. B. King, a great character, they had one of the best fast bowlers cricket has produced. Had he been an Englishman or an Australian he would have been even more famous than he was. A tall, spare, wiry man, he was really fast, had great control of the ball, and made it swing late into the batsman. He also made an occasional delivery 'go with his arm,' and had at his command a good yorker. On his visits to England he clean bowled several of our greatest batsmen.

We also played at Staten Island, New York, and Baltimore, and on our arrival in Baltimore one of the papers wrote: "The hearts of Baltimore girls are going pit-a-pat!" Charming to a degree and very pretty they were, and shall any of us ever forget a delightful dinner and dance, when a 'Darkie' band played the most fascinating tunes? I stayed with the Lurmans. Our host had been wounded on the slopes of Gettysburg, and much interesting talk did I have with him; and it was a delight to experience the comfort and atmosphere of an American country house.

Our games in Philadelphia attracted great crowds, the country houses bringing large contingents; it reminded me of Eton *v.* Harrow, with coaches crowded and all the ladies in their smartest frocks. Old age has its compensations—the greatest of which is memories—and to this day I can recall almost every moment of this tour, and the next, which I was to make a year later. Some of the nicest people in the world live in and around Philadelphia and Baltimore, and I am proud to think that many friends I made then remain to this day. The passing of time has thinned the ranks, but one of them, J. H. Mason, now over eighty, though he does not look it, stands out. It is his custom to send a cablegram before a contemplated visit to England, running something like this: "Dinner Claridge's, Sunday, June — [almost always during a Test Match at Lord's]. Please ask So-and-so." And what memorable evenings they are! Only last summer (1950) Mason gave one of his famous dinners at Claridge's, and on this occasion E. J. Metcalfe, who had taken Incogniti teams to America, made one of the best and most charming speeches I have ever heard, and I have listened to a great many. It was perfect in manner, tone, and substance, and is engraved on my memory. There was another Philadelphian who does not fade from my memory, G. S. Patterson, a fine all-round cricketer—he was called "the W. G. of America"—and an outstanding lawyer, who was Counsel for the Pennsylvania Railroad. He married a relation of Robert E. Lee, and a night or two before the Second World War broke out R. Aird and I dined with him and his wife at Quaglino's. As I knew my Stonewall Jackson, we got on well. I have a great liking, and, indeed, affection, for Americans: a nice American man is as nice a man as one can meet. And the ladies —well, I have tried to describe what grace and charm is theirs.

Thanks to the good offices of A. J. Webbe, I was a pupil of Alfred Lyttelton's at 3 Paper Buildings, Temple, for a year. Lyttelton had been a great cricketer, who had kept wicket for England in the early eighties, and whose batting was described by W. G. as "the champagne of cricket." He was also a fine footballer and tennis-, rackets-, and fives-player—altogether an outstanding athlete. A tall, finely built man, he had that charm of manner which all the Lytteltons I have ever met possess. When he died in July 1913 Mr Asquith paid a wonderful tribute to him in the House of Commons, and during the University Match flags were lowered to half-mast, and for two minutes the members of the M.C.C. and the spectators stood up, and the players stood at attention with their caps off. How can a man die better? Lyttelton, later a K.C., became Colonial Secretary, and when he was appointed, in September 1903, the M.C.C. team were on the eve of sailing to Australia, and *The Times*, in a leading article on the composition of the Government, remarked that his appointment should appeal to our kinsmen across the seas, and especially in Australia, whither a team was about to set out to play cricket of which he was such a notable exponent, or words to that effect. In Lyttelton's chambers were A. T. Lawrence (afterwards Lord Chief Justice of England and the father of Lord Oaksey); Leslie; Trevor Lewis (son of Lord Merthyr), a famous Eton and Cambridge rowing Blue; and Reggie Coventry (later the Hon. Sir Reginald Coventry, Recorder of Stoke-on-Trent). The other pupils, besides myself, were Nigel Playfair and Kenneth Marshall, afterwards a Metropolitan magistrate, before whom I once appeared as a witness on behalf of my son for a very minor motor-car offence. He was a Rugbeian, and when I stood up he almost jumped in his seat on the Bench.

I do not know that I was a very industrious pupil, and the only success I ever achieved at the Bar was when, on entering the chambers one morning, the Clerk said to me, "Mr Lawrence wants you to note this case"—the Lagunas Nitrate Company, in which a million pounds was involved. I cannot recall the name of the defendants. It was a mighty-looking brief, which scared me, but it also interested me, and I worked hard at it and picked out, I believe, the relevant dates and points, with the result that a fortnight or so later the Clerk said, "Mr Lawrence has told me to ask the pupil who noted the Lagunas case to do this one too."

There were many great figures in the Temple in those days—Rufus Isaacs, the youngest 'silk' in terms of length of call ever created to that day, though Lord Simon broke Isaacs' record in this respect, as, perhaps, Sir Raymond Evershed has done to-day, Asquith, Carson, Gill, Marshall Hall, Lawson Walton, Hogg, Avory, Bankes, Sir Edward Clarke, and many another. We pupils were encouraged to watch these great men in court and to study their methods of address. Rufus Isaacs was surely the model to follow: he never overstated his case, as his son records in his book *Rufus Isaacs, First Marquess of Reading*,[1] and his manner was perfect with both judge and jury. I remember one occasion when Mr Justice Wright, I think it was, said, "Mr Isaacs, would you put it quite like that?" "Well, perhaps, if your Lordship pleases, I might be allowed to put it in another way." Simple words, maybe, but the whole tone and manner were wonderful. Anyhow, I have not forgotten them. And, talking of cases, I was once taking a note in which Asquith was leading, with Alfred Lyttelton as his junior, before the Lord Chief Justice, the famous Lord Russell of Killowen. The Lord Chief Justice was in what looked like something of a temper, and I recall Asquith's turning round to Lyttelton and saying, "Alfred, Charles is very testy to-day. What's wrong with him? Has he been losing at cards?" (The Lord Chief Justice was a very keen whist- and, later, bridge-player.) I nearly jumped out of my seat in surprise at the Lord Chief Justice's being referred to as "Charles"! He

[1] Hutchinson (1942–45).

was a keen racing man, and my wife tells me that she walked down to the start with him on the first occasion on which the starting-gate was used at Newmarket.

I spent the Easter vacation in Oporto with a team got up by T. Westray, who, like myself, was elected a member of the M.C.C. when he was still a schoolboy, at Uppingham, where he was Captain of the Eleven. He took us there and back in the *Elbe*, of the line of Coverley and Westray. We were described in the local paper as "afamados jogadores de cricket"—"famous cricketers"—the writer adding that the enthusiasm for cricket in England was almost as great as for bull-fighting in Spain. We stayed in private houses, and had the most wonderful time. We played Oporto not only at cricket, but at lawn tennis and golf, in the evenings danced to beat the band, and fortified ourselves with the wine of the country. Westray's side was: T. Westray (Capt.), F. W. Westray, R. N. Douglas, S. A. P. Kitcat, L. C. V. Bathurst, H. R. Bromley-Davenport, W. N. Fletcher, A. C. Taylor, H. G. Peachey, E. A. Field, and myself.

When the summer arrived I was, I fear, none too regular an attendant in Lyttelton's chambers, the lure of Middlesex cricket being all-compelling. In September and October I was again in the United States and Canada with the following team: P. F. Warner (Capt.), C. J. Burnup, F. Mitchell, C. O. H. Sewell, V. T. Hill, E. H. Bray, G. E. Winter, E. C. Lee, B. J. T. Bosanquet, R. S. A. Warner, E. F. Penn, R. Berens, and J. L. Ainsworth. Though we won both our matches against the Gentlemen of Philadelphia, we had to fight hard for victory, King again bowling very finely. We also played in New York, Baltimore, and Chicago, and in Montreal and Toronto. I shall not forget my first sight of Quebec as we steamed up the St Lawrence.

I had a fairly good season for Middlesex in 1898, scoring 814 runs, with an average of 33·91, and the best innings I played were 46, not out, out of a total of 75, on a sticky wicket, at Lord's against Gloucestershire; 79 against Surrey at Lord's; and 88 against Nottinghamshire at Trent Bridge. C. M. Wells, however, always declares that my actual best this year was 13 against Yorkshire at Leeds, on a piece of very false turf, when we beat Yorkshire by eight wickets. J. T. Hearne and Trott got Yorkshire out for 45, of which Tunnicliffe made 31, in their second innings. It was at Chesterfield in their next match, against Derbyshire,

RUGBY *v.* FREE FORESTERS, 1890

[*See pp. 27–28.*]

MIDDLESEX ELEVEN AT TAUNTON IN 1895

Left to right—Back row: J. T. Rawlin, J. Douglas, R. S. Lucas, J. Phillips. *Middle row:* G. MacGregor, A. E. Stoddart, A. J. Webbe (Capt.), Sir T. C. O'Brien, C. M. Wells. *Front row:* P.F.W., J. T. Hearne.

that Brown and Tunnicliffe put on 554 for the first wicket. Middlesex had a fine side that season, and would probably have won the County Championship had not Trott been unable to play for six weeks at the beginning of the season owing to an injured hand. There were great names in the Eleven—Webbe, Stoddart, O'Brien, Wells, J. and R. N. Douglas, F. G. J. Ford, and MacGregor, in addition, of course, to Hearne and Trott.

D

5

THE TURN OF THE CENTURY
1898–1903

South Africa—George Lohmann—150 v. Yorkshire—The Inns of Court Regiment —The Season of 1900—Webbe and Stoddart—Called to the Bar—A Visit to Paris —The Theatre—New Zealand and Australia—Middlesex Champions

SOON AFTER I returned from the tour in the United States and Canada I received a letter from Lord Hawke asking me to form one of his team to South Africa. If I accepted it meant that I was not pursuing the law seriously, but when I looked round the Temple and saw the tremendous amount of brain-power which was massed there I came to the conclusion that I would in all likelihood never get into even the 'Fourth' or 'Fifth Eleven,' and as "The Baron" emphasized the educational value of such a tour, after some hesitation I accepted. He had got together a good side—seven amateurs (Lord Hawke, (Capt.), F. Mitchell, H. R. Bromley-Davenport, C. E. M. Wilson, F. W. Milligan, A. G. Archer, and myself) and five professionals (J. T. Tyldesley, A. E. Trott, W. R. Cuttell, J. H. Board, and S. Haigh)—and we went through the tour unbeaten, winning fifteen of the seventeen matches, several of the games being against odds. We met South Africa twice, at Johannesburg and Cape Town. At Johannesburg we won a terrific fight by 32 runs, and in the second innings I carried my bat through the innings for 132, "The Baron" giving me a signet-ring with these words inside:

Lord Hawke's XI *v.* South Africa, 1899
P.F.W., 132. From H.

We won the Cape Town match easily, after being behind on the first innings, Tyldesley playing a great innings of 112. Trott and Haigh bowled very finely on the matting wickets which were prevalent through South Africa in those days. South Africa were not so good a side as they are to-day, but they had three outstanding cricketers in Halliwell, Sinclair, and Llewellyn, each one of whom would have adorned any eleven, Halliwell being one of the greatest of wicket-keepers and Sinclair and Llewellyn fine all-rounders.

The travelling was often tiring. For example, we left Kimberley at nine o'clock on a Friday morning, and did not arrive at Bulawayo until four o'clock on Sunday afternoon; and the railways were not then so comfortable as they are now. The town was in its infancy. Two or three years earlier it had been the capital of a savage nation, where life depended on the temper of the King, Lobengula. The ground on which we played had been the camp of Lobengula's army, but there was a fairly good matting wicket and a large, if rather rough, outfield. We were driven into the Matopos, and from a kopje saw the famous World's View. It is here that Cecil Rhodes lies. I am writing of over fifty years ago, and to-day Bulawayo is a large and well-laid-out town, but even in its earliest beginnings it was possible to dine very well, as may be gathered from the menu of a dinner given to us on the last evening of our stay, at the Bulawayo Club:

Oysters
Clear Turtle Soup
Scotch Salmon   Shrimp Sauce
Cream of Chicken
Lamb Cutlets and Spinach
Roast Turkey and Ham
Pheasant   Grouse   Wild Duck
Fruit Jelly   Gipsy Trifle
Anchovy Titbits
Strawberry Cream Ices

Not a bad dinner for what was then almost the wilds of South Africa, and one which to-day would give most of us a severe attack of indigestion!

I had seen Lohmann play on many occasions, and I got to know him very well on this tour. Many an interesting conversation did I have with him during our long railway journeys. Because of lung trouble he had been forced to make his home in South Africa after the end of the 1896 season, and he acted as manager of the team. A tall, fair, good-looking man—he was of German origin—he loved cricket with tremendous enthusiasm, and, sensing a kindred spirit in me, used to tell me, on my prompting, of his own and others' cricket. He was a medium-paced bowler with perfect control of length and a most deceptive flight, who could turn the ball both ways, and who made use of both sides of the crease. He was also a dashing batsman, who did not worry much about runs unless they were needed, and a magnificent second slip, the equal of anyone in that position before or since. Some of his catches are historic. In an obituary notice of him in *Wisden* of 1902 S. H. Pardon, the famous editor, refers to a "miraculous" catch by him which had got rid of A. C. Bannerman, off Peel's bowling, in the Test Match at the Oval in 1888. "It was said at the time that Bannerman talked of nothing else for the rest of the day." Of Lohmann's bowling C. B. Fry wrote in the same issue of *Wisden*:

> He was what I call a very hostile bowler; he made one feel he was one's deadly enemy, and he used to put many batsmen off their strokes by his masterful and confident manner with the ball. He was by far the most difficult medium-paced bowler I ever played on a good wicket.

Lohmann died on December 1, 1901, at Matjesfontein, in Cape Colony, and over his grave is a handsome memorial erected by the Surrey County Cricket Club.

I returned very fit after four months in the glorious climate of South Africa, and on May 30, 1899, made 150 for Middlesex against Yorkshire at Lord's, which *Wisden* described as "emphatically the innings of his life." It was a perfect batsman's wicket, but one had to face Rhodes, Hirst, Haigh, Jackson, and Wainwright. I was 131, not out, at lunch on the second day, and in the first over after lunch, bowled by Jackson from the Pavilion end, I hit three fours—an off-drive, an on-drive, and a late cut (there were five balls to the over then)—and I remember each one of those strokes as if it were yesterday, and Jackson saying to me, "Look here, what the devil are you doing, Plummy?" Frank Mitchell remarked that "I played forward as hard as some men hit." This sounds as if I had a proud stomach, but, after all, it is over fifty years ago, and may not an old man recall with pride a big event in his cricketing life? When one is an active participant in the game a modest mind is essential, but when one has cast aside one's armour a certain latitude may perhaps be permitted.

In this game Albert Trott played a remarkable innings of 164, at one period scoring 137 out of 181 in an hour and a half. He made one tremendous drive which hit the pavilion rails so hard that Jackson picked it up at mid-on. At this period of his career Trott was a great all-round cricketer, and in this season scored 1175 runs and took 239 wickets. He was also a dead-sure catch at second slip. He gave his name to articles in a weekly paper, but he never wrote a single word of them. He was not a literary genius! On one occasion the newspaper in question stated that "the beer gave out before lunch on Whit Monday." So Trott was hauled before F. E. (later Sir Francis) Lacey, the Secretary of the M.C.C., when the following conversation is alleged to have taken place:

F.E.L.: I see you have been criticizing the Club.

TROTT: I never wrote it, sir.

F.E.L.: So I understand. As a matter of fact, what was written is not correct . . . and in any case you cannot be both a servant and a critic of the M.C.C.

TROTT: I know nothing about it, sir.

F.E.L.: Well, that's all right, but you must ask your friend, whoever he may be, to be more accurate in future.

Just comes of having a 'ghost'!

It was on July 31 this season that Trott hit M. A. Noble, the Australian, over the pavilion at Lord's when playing for the M.C.C. No one had ever before done this, and so far no one has equalled this tremendous drive, though F. T. Mann, for Middlesex against Yorkshire, only just failed to do so, as did Miller playing for the Dominions team against England in 1945.

Among some of the pleasantest matches I took part in outside first-class cricket were those at Burton Court against the Household Brigade and those during a week at Woolverstone Park, in Suffolk, at the Berners's, where the cricket was excellent and very keen, the hospitality unbounded, and where, as the house was full, we danced every night. I have always loved dancing, and 'the polished floor' is good for one's cricket, for it teaches rhythm, balance, and footwork and keeps one young. Did not J. T. Tyldesley say, "Get into the ballroom as often as you can"?

I stayed, too, at Linton Park, near Maidstone, with the Cornwallis's. The squire was one of the most charming men and greatest gentlemen it is possible to imagine. Here we had good and keen cricket and dancing in the evening. Linton is a lovely place: "The whole county is its garden."

I joined the Inns of Court—"The Devil's Own"—in January 1900. The South African War was on, and after the "Black Week," when we suffered reverses at Colenso and Magersfontein, nearly everybody in the Temple and Lincoln's Inn joined the Regiment, which was subsequently turned into an Officers' Training Corps by Lord Haldane, "the greatest Secretary of State for War England has ever had," as Field-Marshal Lord Haig called him on a page at the beginning of a volume of his Dispatches which he presented to him. The Regiment has a notable history, going back to the days of Queen Elizabeth, and when George III reviewed the Volunteers in Hyde Park, as the Inns of Court marched past he asked Erskine, the Lord Chancellor, "Who are these?" "They are all lawyers, sir," replied Erskine. "Lawyers, lawyers," said the King. "Call them the Devil's Own." And the name remains to this day. We used to drill during the luncheon interval, and, as the days lengthened, after four o'clock. Every one wore a black top-hat in the Temple and Lincoln's Inn, but we succeeded in sloping arms without knocking them off. There was some rather complicated drill, and "Rear Form" tested even the keenest brains. It was later abolished.

Lord Robert Cecil, K.C., now Lord Cecil of Chelwood, was one of us. He had a pronounced stoop, and the Adjutant, Captain B. A. T. Kerr-Pearse, coming on to parade, went for him:

THE ADJUTANT: Who is that man? As long as I am Adjutant of this Corps I will have no man standing on parade like that.

SERGEANT-MAJOR: Lord Robert Cecil, sir, a K.C., sir. Joined as an example, sir.

THE ADJUTANT: I don't care. I will have no man standing like that. Hold your head up.

SERGEANT-MAJOR: Please, sir, don't talk to him like that, sir—a K.C., sir, etc., etc.

—the Sergeant-Major was almost in tears by this time. When the parade was dismissed all Lord Robert said was: "I thought he was a little hard on me, didn't you?" Many years afterwards I met Captain Kerr-Pearse in the Weld Club at Perth, where he was Military Secretary to the Governor, and during a pleasant dinner I ventured, tactfully, to refer to the incident. He recalled it, and we had a good laugh. "What an ass I must have been!" he said. He was very far from that, and was an exceedingly smart officer —he was in the Rifle Brigade or the 60th Rifles, I forget which

—but perhaps, at the time, he did not quite realize that with so many 'learned friends' in the ranks we could not be treated like ordinary 'rookies.' He made us jump to it, however, which was right, and good for us.

At Easter we marched away some 800 or 900 strong, and spent four or five days at Winchester, where we were billeted in the College and dined in Hall, and there you might find a K.C. in the ranks and a briefless, or nearly so, barrister an officer. It was a great Corps, with a wonderful spirit, and when we escorted an imaginary convoy into Winchester we earned the approval of the German Military Attaché, who had come to have a look at us. On the way back from Winchester we made an attack with loaded rifles and fixed bayonets on the targets at Pirbright, ending up with a charge punctuated with yells which nearly equalled the famous "Rebel Yell" of the Southern troops in the North and South War in the United States. The markers came out of their dug-outs and, pointing to the targets, made complimentary remarks in comprehensive soldier language: "My G—, if you gentlemen can shoot like this after only short training I am b— well sorry for any enemy you ever meet." Result, lots of cigarettes and not a few half-crowns, and we returned to London thinking we were pretty good! My Company Commander was Captain Sankey (later Colonel Sir Stuart Sankey), who gave us a great dinner in the Mess, when champagne and punch flowed, and he eulogized us. "So long as we have men like you to officer England we have nothing to fear!"

I was promoted Lance-Corporal after a field day on Wimbledon Common, when I was the pivot of a long line which was extended at ten paces interval. I recall distinctly the Adjutant's shouting out, "Where the h— is that man going?" but I got my bearings right, and, anyhow, I was promoted "for gallantry on Wimbledon Common"! All of us were, of course, more or less educated men, and, I suppose, picked up things pretty quickly, but, though free and easy in a way, and not having the parade polish of the Brigade of Guards, we realized the value of discipline, and were keen and anxious to learn.

I was very fit when the season of 1900 began—I put it down to the many hours of drill with the Inns of Court—and started in great form, scoring 83 and 69 for the M.C.C. against Yorkshire, 114 for Middlesex v. Sussex, and 146 v. Lancashire, all at Lord's;

but towards the end of my innings against Lancashire I received a blow on a vein on my left shin from Mold, one of the great fast bowlers of the day, who used to make the ball 'fizz' off the pitch with rare venom. I was as lame as the proverbial dog, and was kept out of the field for three weeks, missing four Middlesex matches. I finished with an aggregate of 1727 runs and an average of 45·44 for 39 innings (one not out), and *Wisden* remarked that "Warner was quite one of the best bats of the season, his play being a model of consistency. . . . His remarkable skill in playing fast bowling was as conspicuous as ever."

Middlesex fared badly during the first half of the season, but, reinforced by C. M. Wells and J. Douglas, we lost only one match, against Yorkshire at Leeds in August, by 63 runs. In this game Wells obtained thirteen wickets for 68 runs, and Douglas made one of the finest catches I have ever seen in the deep field, holding a low skimming drive from Rhodes high up with his left hand while running sideways. Then in the second innings Tunnicliffe had me, at slip, off Hirst, before I had scored, with a catch so fine that as I walked away I heard Lord Hawke say, "Ten shillings for that one, John." These were the days of 'talent money,' as it was called, for a particularly good piece of batting, bowling, or fielding.

I played once for the West Indies, against Leicestershire at Leicester, and 'came off,' scoring 113, but Woodcock hit me on the same spot as Mold had done, and I was again out of action, but on this occasion for only a few days.

Two great Middlesex cricketers bade their farewell to first-class cricket at the end of the year—A. J. Webbe, our captain, and A. E. Stoddart. Webbe was the life and soul of Middlesex cricket, and was one of the nicest men I have ever met. I owe him more than I can ever say or repay, and his memory does not fade, nor ever will. Stoddart was a name to conjure with both in England and Australia, and was a great batsman, some of his finest innings being played on difficult wickets. He was also a great Rugby three-quarter back, and was Captain of both England and Blackheath. It was only in the proper sequence of things that both should retire in a blaze of glory, Stoddart scoring 221 against Somerset at Lord's[1] and Webbe 59, not out, on a sticky wicket

---

[1] This was J. T. Hearne's benefit, and, out of compliment to Hearne, Stoddart took his place in the side.

against Worcestershire at Worcester, an innings which saved us when defeat stared us in the face.

In the autumn of 1900 I was called to the Bar at the Inner Temple, and became by courtesy, if not in achievement, 'my learned friend.'

Although I have what I am told is an almost uncanny memory for cricket events and scores, yet to-day my own successes seem to me quite impersonal, and I think of them as if they were another's. Watching the game, I feel I cannot have made the runs *Wisden* credits me with, and, talking to P. Perrin, one of the Selectors, during a trial match, I once asked him, "Did I bat as well as this fellow?" "About twice as well," he replied, in his blunt and characteristic manner. Yet somehow I cannot imagine that I made a lot of runs in my time, and in looking up old scores I have honestly a completely detached attitude. I like not the man who has too much ego in his cosmos, but in writing one's own reminiscences it is obviously impossible to avoid the personal pronoun. Therefore, if I quote from the descriptions of cricket-matches in which I took part, the blame is not mine, but the writer's. As I have tried to explain, I feel as if he were commenting on another's play.

The season of 1901 was another good one for me, for I scored 1680 runs in 39 innings, with an average of 45.40, and in fifteen innings at Lord's was not once dismissed for a single-figure score. Writing in the *Daily Telegraph*, Captain Philip Trevor said this of an innings of 197, not out, which I played for Middlesex against Somerset at Lord's:

> He appeared to score with almost equal facility from all bowlers brought against him. At one time his cutting would be particularly noticeable, at another his placing on the on-side appeared the feature of his play, and then came a period during which onlookers had to wonder how a man of such comparatively slight physique could get so much power into his drives. Yesterday he got most of his runs by cuts, but he brought off some very big drives.

My mentor at Rugby who urged me to keep a modest mind would give me half a dozen or 1000 lines for writing like this; and this reminds me that the science master at Rugby once gave a boy 10,000 lines—it sounded like a life sentence—which were reduced next day, when the atmosphere was less heated, to 100!

It was in this season that I made my first appearance for the

Gentlemen against the Players at Lord's. Two very powerful sides took the field: G. MacGregor (Capt.), C. B. Fry, K. S. Ranjitsinhji, R. E. Foster, J. R. Mason, G. L. Jessop, A. O. Jones, D. L. A. Jephson, C. M. Wells, W. M. Bradley, and myself for the Gentlemen, and R. Abel (Capt.), H. Carpenter, J. T. Tyldesley, T. Hayward, L. C. Braund, W. Storer, W. H. Lockwood, G. H. Hirst, J. Gunn, A. E. Trott, and W. Rhodes for the Players, who won by 221 runs, the scores being 394 and 256 for six wickets, declared, to 245 and 184. Tyldesley (140) and Fry (126) batted splendidly. Fry and myself put on 105 runs for the Gentlemen in the first innings for the opening partnership, and I made 37 and 48.

I spent nearly three months that winter in Paris with a charming family who had a flat in the Rue Chezy, and got so far as almost to begin to think in French. I saw "the divine Sarah" in *Phèdre*, *La Dame aux Camélias*, and *L'Aiglon*, explored the Louvre and other picture-galleries, and Notre-Dame, and was often at Versailles, and once or twice at Fontainebleau; and the more I saw of those palaces the more I wondered why there was no King of France. The English were not exactly popular in France at the time of the South African War, and often I heard a not too friendly comment—"Un anglais," with a good bit of sneer in it. There were some monstrous cartoons of Queen Victoria, and our Generals were described as butchers!

Writing of Sarah Bernhardt, I remember asking James Agate, whom I knew fairly well, and in whose *Ego* volumes I occasionally figure, who was the most beautiful woman he had ever known, and he replied, "Sarah Bernhardt." I suggested that she was far from that, and then he gave a long discourse on what true beauty really meant, and waxed enthusiastic over her wonderful *voix d'or*, her grace, her charm, and her personality, and stuck to his point. Agate was a character, and, of course, a brilliant dramatic critic, but in some quarters he was thought to be far too harsh, and when I asked him if there was anything in this he replied, "I don't think so. I aim at the highest possible standard" —like the Sergeant-Major's "A thing should be done not only as well as possible, but even better than that, sir." Agate was a keen cricketer, with a memory for facts and figures, and I enjoyed his company and his vivid and lively conversation.

I am a great lover of the theatre, and am old enough to remember Henry Irving, Ellen Terry, Bancroft, Tree, Wyndham, Mary Moore, Alexander, Aynesworth, John Hare in *The Gay Lord Quex*, with the charming Irene Vanbrugh, Lewis Waller, Mrs Patrick Campbell, H. B. Irving, Evelyn Millard, and many another famous figure of the far past; and I agree with my friend G. J. V. ("Gerry") Weigall that the best day one can have is to make a big score in a big match at Lord's and thence to a play. "Cricket and the drama, sir, those are the two things." Here *was* a lovable character, and if he had unusual views on cricket, and was, perhaps, over-enthusiastic and not always logical, no one ever heard him say an unkind word of anyone. He considered Woolley the best of all batsmen, and when he was left out of the England Eleven at Lord's in 1934, and of the M.C.C. team to Australia in 1928–29, he never ceased calling to heaven to witness what an injustice had been done, brandishing his stick meanwhile, to the grave danger of those who had gathered around to listen to his dicta.

The summer of 1902 was very wet, and for various reasons I did not play as much as usual. On November 12 I started on my sixth tour abroad, to New Zealand and Australia with Lord Hawke's team, but, as I have already said, Lord Hawke was unable to lead the side, and he made me captain in his stead. We were, of course, known as his team, and wore his colours—light blue, dark blue, and yellow. We had a good side, eleven amateurs (P. F. Warner (Capt.), C. J. Burnup, F. L. Fane, T. L. Taylor, E. M. Dowson, B. J. T. Bosanquet, P. R. Johnson, J. Stanning, A. E. Leatham, and A. D. Whatman) and two professionals (S. Hargreave, of Warwickshire, and G. J. Thompson, of Northamptonshire). We travelled via New York and San Francisco, arriving at Auckland a week before Christmas. We played from Auckland to Invercargill and back again, in Sydney, Melbourne, and Adelaide, and then home by the Suez Canal. Altogether we covered over 30,000 miles by land and sea. In New Zealand we played eighteen matches, eleven against odds, and won them all. Cricket in New Zealand had not then attained its present excellence. The representative New Zealand team was a very fair side, with some particularly good bowlers—Frankish, Downes, Upham, and Callaway, an Australian, who had played for Australia against Stoddart's 1894–95 side—but they had no Donnelly or Sutcliffe. Charles Bannerman, who was a member of, and the best batsman in, David Gregory's team to England in

1878, umpired in many of our matches, and was impressed with the possibilities of Bosanquet's bowling, and prophesied that his off-breaking leg-break would one day win a Test Match for England. How true a prophet he was was soon to be proved. It was in New Zealand that I first saw the word 'googly' in print.

Reinforced by Albert Trott, who had been coaching at Napier, we proceeded to tackle the three great Australian states. We were beaten after good fights by Victoria and South Australia, but we held the powerful New South Wales team to a draw. At Sydney we met the great Victor Trumper, and Bosanquet clean bowled him with the first googly ever sent down on that famous ground, and even to this day the googly is often referred to as the 'bosey,' in honour of the inventor of what was then a new style of bowling. In two of my books, *Cricket across the Seas*,[1] and *My Cricketing Life*,[2] I have written fully of this delightful tour, which was destined to mark a big change in my cricketing career, for soon after it I was promoted to a position which I had never dreamed of attaining. How it came about I will tell in the next chapter.

The season of 1903 was a great one for Middlesex cricket. It was one of the wettest seasons, even worse than that of 1902, and in two matches, against Kent and against Essex, at Lord's, not a ball was bowled, while there was very little play in two or three other games. We won eight matches out of sixteen, drew seven, and lost only one, to Yorkshire at Leeds. Some critics called us a lucky side, but the fine form we showed against a strong Rest of England side[3] at the Oval gave a complete answer to those who had decried us. As *Wisden* put it:

> The batting strength was remarkable and would of course have been still more apparent in a normal summer. The bowling was abundant and well varied and from first to last the fielding was maintained at a pitch of quite exceptional smartness. Indeed, to their fine fielding more than to anything else the eleven owed their triumph.

Here is the batting order: P. F. Warner, L. J. Moon, G. W. Beldam, J. Douglas, B. J. T. Bosanquet, C. M. Wells, E. A. Beldam, G. MacGregor (Capt.), A. E. Trott, J. H. Hunt, and J. T. Hearne.

[1] Longmans, 1903.   [2] Hodder and Stoughton, 1921.
[3] In the order of batting: T. Hayward, E. G. Hayes, J. T. Tyldesley, E. Arnold, G. H. Hirst, K. S. Ranjitsinhji, L. C. Braund, J. Gunn, Lord Hawke (Capt.), W. Rhodes, and H. Strudwick.

6

CAPTAIN OF THE FIRST M.C.C.
TOURING TEAM
1903–5

The M.C.C.'s First Tour abroad—R. E. Foster—My Marriage—The "Westminster Gazette"—The Season of 1905

WHEN WE were in Melbourne a dinner was given in our honour, and during his speech Major B. J. Wardill, of the Melbourne C.C., suggested that I should bring out the next team to Australia. The Major was a big figure in Australian cricket, and had broached the idea privately in a letter some weeks before this. My reply was, "Ask the M.C.C. They are the proper body." The Melbourne C.C. then asked me to approach the M.C.C. on my return home, which I did as soon as I arrived back in England early in May. F. S. Jackson was asked if he would captain the side, but declined.

On Thursday, June 4, Middlesex were playing Yorkshire at Lord's. I had just got out, caught at the wicket, for 39, when W. H. Patterson, a member of the M.C.C. Committee, came up to the Middlesex dressing-room and said that the Committee wished to see me. I followed him into the Committee Room, feeling a bit nervous and wondering what I had done! I never dreamed that I was to be asked to be captain, but so it was. It is important to remember that I had never played for England in a Test Match, and it took me some days before I made up my mind to accept. I was urged to this decision by several members of the M.C.C. Committee, who stressed that, even if I had not hitherto played for England, they thought I would do the 'job' well, and were generous enough to add that they had regarded with favourable eyes my captaincy on tours abroad and of Middlesex whenever MacGregor, our regular captain, was unable to play. They also added that I could bat a bit! I think Lord Hawke had his say, and I fancy Australia, in private correspondence, had been generous enough to consider that I would be welcomed as a leader.

When the announcement was made there was a storm of criticism, but only a three-knot breeze compared to the whirl-wind of criticism which might be expected to-day! It was urged that there was only one man to captain England—A. C. MacLaren —but *The Times* expressed the opinion that "Mr MacLaren has no prescriptive right to captain England." It was all very embar-rassing, but, of course, I did not enter into it, and the M.C.C. stuck to me, as they always do to those to whom they have given their confidence.

We were without MacLaren, Ranji, Fry, and Jackson, all indispensable choices for an England Eleven of those days, but R. E. Foster and Bosanquet were fine, and young, cricketers, and with myself formed the three amateurs in the team. We did have, however, the best professionals in England—Lilley, Hirst, Hayward, Rhodes, Braund, J. T. Tyldesley, Strudwick, Arnold, A. E. Relf, Fielder, and Knight—their names read well!—and, as fate decreed, we were destined to 'recover the Ashes,' after many long years of waiting and disappointment. By the time we sailed on September 25 opinion had veered round in our favour, though one critic had written that "when they return beaten five-love they will be more than ever the laughing-stock of cricketing England."

We had a wonderful send-off from St Pancras, and there was so much cheering that a porter remarked, "There could not have been more noise if Jessop had hit six sixes in one over." On the day we left Fry wrote me a charming open letter in the *Daily Express*, and urged me to "persuade that Bosanquet of yours to practise, practise, practise those funny googlies of his," and added, like Charles Bannerman, that "that leg-break of his which breaks from the off might win a Test Match." What seers they both were!

We had a very pleasant voyage. Bishop Welldon was on board. We made friends with him, and I offered him the Chaplainship of the Forces, which he was graciously pleased to accept. I got to know him well, and once asked him, "Bishop, is it wrong to pray to beat the Australians?"

His answer was, "My dear Warner, anything which tends to the prestige of England is worth praying for."

"I shall pray night and morning and on the field," I replied.

The Bishop used to preach on Sundays, and invariably drew a big 'gate.' "You who are going out tó play cricket for England carry with you a great responsibility. Every word, every gesture, every action, of yours will be criticized. . . . Therefore you will realize that in your hands lies the honour, not only of cricketing England, but of the whole of England." Impressive words, which we did not, I hope, forget!

The story of that tour has often been told, and when at twenty minutes to six on the afternoon of March 3, 1904, at Sydney, Hirst clean bowled Cotter, and England had won by 157 runs, my feelings may be imagined. Here is the full score of this match:

AUSTRALIA v. ENGLAND

Played at Sydney, February 26, 27, and 28 and March 1, 2, and 3, 1904

Result: England won by 157 runs

ENGLAND

First Innings		Second Innings	
P. F. Warner (Capt.), b. Noble	0	not out	31
T. Hayward, c. McAlister, b. Trumble	18	l.b.w., b. Trumble	52
J. T. Tyldesley, c. Gregory, b. Noble	16	b. Cotter	5
R. E. Foster, c. McAlister, b. Noble	19	c. Noble, b. Hopkins	27
A. E. Knight, not out	70	c. McAlister, b. Cotter	9
L. C. Braund, c. Trumble, b. Noble	39	c. McLeod, b. Hopkins	19
G. H. Hirst, b. Noble	25	c. Kelly, b. McLeod	18
B. J. T. Bosanquet, b. Hopkins	12	c. Hill, b. McLeod	7
E. G. Arnold, l.b.w., b. Noble	0	st. Kelly, b. Noble	0
A. A. Lilley, c. Hopkins, b. Trumble	24	b. McLeod	6
W. Rhodes, st. Kelly, b. Noble	10	c. McAlister, b. Cotter	29
Byes 6, leg-byes 7, no-ball 1, wides 2	16	Leg-byes	7
Total	249	Total	210

AUSTRALIA

V. T. Trumper, b. Braund	7	l.b.w., b. Arnold	12
R. A. Duff, b. Arnold	47	b. Arnold	19
C. Hill, c. Braund, b. Arnold	33	st. Lilley, b. Bosanquet	26
P. A. McAlister, c. Arnold, b. Rhodes	2	b. Hirst	1
A. J. Hopkins, b. Braund	9	st. Lilley, b. Bosanquet	0
C. E. McLeod, b. Rhodes	18	c. Lilley, b. Bosanquet	6
J. J. Kelly, c. Foster, b. Arnold	5	c. Foster, b. Bosanquet	10
M. A. Noble (Capt.), not out	6	not out	53
S. E. Gregory, c. Foster, b. Rhodes	2	l.b.w., b. Bosanquet	0
H. Trumble, c. Lilley, b. Rhodes	0	st. Lilley, b. Bosanquet	0
A. Cotter, c. Tyldesley, b. Arnold	0	b. Hirst	34
Bye 1, wide 1	2	Byes	10
Total	131	Total	171

BOWLING ANALYSIS
AUSTRALIA

First Innings					Second Innings				
	O.	M.	R.	W.		O.	M.	R.	W.
Cotter	14	1	44	0	Cotter	18.3	3	41	3
Noble	41.1	10	100	7	Noble	19	8	40	1
Trumble	43	20	58	2	Trumble	28	10	49	1
Hopkins	8	3	22	1	Hopkins	14	5	31	2
McLeod	8	5	9	0	McLeod	20	5	42	3

ENGLAND

	O.	M.	R.	W.		O.	M.	R.	W.
Hirst	13	1	36	0	Hirst	12.5	2	32	2
Braund	11	2	27	2	Braund	16	3	24	0
Rhodes	11	3	33	4	Rhodes	11	7	12	0
Bosanquet	2	1	5	0	Bosanquet	15	1	51	6
Arnold	14.3	5	28	4	Arnold	12	3	42	2

Umpires: R. W. Crockett and P. Argall.

Of the five Test Matches two were won by the toss—the second game, at Melbourne, by England, and the fifth, also at Melbourne, by Australia. Four times during the tour I helped in an opening partnership of over a hundred, two of these occasions being with Hayward in Test Matches—at Melbourne, 122; at Adelaide, 148. Hayward and I also made 122 together against South Australia in the opening match of the tour, and Foster and I 117 in the last match, also against South Australia. We not only won the rubber, but defeated New South Wales and Victoria twice each, and drew one and won one game against South Australia. In the second match against Victoria we got them out for 15 in their second innings, but it was an impossible wicket after rain. Rhodes took five wickets for 6 runs and Arnold four wickets for 8 runs; and Victoria had McAlister, McLeod, Armstrong, H. Trott, Laver, and Saunders, all Test players, and Ransford, who was destined to be one.

On the voyage home several ships altered course and passed so near us that we could hear their cheers, and many a signal was made: "Well played! Warmest congratulations!" We were given a dinner by the M.C.C. at the Trocadero, with Lord Alverstone, the Lord Chief Justice and President of the M.C.C., in the chair. It was a bit of an ordeal for a briefless barrister to have to reply to the Lord Chief Justice. And here I would utter a word of warning: a victorious captain has a great many compliments paid him, and it is not always easy to keep one's head. I fear that I may have for a while failed to maintain an

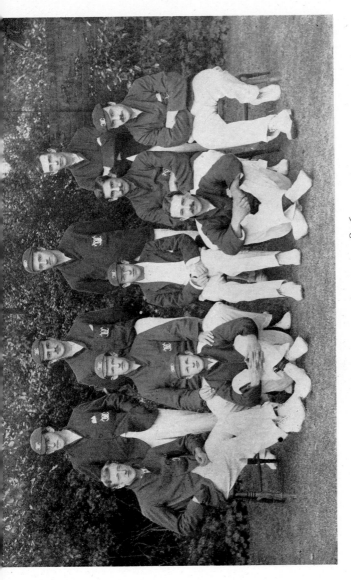

OXFORD ELEVEN, 1896

Left to right—Back row: F. H. E. Cunliffe, J. C. Hartley, P. S. Waddy, G. O. Smith. *Middle row:* H. K. Foster,
G. R. Bardswell, H. D. G. Leveson Gower (Capt.), G. J. Mordaunt, R. P. Lewis. *Front row:* P.F.W.,
C. C. Pilkington.

[*See pp.* 39–40.]

LORD HAWKE IN 1899

altogether modest mind, but a remark from Lord Hawke, "Is it quite the same Plum who left us last September?" set my feet, I hope, on the right track. Flattery like "Has England discovered a Great Leader?" as the *Daily News* put it, is intoxicating wine!

At the beginning of the 1904 season Foster and I were made members of the M.C.C. Committee, and I began a long connexion with what may be called the government of cricket, which has lasted to this day. Foster died in 1914. His is one of the great names in the science and art of batsmanship. He was a beautiful player to watch, with wrists of steel and the eye of an eagle, and, like the great West Indies batsmen Worrell, Weekes, and Walcott, he used a very light bat—"I can waggle it quicker," he said. His ever-famous innings of 287 against Australia at Sydney was one of the main causes of our success, and he was also a superb slip fielder. I never saw him miss a catch.

On June 7, 1904, I married Agnes Blyth, daughter of Henry Arthur Blyth, of Stansted, Essex, at the Parish Church of St Marylebone. Bishop Welldon gave the address, and Field-Marshal Lord Roberts signed the register, and presented my wife with a beautifully bound signed copy, with some nice words inside, of his *Forty-one Years in India*.[1] Lord Hawke was my best man, and there was a huge crowd, including some of the M.C.C. Australian team. The game at Lord's between the Gentlemen of England and I Zingari was interrupted for an hour or so to enable some of the players to come to the wedding.

My wife has always been fond of cricket, and is a really good judge of the game, with a flair for spotting true ability. Did not W. H. Patterson say, "If you cannot have Warner on the Selection Committee you should ask his wife"? She was a keen rider to hounds in her youth, but in recent years ill-health has been her untoward fate, and I have never met a braver woman. Fond of every sort of game, including bridge, at which she is no mean player, she had wonderfully good health until recent years; and she has borne this misfortune with remarkable courage and patience, and with an increasing cheerfulness and spirit, helped by the wireless and television, plus an occasional flutter on a horse, and by a most devoted maid, Doris Smith, who, incidentally, is one of the nicest women I have ever known.

[1] John Wisden and Co. gave me a set of magnificently bound volumes of the *Cricketer's Almanack* from 1864, the first year of publication, to 1904, and I now possess the whole series bound in similar fashion.

E

My mother-in-law had a house in Portland Place which was full of beautiful things, and there it was her pleasure to welcome her married daughters and sons-in-law. Her hospitality and kindness knew no bounds. She died in 1914, at the age of seventy-seven, leaving behind her the happiest of memories. She was never happier than when she had the house full. She had a wonderful butler, Walter Amner, one of the old type, who was with her for over forty years—a friend indeed to all the family.

Soon after we were married we bought a house—15 Tedworth Square, Chelsea—from Lady de Bathe (Mrs Langtry). Sir Henry Dickens, K.C., afterwards Common Serjeant of London, son of the great novelist, had lived there before Lady de Bathe, who changed the entrance to the house and made it quite beautiful inside, with a marble floor in the drawing-room and a lovely hall leading into the dining-room, which had very old oak panelling. When we bought the house the lease had forty-six years to run, to June 1950. I found Mrs Langtry very pleasant to deal with: "I hope you will never get out at cricket," and "I hope you will win all your bets on the turf." I was fortunate enough to let the house when I was in South Africa and Australia. Later we lived at Leeds, near Maidstone, and at Datchet, and eventually sold the house. It was a difficult house to run, for it meant having a good many servants.

In the garden of Tedworth Square I occasionally played cricket with my younger son, John, with his boy's bat and an india-rubber ball: he was then about eight. On one occasion he was bowling to me, and, when I off-drove him into a flower-bed, said, "I knew you were pretty good, Daddy, but I had no idea you were as good as this!"

I had a good season in 1904, and recall hitting a ball of John Gunn's on to the top of the pavilion at Trent Bridge with a bat given me by an Eton boy with whom I had been playing cricket on the lawn of a house at Bray. Never was there such a bat! I have not forgotten it, and happily it lasted a long time. I owe that boy, who was a relation of my wife's, a debt of gratitude. I reminded him of this only last summer at Lord's, during Eton v. Harrow, when I met him with his wife and one of the nicest-looking boys I have ever seen, with a merry twinkle in his eye, who had just gone to his father's old school.

Just about this time—to be exact, it was in the previous year—

J. A. Spender, the famous editor of the *Westminster Gazette*, asked me to write weekly cricket articles, and I continued to do so until the paper passed out, to the great regret of all, whatever their political views. It was a Liberal organ, was printed on a sort of sea-green-coloured paper—it was called "the Sea-green Incorruptible"—and was read by men and women of all parties and in every Chancellery in Europe. There F. C. G. (Sir Francis Carruthers Gould) drew his inimitable cartoons, and invariably in the best of taste.

I wrote weekly letters to the *Westminster Gazette* on my tours in Australia and South Africa, and no one made any fuss about it! To-day members of a touring team are not allowed to have any connexion with the Press—and rightly so—but in my time things were different. One was asked to write about *cricket*, and not to enter into any sort of personalities; and there was no band of cricket correspondents from England accompanying the team. *The Times* and Reuter each had a representative on the Australian tours in 1903-4 and 1911-12, and both were living in Australia.

It was at a luncheon party in Spender's flat in Sloane Street that my wife and I met Lloyd George, Winston Churchill, and McKenna, who were then leading lights in the Liberal Party. Winston Churchill was on his way to play polo at Hurlingham, and was in polo kit, and I remember his talking of his forthcoming book on his father's life. I sat next to Lady Dorothy Nevill, a charming old lady, and a prominent figure in London Society, who confided in me that she was a Tory, but "I like these Liberals. They are so clever." I suppose the Liberals of 1905 would be called Tories of the worst type by the Socialists of the present day, while the Tories of 1905 would regard the Conservatives of to-day as "d— Radicals," as King, the Oriel groundsman, called my Rugby and Oxford friend Ronald Walker, who was a Liberal: "How comes it, sir, that such a nice gentleman as Mr Walker is such a d— Radical?" How times change, and political views with them!

I think I batted as well as I ever did in 1905, with some reservations, for between scores of 204 for the M.C.C. against Sussex, 85 for the Gentlemen of England against the Australians, 60 for Middlesex against Nottinghamshire, and 49 and 86 against Sussex, I made no fewer than five ducks, once run out, including a pair of spectacles against Gloucestershire at Lord's. This pair followed immediately on the double century, which, if disappointing, is very good for one's character, for just as one is beginning, perhaps, to think too much of oneself, down comes a salutary reminder to keep a modest mind.

My score of 204 produced a text for Prebendary Carlile's sermon, "Warner's double century," and I went to hear him with a sister of mine. I had a real shock when he opened with "We are all thinking of Warner to-day," and he went on to say how the 204 set my feet on the right path, but he had also noted the 0 + 0, and so came a heavy fall from grace—sort of temptation by the devil! It was his custom to shake hands with every one as they came out of the church, and when he shook hands with me he said, "I seem to know your face," and I answered, "You have just been preaching about me, sir."

My highest innings for Middlesex was 166 against Lancashire at Lord's, on which *Wisden* was good enough to comment in very favourable terms, but perhaps my best innings was 48, out of a total of 87, on very false turf at Bradford, when Rhodes was on the warpath and David Hunter, the famous wicket-keeper, paid me a rare compliment: "Ah, Mr Warner, you play Wilfred better than anyone else." A few minutes later I was c. Hunter, b. Rhodes!

7

SOUTH AFRICA AGAIN
1905–6

We lose the Rubber—Splendid South African Bowling—The Season of 1906

THE South African team which visited England in 1904 under
the captaincy of F. Mitchell, the old Cambridge and Yorkshire cricketer, who had settled in South Africa, was a thoroughly
good side. They were not given Test Match status, but they
defeated in a very convincing manner the following England
Eleven at Lord's: MacGregor, Ranjitsinhji, Jessop, Rev. F. H.
Gillingham, J. Gunn, W. H. B. Evans, G. W. Beldam, Vine,
Wass, J. T. Hearne, and King. Their bowling, in the hands of
Kotze, Sinclair, Schwarz, and White was of high quality, and
they could bat down to No. 10. I do not think, however, that
their real strength was fully recognized, and when the M.C.C.
decided to send a side to South Africa during the winter of
1905–6 there was not the same meticulous care in the selections
as was given to the team to Australia two years previously. It
was not realized what strides the game had made in South Africa,
and it was in no sense a representative side, the idea being to get
together "a team which would give South Africa a good game."

As the sequel proved, we were in no sense their equals. I had
my misgivings about our strength, as had others, but there it was.
We were beaten by only one wicket in the first Test, at Johannesburg, in the best-fought match, everything considered, I have
ever taken part in, but we were decisively defeated in three Tests,
and won only one, the fourth, at Cape Town. The South Africans
had eleven good batsmen, none of them at that time great batsmen, for A. D. Nourse and G. A. Faulkner had not developed
their subsequent skill, but their last batsman was P. W. Sherwell,
who eighteen months later was to score an unforgettable century
at Lord's against the full strength of England. It is not difficult,
therefore, to imagine that they were by no means an easy side

to get out for a reasonable score. Sherwell was also a wicket-keeper of the first rank, and a most able captain, and the fielding was so good that hardly a catch was missed in the five Tests.

The same eleven played in every match, but it was their bowling which was the real cause of their success—Schwarz, Faulkner, Vogler, White, all googly bowlers, though Schwarz turned the ball only from the off, with, however, a pronounced leg-break action, and Sinclair, Nourse, and Snooke. On the matting wickets the googly bowlers were very difficult to play. Under these conditions, indeed, they not only kept a good length, but turned the ball quickly and often made it get up. If one was not in form the others were, and Sherwell seemed to have an uncanny instinct as to whose day it was. Who that took part in, or saw, that tremendous finish on the Wanderers ground on January 4, 1906, will ever forget it? It was a red-letter day in South African cricket, and emphasized their undoubted right to throw down the gauntlet to England and Australia.

F. L. Fane and J. N. Crawford, the wonderful Repton boy cricketer—he was but nineteen—were the only two with any success to cope with all this exceptionally fine bowling. I myself was a bitter failure after the first Test, and in ten innings scored only 89 runs, 51 of them in one innings. I have no excuses to make, except, perhaps, one. I was smitten with a debilitating internal trouble, and lost a great deal of weight, but *I freely admit that the googly bowlers, on the matting wickets, were my masters.*

At the end of the tour we all agreed that it would have taken the best eleven in England to defeat the South Africans on the Wanderers ground, where the matting was laid on the red sand. At Newlands, Cape Town, the matting was laid on grass, was slower, and did not favour the googly bowlers so much. We ventured to suggest that the South Africans would be better able to compete with England and Australia if grass wickets could be made all over South Africa, but the reply was:

Turf without matting is not possible, no matter what experiments are made. The unprotected wicket would not be worth playing on, with alternate showers and sunshine, and would crumble to dust in fine weather. Please, therefore, do not advocate its necessity for the salvation of South African cricket, otherwise, we are afraid, South African cricket must go without salvation.[1]

[1] I quote from an open letter to me in the *Cape Times* on our arrival at Cape Town.

To-day these then insuperable difficulties have been overcome, and all over South Africa grass wickets are the rule. Modern science seems able to do anything.

Our programme was a heavy one. Between December 2 and April 2 we played twenty-six matches, which meant sixty-six days' cricket, and travelled 6348 miles by railway, in addition to a voyage between Durban and East London. No fewer than twenty-two nights were spent in the train.

On the way to Kimberley, a few miles north of the Modder river, the train was brought almost to a standstill by a swarm of locusts which rained upon the line, and they were in evidence too at Kimberley. It was very hot, over ninety degrees in the shade, but the atmosphere was dry and bracing. There had been practically no rain in Kimberley for eight months, and we were told that no rain had fallen near the Orange river for four years, and that when it did fall the children were frightened and cried.

During the match at Pretoria my wife and I stayed with Sir Godfrey Lagden, renowned for his tactful and wise rule in Basutoland, and before breakfast we were picking nectarines and peaches off the trees. Another kind host and hostess were Sir Richard and Lady Solomon, who showed us the pen with which the Treaty of Vereeniging was signed. At Pretoria I first met Jack Lyttelton (afterwards Lord Cobham), who was A.D.C. to Lord Selborne, the Governor-General, and of whom I was to see much in later years, when he was President and Treasurer of the M.C.C. But all over South Africa it was the same, and we greatly enjoyed and appreciated the hospitality shown us. And what a glorious climate it is! South Africa, as Kipling wrote, is a jealous mistress, and if you have once known her you just have to return to her.

The season of 1906 in England was fine and warm, and was marked by the great all-round cricket of Hirst, Hayward's superb batting, and the fast bowling of Knox and Fielder. Hirst scored 2385 runs, and took 208 wickets, Hayward 3518 runs, with an average of 66·37, and his remarkable skill in playing fast bowling was never more emphasized than in Gentlemen *v.* Players at Lord's, when he faced a terrific onslaught by Knox and Brearley. Knox was tall and loosely built, and had an intimidating run up to the crease, bounding like a kangaroo, with his fair hair flying in the breeze. He combined a deadly off-break with the power of making the ball rise even on the best of wickets. Brearley was fast, with a short approach to the crease, and could make the ball go with his arm and also come back. He never gave in, and, indeed, would have liked to bowl from morning to night. Fielder was fast, if not so fast as Kortright, Kotze, of South Africa, or Knox, and some others, but he bowled a most difficult ball which went with his arm, and occasionally brought one back. Like Lockwood, he was especially effective at Lord's, and for the Players *v.* the Gentlemen this season took all ten wickets in the first innings. Of all the fast bowlers I played I disliked Fielder the most, for the reason that the way he made the ball move away from the bat worried me far more than Lockwood's or Richardson's off-break. I preferred the ball to turn into me, rather than go away.

I came back a bit shattered after my failure in South Africa, but I put on weight during the voyage home, and finished the season with an average of 41·90; but I did not approach the form of 1905, or of the years 1907 and 1908.

8

CRICKET IN KENT AND ELSEWHERE
1906–7

Caring House, Kent—An Historic Game at Bearsted—The South Africans in England—Third in the Averages—Nottinghamshire Champions

WE LET Tedworth Square, and in the autumn of 1906 went to live at Caring House, about three or four miles from Maidstone, and two from Bearsted, on the green of which such famous cricketers as Alfred Mynn ("the Lion of Kent"), Fuller Pilch, Edgar Willsher, and W. Martingell had played. Caring was a charming old house, with beautiful oak beams. There was a walled garden at the back, and one went through a door into a cherry and apple orchard which in the spring was a fairyland. In the orchard I made a most excellent practice wicket—and a tennis-court—and before the start of each season I used to collect many of my cricketing friends. It became a sort of 'training camp,' and what happy times we had, and how fit we were after all the strenuous exercise! When we were not eating or sleeping we were busy with cricket, tennis, golf on the links at Bearsted, and bridge!

We used to play two or three matches, on the Green, at Milgate Park, which was just opposite, at Leeds Castle, and, once, at Gore Court, when our opponents included in their eleven Barnes and Blythe—and the wicket was sticky! Many famous names are to be found in the score-book, and Bearsted recovered some of the glories of former days.

My Oriel friend W. H. Whitehead was a prominent personage in the village, as was F. R. Howlett, and between us we created considerable enthusiasm, and round the Green used to gather a goodly company of spectators. When, two years later—in 1909 —Captain J. M. de Robeck brought a side from H.M.S. *Dominion*, which was lying at Chatham, there was a dense circle round the Green. People came in cars, on bicycles, and on foot, and half the countryside seemed to be present. Sir John Jellicoe was one of my side, and when we were fielding, in backing up at mid-on he let a ball through his legs, and an irreverent sub-lieutenant shouted to his partner, "Come on; we've torpedoed the Admiral!" I give the score of this match, for it seems to me to be of historic interest, seeing that Jellicoe became Commander of the Grand Fleet from 1914 to 1916, and an Admiral of the Fleet; de Robeck C.-in-C. of the Mediterranean Fleet from 1919 to 1922, C.-in-C. of the Atlantic Fleet from 1922 to 1924, and an Admiral of the Fleet; Forbes C.-in-C. Home Fleet from 1938 to 1940, and an Admiral of the Fleet; and Syfret C.-in-C. Home Fleet from 1945 to 1948. The score, which I take from the *South-eastern Gazette* of May 11, 1909, is incomplete as regards the ranks and initials of *Dominion's* Eleven, but they were all officers. Seldom can so many distinguished sailors have played in the same match. Captain Morgan smote the bowlers all over the field, and the game ended five minutes before time, amid great excitement, the ship's band, who had delighted the crowd during the afternoon, playing us off the ground with a stirring march. The village was decorated, and altogether it was a memorable day.

CRICKET ON THE VILLAGE GREEN

BEARSTED v. H.M.S. "DOMINION"

Played at Bearsted, Saturday, May 8, 1909
Result: P. F. Warner's XI won by 53 runs

P. F. WARNER'S XI

F. L. Fane, st. Godfrey, b. Syfret	20
L. H. W. Troughton, c. and b. de Robeck	8
B. D. Bannon, st. Godfrey, b. Mornement	14
B. J. T. Bosanquet, c. Brooke, b. Syfret	12
P. F. Warner, c. Brooke, b. Elstob	73
Rear-Admiral Sir John Jellicoe, c. Bigg-Wither, b. Mornement	6
K. G. Macleod, b. Elstob	19
W. H. Whitehead, l.b.w., b. Mornement	7
A. Brownscombe, b. Dutton	45
G. C. Mercer, not out	20
J. J. Ellis, b. Brooke	1
Extras	23
Total	248

H.M.S. "DOMINION"

Captain de Robeck, b. Bosanquet	18
Lieutenant-Surgeon Jones, b. Bosanquet	7
Mornement, b. Macleod	1
Bigg-Wither, b. Bosanquet	6
Godfrey, c. Brownscombe, b. Macleod	0
Elstob, b. Bosanquet	13
Syfret, b. Bosanquet	4
Forbes, b. Bosanquet	0
Morgan, not out	84
Dutton, c. Brownscombe, b. Bosanquet	6
Brooke, b. Ellis	33
Extras	23
Total	195

I like to dwell on those happy days at Caring. The garden and the orchard were a delight, and my small daughter, Elizabeth, and my son, Esmond, were a great joy to us. My boy used to get very upset when we picked the flowers or pruned a tree; he used to think that we hurt them, and often exclaimed, "Oh, Daddy, don't do that; it hurts them."

And the dogs! I love dogs—I even like other people's dogs— and from my Oxford days until recently I have always had a dog—collies, spaniels, fox-terriers—and in "Jim" we had a wonderful fox-terrier. He was the most active and intelligent little fellow I have ever met, equalled only by "Judy" of a later date. Jim could catch any tennis-ball at any angle and however high, and we also taught him to play Rugger with a tennis-ball. He used to dodge his way through a defending line of three-quarter backs, one of whom was no less a personage than K. G. Macleod, the ever-famous Fettes, Cambridge, and Scottish three-quarter back, who was also a great sprinter, and an all-round cricketer who played for the Gentlemen at Lord's in 1909. There were shouts of "Tackle him, tackle him," but Jim generally got through, and, as Geoff Hopley said, "However keen the tackling, Jim never, never bites." In the end he fell in a hunting foray, and we put up a tablet to him on the wall facing the orchard:

TO

THE MEMORY OF

JIM

a faithful adherent of the house of Warner,
the greatest three-quarter back of his time,
and a superb slip, this tablet is erected in
his memory by those who knew and loved him

We had made him a pair of white shorts, with a hole in them for his tail and red ribbon for his legs, in honour of Macleod: the Fettesian-Lorrettonians so garb their sturdy legs. He also had a blue blazer with "England, 1907" on it, and his excitement when he was being prepared for the fray was terrific. If ever there was a human being of a dog it was Jim!

The South Africans were here in 1907, and though they did not win one of the three Test Matches—two were drawn—they ran us hard, and not since the days of the earlier Australian teams have any bowlers been more talked about than Vogler, Schwarz, Faulkner, and White. People used to flock to see them bowl. On the sticky wickets which were so prevalent that season they were very effective, but on hard, true wickets they were not, in proportion, so difficult; and it is generally conceded that the googly, if bowled to a length, is most dangerous when the turf is false or on matting wickets. This was a great South African team: they could all bat, Sherwell was a superb wicket-keeper, and the catching was remarkably safe, especially so in the deep field.

R. E. Foster was elected Captain of England in preference to C. B. Fry and G. L. Jessop, who were senior to him, and his slip fielding was as fine as ever. Fry's innings of 54 at Leeds, on a very difficult wicket, and of 129 at the Oval saw that great batsman at his greatest, and at Lord's Jessop scored 93 out of 145 in an hour and a quarter without a chance, and Braund a very good 104. The Leeds game was rather a desperate affair, but Blythe's magnificent bowling—he took fifteen wickets for 99 runs—pulled us through. In England's first innings Faulkner's analysis was:

O.	M.	R.	W.
11	4	17	6

and Lilley, our wicket-keeper, said, "It was like playing Briggs through the air and Richardson off the pitch." The South Africans, if they did not win the rubber, left a great name behind them.

The more I work at this book the more I dislike the personal pronoun, but if it is to be an accurate recording of my life I must perforce mention that I had a very successful season, scoring 1891 runs in 47 innings, with an average of 46·12, and coming out third in the averages, being only a decimal-point below C. B. Fry, who averaged 46·74 in 34 innings, and F. H. B. Champain, with 46·60 in 11 innings.

I had learned a great deal of how to bat on sticky wickets from watching closely the methods of such men as Fry, Tyldesley, and Ranjitsinhji. There were very few hard, true wickets during this summer, but on one of these I scored 149 against Surrey at the Oval, and this I believe to be the best innings I have ever played on a good wicket, for Knox, Lees, J. N. Crawford, and Rushby were the bowlers against us. J. Douglas and I put on 232 runs for the opening partnership in two hours and a half. At Taunton Douglas and I put on 110 runs in fifty minutes, of which I claimed 77. I hit Braund for *44 runs in three overs*, but in the next over he had me caught at short leg. At lunch he remarked to me, "I trapped you in the end," and I replied that I had enjoyed myself so much that I did not care how often he 'trapped' me if I could always have those three overs. Braund was a great all-round cricketer, and in his prime an indispensable choice for an England Eleven. Fortune has dealt hardly with him, but he has borne the loss of both legs with rare courage and cheerfulness. He is often at Lord's in a special place in his bath-chair, and I am glad to think that he is invariably very welcome, and that everything is done in order that he should watch the cricket in comfort. His chair is surrounded by his many old cricketing friends and colleagues, and he delights in recalling past days, as old men like to do.

Nottinghamshire were champions this year. They were splendidly captained by A. O. Jones, and Hallam and Wass, on the many sticky wickets, were a formidable pair. They did practically all the bowling, taking 298 wickets between them and sending down 1565 overs. Hallam has passed away, but Wass is still to be seen at Trent Bridge, and we fight again our old battles. On any wicket he was a fine bowler, but on a sticky one he was a bit of a terror, as he bowled a fast leg-break. We had many duels: more than once he clean bowled me in the first over or two, but now and then I got my own back, and we talk of, and laugh over, these things. Hallam was accuracy incarnate at medium-pace right-hand, and, that season, a great bowler.

9

THE NAVY AND THE ARMY

1908–11

A Great All-rounder—MacGregor—Cruise with the Home Fleet—I play for the Navy at Oporto—The School of Instruction at Chelsea—Cricket in Spain—Army Manœuvres

IN ON Tuesday, not out on Saturday. At the beginning of the season of 1908 I had an unusual experience at Lord's. I went in to bat on Tuesday evening at six o'clock, and was still not out on Saturday evening! What happened was this: I went in first for the M.C.C. against Yorkshire, and was 7, not out, at the drawing of stumps; next morning I carried my bat through the innings for 64, out of a total of 95. On the Thursday, for the M.C.C. against Kent, I was not out 4 when rain stopped further cricket until after lunch on Saturday, when I again carried my bat for 64, out of a total of 124. The M.C.C. gave me a couple of bats. This innings against Yorkshire and those of 58 for Gentlemen *v.* Players at Lord's in 1909 and 24 in the same match in 1913 were, I consider, the best innings I ever played on sticky wickets, the bowlers I met being Hirst, Rhodes, Haigh, Barnes, Tarrant, and Buckenham.

A fine all-round cricketer, F. A. Tarrant, a relation of George Tarrant, the famous fast bowler of the sixties, was now playing a great part in Middlesex cricket. He was born in Victoria, and when I was in Australia in 1903 I was informed that he was anxious to make his cricket career in England. Correspondence followed with the Middlesex authorities, with the result that Tarrant arrived here, and was duly qualified to play for Middlesex after he had completed the necessary two years' residence. In his first season (1907) he came right to the front, scoring 1552 runs, with an average of 32·33, and taking 183 wickets for 15·70 runs each, and in 1908 he averaged 41·04, with an aggregate of 1724 runs, and took 169 wickets for 16·68 each. He was almost the only Australian I have known who could not throw, but he was a very fine fielder at extra slip, a right-handed batsman, and a slow left-hand bowler of considerable variety, who could spin the ball. In proportion he was a better bowler on a good wicket than on a difficult one, for he sometimes tried to spin the ball too much when the turf was in his favour, and was apt, on occasion, to lose his length. As a batsman he was at first inclined to be over-cautious, but he soon adopted more forcing methods, and, though he always had a strong defence, became a magnificent cutter and hooker, who also used the on-drive. He was on the M.C.C. staff, was an automatic choice for the Players, and was good enough for any England Eleven of his time. But he was a sort of 'No Man's Land-er,' for the rules of qualification were then strict, perhaps too strict according to modern ideas, and he could not play for either England or Australia, though he was good enough for a World Eleven. I think the regulations were a bit too severe, for he had not played for Victoria in a first-class state match, though he had played for Victoria against Tasmania, which was not then in the Sheffield Shield competition. Any-way, he was a great cricketer who rendered magnificent service to Middlesex between the years 1907 and 1914.

I succeeded MacGregor in the captaincy of the Middlesex Eleven at the beginning of 1908. MacGregor was a most able captain, who believed in encouraging his men, and under whom it was a great pleasure to serve. He knew all there was to know about the tactics and strategy of the game, and was an uncanny judge of the exact state of a wicket. More than once I heard him say to J. T. Hearne or Trott, "The pitch is a bit slower than you think; you need to bowl a yard farther up"—and, indeed, he missed nothing. He was one of the greatest of wicket-keepers, very quiet in his methods—"sphinx-like in his calm fixity," as Ranjitsinhji wrote of him in the *Jubilee Book of Cricket*. His catch, standing up to Kortright, one of the fastest of bowlers, in the Gentlemen *v.* Players match at Lord's in 1893 will never be forgotten by those who saw it, for it was made within two or three inches of the ground; and in his Cambridge days his keep-ing to S. M. J. Woods, another fast bowler, was a constant theme of admiration. It was no easy task to follow such leaders as Webbe, Stoddart, and MacGregor, and it would have been folly on my part not to seek, as I invariably did, their counsel and advice.

Middlesex were a good side, with our full team, in 1908, the batting being "very fine indeed," as *Wisden* put it, but the bowling was not strong, for the great J. T. Hearne and Trott were past their best, though Hearne was to 'come again' with a vengeance in 1910 and 1911. My own figures were 1822 runs in 44 innings, with an average of 45·55, and for Middlesex I averaged 54·08, Bosanquet 50·84, and Tarrant 48·24.

At the end of February 1910 I was very fortunate indeed to be invited to go on the Spring Cruise with the Second Division of the Home Fleet, which comprised seven battleships, five cruisers, two light cruisers, and a repair ship. The battleships were of the pre-Dreadnought class, and the Fleet was commanded by Vice-Admiral Sir Berkeley Milne. I was the guest of Captain John Bush, R.M.L.I., in H.M.S. *Commonwealth* (Captain Ballard). We were away from England about five weeks, and visited Vigo and Arosa Bay. A match with Oporto was arranged, and I was one of those selected. I am the only civilian, so far as I know, who has had the honour of playing cricket for the Royal Navy, and I am very proud indeed of the distinction. I have the Naval Signal to this day. I was described as just Warner—no P. F. or A.B.—plain, unadulterated Warner. We won our match—I was top scorer with 41, run out—and the sailors thrived on the white port we drank at lunch, and at other times, and the British Club gave a dance in our honour.

I stayed a few days with the Rupert Coverleys in their charming house Casa de las Figueras (the "House of the Figs"), and rejoined the Fleet at Arosa Bay, driving from Pontevedra to Villagarcia. I sat on the box with my Jehu, who would have it that I was an "oficial inglés" and a "primer teniente" ("lieutenant") in the "escuadrón inglés," and, with my extremely limited knowledge of Spanish, I failed to make him understand that I was only a guest in the Fleet. He insisted on stopping at every wine-shop, and as we proceeded on our way I went up in rank, and finally finished up a "capitán de fragata." The peasants had the most delightful manners, and always took off their hats when I went in and left the wine-shops. They refused to let me pay for drinks, of which I had a few, and my Jehu a good many. He was very good to his horses, "Arragante" and "Ninon," and urged them on by name—never with a whip—saying, "Galopea," "Alto," "Trota," and they obeyed on the instant. He was obviously very proud of them. He was a character!

P.F.W. AS SECOND-LIEUTENANT IN THE 4TH WEST
KENT REGIMENT

Taken at Caring in 1909.

MY WIFE, ABOUT 1910
From a portrait by Maud Hall-Neal

There was a German training cruiser lying in Vigo, and we met several of her young officers. They looked—or nearly all of them —exactly like our own midshipmen, and the men were a fine-looking lot, several of the petty officers wearing imperials. There can be no doubt that the German Navy was splendidly officered and manned. I lunched and dined in several ships, and renewed acquaintance with Captain de Robeck and Captain Hickley, who had stayed with us in Trinidad when he was a midshipman in the eighties. De Robeck was Captain of H.M.S. *Dominion*, one of the battleships, and Hickley of H.M.S. *Cochrane*, a cruiser.

In spite of this health-giving cruise and a lot of practice at Caring I began the season of 1910 with a pair of spectacles against Kent at Lord's, clean bowled by Morfee in each innings, and telegrams of condolence and chaff rained on me from H.M.S. *Commonwealth*. Huish, the splendid Kent wicket-keeper, always insisted that they were two "beastly" good balls which defeated me, and I thoroughly agree with him, for one swung very late from leg, and the other, a good length outside the off stump, kept very low and sent my middle stump somersaulting—and Morfee was a fast bowler! He did not last long with Kent—he retired to the League—and a few years later, when I asked Humphreys, of Kent, who was the best bowler in England, he replied, "Your old friend Morfee!" Morfee had enormous hands, in which he seemed to wrap the ball, and I have seen a photograph of him with five cricket-balls in his hand. He was a bowler of great natural talents, but somehow never quite 'got there.'

In spite of my elimination by Morfee I had a better season in 1910, but my duodenum had been on the warpath, especially in 1909, when I suffered agonies of pain at various times. In 1910, however, I finished, according to *Wisden*,

in magnificent style, scoring in his last three matches at Lord's 101 not out against Essex, 145 not out against Hampshire, and 137 against Surrey. In these closing weeks of the season, Warner stood ahead of all other batsmen except Tyldesley.

The Hampshire match was finished just before luncheon on the third day. F. T. Mann and I were staying at the Great Central Hotel, and we were reading the evening papers, in which it was stated that Crippen was arriving at Euston that evening about 6.30. After some hesitation we decided to go and see him arrive,

F

but before doing so we removed the Free Forester ribbons which adorned our straw hats and substituted black ones. We were a little ashamed of ourselves—but go we did! Somehow we got on to the platform, but actually saw little, or nothing, of Crippen, who was hurried out of the train to a waiting police van and driven away. Writing that evening to my mother, I said, "What do you think Frank Mann and I did this afternoon? We went to see [and then, on the other side of the page, in block letters] Crippen arrive at Euston." Our letters crossed, and next day I received a letter from her saying, "I can't think what England is coming to. A lot of vulgar people going to see Crippen arrive!" Crippen was a murderer, and, I suppose, deserved his fate, but in Edward Marjoribanks's book *The Life of Sir Edward Marshall Hall*[1] Lord Birkenhead is quoted as having said: "He was, at least, a brave man, and a true lover." Marshall Hall, in his appreciation, wrote: "Of one thing both Irving and I felt convinced, that if Crippen had cared to throw over the companion who was eventually arrested with him, he might have made good his escape"; and "one witness in the case referred to Crippen as the nicest man she ever knew." Some months after the trial I was shown over Scotland Yard, and my guide, talking of the case, said much the same thing of Crippen, but his opinion of his wife was damning: "A very unpleasant person, sir." Crippen was hanged in November 1910. At the time I was doing a course of instruction for Territorial officers at Chelsea Barracks, and before we fell in for parade at eight o'clock one of the Drill Sergeants said to me, "Nasty morning to be hanged, sir. Very raw and cold, sir. Very sorry for Crippen, sir."

Early in 1908 I had been given a commission in the 4th Royal West Kent Regiment, and in the autumn of 1910 I was at Chelsea Barracks for a month. Every morning except Saturdays and Sundays we were on the square from eight to nine, and in the evening we had more drill and lectures.

Sergeant-Major J. H. Levy (now a Lieutenant-Colonel, a C.B.E., and a D.S.O.) was a remarkable man. He possessed a great knowledge of military history, was a born lecturer, and woe betide if you did not jump to it on parade! His motto was that a "thing should be done not only as well as possible, but even better than that, sir." So good a lecturer was he that had he been

[1] Gollancz, 1929.

a Don at Oxford or Cambridge he would have had not only a University but a European reputation. We used to drill with the Guardsmen, and the stern discipline and wonderful efficiency were very good for us. Chelsea, indeed, was a physical and mental tonic. Levy had been at one time attached to the War Office, and in that capacity went to France and Germany, where he saw something of the French Army and the Prussian Guard. I questioned him about the Prussian Guard, and he said, "Pretty good, sir, pretty good." "Not better than our Guardsmen?" "No, I wouldn't say that, sir, but if ever we meet them we shall meet foemen worthy of our steel."

There were about seventy to eighty Territorial officers at this course, all except one subalterns, and at the end of it we were examined in drill, both practical and on paper, in infantry training, etc., and we all managed to pass. My month there increased my interest in military history, and I read several books on the Franco-Prussian War, the Russo-Turkish War, and the North and South War in America; and I believe that reading military history is a help towards captaining a cricket team.

In February of 1911 I was at Algeciras for a few weeks with a sister of mine who had been ill, and I got up a side to play the Navy and the Army on what was the jumping-ground of a Spanish cavalry regiment. The wicket was matting, stretched on rather coarse grass, and just beyond mid-off was a sort of open ditch, into which our mid-off fell! Many people came over from Gibraltar to see the match, and the local newspaper described me, in Spanish, as "the champion." I made 32 not very good runs, but it was the sort of pitch that would have tested a Grace, a Hobbs, a Hammond, a Bradman, a Hutton, or a Compton. At the suggestion of Mr Harry Smith, who had a lovely house at Algeciras—the wistaria was a wonderful sight—and an aviary of birds, I called with him on the Governor of Algeciras in order to thank him for having lent us the ground, and he was very interested when I told him that my grandfather on my mother's side was a Spaniard. Admiral Jellicoe was at that time C.-in-C. of the Atlantic Fleet, with his flag in H.M.S. *Prince of Wales*, and I again raised an eleven, the match being played on the dock-yard ground. I made 1—yorked by Syfret, a slow left-hander, who had played at Bearsted, as already mentioned—and missed a catch, so I did not add to my reputation in Spain!

About this time I used to speak for Lord Roberts in his campaign for National Service and went to Charterhouse, where Brian Robertson,[1] son of the Field-Marshal, whom I was subsequently to meet at the War Office during the First World War, was at school. He was on our side, and we carried the day by, I think, 110 votes to 14. Later M. Falcon, the Harrow, Cambridge, and Norfolk cricketer, and I went to King's Lynn, where we faced a big crowd and again won. I recall vividly a speech by a soldier who, like some seer, inquired whether sufficient attention was being paid to the perils in the air and beneath the waters. One way and another I was pretty busy, and I do not recall being ever bored in my life.

Both in 1909 and 1910 I went on Army manœuvres, being attached to the Northamptonshire Regiment in the first instance and to the Worcesters in the second. In the former year we were camped at Cumnor, near Oxford, for a couple of days, so I called on the Dean of Oriel, the Rev. F. H. Hall, who in his day had coxed the Varsity Eight, and, as a result, he asked me to dine in the Common Room and to bring with me two or three of the officers in my battalion the next evening, when the finest of wines and a sumptuous dinner were our happy lot. Dons and soldiers got on wonderfully well, and it was pretty late in the evening before we separated.

The next day the final 'battle' of the manœuvres was fought. We rose at 2 A.M. from our tents, marched sixteen miles before breakfast, did another twelve miles afterwards, the last two of which I walked in my sleep alongside my Company Commander, Arthur Capel, a charming man and a fine officer, if ever there was one, who, like so many of the best, was destined to fall in the First World War. I never knew before what it was to be really tired! In 1910 we were near, or on, Salisbury Plain, which is really not quite a plain, and I heard a private remark, "They told us this was a plain. It seems to me more like the side of a house!"

---

[1] Later General Sir Brian Robertson, Commander-in-Chief and Military Governor, C.C.G.

10

ILLNESS AND RECOVERY

1911–14

The Australian Tour of 1911–12—The M.C.C.'s Great Side—A Memorable Match—The Triangular Tournament—The Seasons of 1913 and 1914

THE MINDS of the M.C.C. Committee were set on getting together a side good enough, with ordinary luck, to recover the Ashes from the Australians, who had defeated us in Australia in 1907–8 and in England in 1909. With this idea in view two Test Trials were played, one at Sheffield and one at Lord's, while Gentlemen *v.* Players at Lord's brought together the cream of our talent. Of the sixteen players eventually selected, ten were new choices, the younger generation being represented by F. R. Foster, Woolley, Mead, J. W. Hearne, and E. J. Smith, all of whom were under twenty-five years of age, while Hitch was only just twenty-five. Neither C. B. Fry, who was originally asked to be captain, nor R. H. Spooner was able to go, but with the exception of these two great batsmen we had just about our best side, though there were others who knocked loudly on the door, clamouring for admission.

It was a gloriously fine and warm summer, but the international situation was tense, and only a fortnight before we sailed the Adjutant of the 4th Royal West Kent Regiment informed me that it was doubtful if I should be given leave. However, the crisis passed for the moment—until 1914.

The records of that summer show that I made over 2000 runs for the first time in my life, but towards the end of it I was far from well, and in the final match of the season, Warwickshire *v.* England at the Oval, before going in to bat I had to fortify myself with a strong brandy and soda before the sun was over the yard-arm, and another equally strong one at lunch. I most emphatically do not recommend such a prescription in the ordinary way, but on this occasion it was a great tonic, for I scored

244 and hit thirty-five fours. I made a rather unsteady start, but
the second brandy and soda made me feel as strong as Sandow!
I was missed once, at slip, when 94.

There was a tremendous crowd at St Pancras to see us off to
Australia, Lord Harris and many members of the M.C.C. and
the general public, and there, too, on the platform, in full uni-
form, were Sergeant-Major Levy, Sergeant Grey, and Sergeant
Badger, of the School of Instruction at Chelsea. I introduced
them to Lord Harris, and as the train started they saluted us as
only Guardsmen can salute. My wife and my girl and boy, aged
six and four, came with me, and we had a delightful voyage.
Stopping at Colombo, we played a one-day match before a big
crowd clad almost entirely in white, with green umbrellas above
them to shade them from the fierce rays of the sun. We all wore
large pith helmets. We won easily, Barnes, Foster, and Woolley
being too much for our opponents on a sticky wicket, but Ceylon
were a very fair side with V. F. S. Crawford (Surrey), W. T.
Greswell (Somerset), and Dr G. Thornton (Middlesex) among
them. The two de Serams and Horan were good bowlers, and
Rozayro stumped Hobbs (45) very smartly. We ended the
evening with a big dinner, at which many of the local notabilities
were present, and so back to the Orient liner all the better for
having stretched our legs. The scores were: M.C.C. 213,
Ceylon 50.

When we arrived at Adelaide the weather was perfect, and we
enjoyed splendid practice in the Adelaide Oval, one of the best
and most beautiful grounds in the world, on the University
ground, and at St Peter's College, whose headmaster, the Rev.
H. Girdlestone, had stroked the Oxford crews of 1885 and 1886.
I had a memorable quarter of an hour on the Oval with Barnes,
Foster, and Douglas bowling their hardest and best. We won our
first match against South Australia, who were captained by the
famous Clem Hill—

> Sir Clement of the flashing blade,
> The pride and joy of Adelaide—

by an innings and 194 runs—M.C.C. 563, South Australia 141
and 228. We had some good bowlers to play—W. J. Whitty,
J. N. Crawford, and R. B. Rees (a googly bowler)—but Barnes,
Foster, and Douglas were always on top of their batsmen.

Foster (158), myself (151), and Gunn (106) were our successful batsmen.

This was the last time I was to put my pads on in Australia, for on the train to Melbourne I had a complete breakdown, and later, after reaching Sydney by ship, spent some six weeks in a nursing home. I was desperately ill, and I owe my life to the skill of Mr Blackburn (now Sir Charles Blackburn) and the most devoted nursing and care. And the kindness of every one! Lord Chelmsford, the Governor of New South Wales, and Mme Melba, who had an opera company in Australia that year, and who very kindly gave my wife a pass to all her operas, were constant visitors, as well as Clem Hill and other members of the Australian team and my own side—and many another, including Arthur Allen, an uncle of G. O. Allen. Letters and telegrams arrived from every part of the world, and all this kindness helped me enormously.

I appointed Douglas my successor as captain, and if, perhaps, he did not have the side in hand by the time of the first Test Match—he made the mistake of not giving the new ball to Barnes —subsequently he did splendidly. Douglas was a man of character. He possessed courage and determination in a marked degree, and was always the essence of fitness. He inspired the side with remarkable zeal and strenuous endeavour, and thoroughly deserved the great triumph which was to be his, England winning the rubber by four matches to one, after losing the first Test, at Sydney. Hobbs and Rhodes were a great opening pair, with Gunn, Hearne, Woolley, and Foster to follow, and in Barnes and Foster we had, in Australian opinion, "the best pair of bowlers England has ever sent to Australia." Douglas gave them strong support, and between them they took 81 wickets in the Test Matches—Barnes 34, Foster 32, and Douglas 15. The attack was almost entirely concentrated in their hands. But have not all these things already been told in *Wisden* of 1913 and in other directions? I will say no more, except to give the score of the fourth Test Match, at Melbourne, that by which the Ashes were regained for England:

AUSTRALIA v. ENGLAND

Played at Melbourne, February 9, 10, 12, and 13, 1912
Result: England won by an innings and 225 runs

AUSTRALIA

First Innings		Second Innings	
C. Kelleway, c. Hearne, b. Woolley..	29	c. Smith, b. Barnes.................	5
H. V. Hordern, b. Barnes...........	19	c. Foster, b. Douglas...............	5
W. Bardsley, b. Foster.............	0	b. Foster..........................	3
V. Trumper, b. Foster..............	17	b. Barnes..........................	28
C. Hill (Capt.), c. Hearne, b. Barnes..	22	b. Douglas........................	11
W. W. Armstrong, b. Barnes.......	7	b. Douglas........................	11
R. B. Minnett, c. Rhodes, b. Foster ..	56	b. Douglas........................	7
V. Ransford, c. Rhodes, b. Foster....	4	not out...........................	29
T. J. Matthews, c. Gunn, b. Barnes...	3	b. Foster..........................	10
A. Cotter, b. Barnes................	15	c. Mead, b. Foster.................	8
H. Carter, not out.................	6	c. Hearne, b. Douglas..............	38
Bye 1, leg-byes 5, no-balls 7...	13	Byes 9, leg-byes 2, no-balls 7...	18
Total................	191	Total................	173

ENGLAND

J. B. Hobbs, c. Carter, b. Hordern...................	178
W. Rhodes, c. Carter, b. Minnett...................	179
G. Gunn, c. Hill, b. Armstrong...................	75
J. W. Hearne, c. Armstrong, b. Minnett..............	0
F. R. Foster, c. Hordern, b. Armstrong..............	50
J. W. H. T. Douglas (Capt.), c. Bardsley, b. Armstrong.	0
F. E. Woolley, c. Kelleway, b. Minnett..............	56
C. P. Mead, b. Hordern...........................	21
J. Vine, not out...................................	4
E. J. Smith, c. Matthews, b. Kelleway................	7
S. F. Barnes, c. Hill, b. Hordern.....................	0
Byes 2, leg-byes 4, no-balls 9, wides 4..........	19
Total..............................	589

BOWLING ANALYSIS

ENGLAND

First Innings	O.	M.	R.	W.	Second Innings	O.	M.	R.	W.
Foster...............	22	2	77	4	Foster..............	19	3	38	3
Barnes...............	29.1	4	74	5	Barnes..............	20	6	47	2
Woolley.............	11	3	22	1	Woolley............	2	0	7	0
Rhodes.............	2	1	1	0					
Hearne.............	1	0	4	0	Hearne.............	3	0	17	0
					Douglas.............	17.5	6	46	5

AUSTRALIA

	O.	M.	R.	W.
Cotter............................	37	5	125	0
Kelleway..........................	26	2	80	1
Armstrong.........................	36	12	93	3
Matthews..........................	22	1	68	0
Hordern...........................	47.5	5	137	3
Minnett...........................	20	5	59	3
Ransford..........................	2	1	8	0

Umpires: R. W. Crockett and W. Young.

On Christmas morning I was well enough to be carried on board
ship for the voyage to Melbourne, and that evening Mme Melba's
opera company sang many of the Christmas hymns and carols,
and at midnight they went on to the boat deck, the ship reduced
speed, and John McCormack sang *Hark! the Herald Angels sing*.
I was below in my cabin, but was told that it was moving to
a degree.

On my return to England I was told that I might attempt first-
class cricket, and I began in great form, scoring three hundreds,
all at Lord's, within ten days, but it was too great an effort, and
by the end of June I was in bed, and stayed there, on and off, until
October. One of those centuries (126) I may, perhaps, be allowed
to recall, on May 23, for the M.C.C. Australia team against the
Rest of England. The large crowd gave me a tremendous welcome, and Tom Pawley, our splendidly capable manager, wept
with joy on my return to the dressing-room. I see him now with
the tears running down his cheeks as he held out both hands to
me. I was completely overcome. We won by an innings and
10 runs—509 (Woolley, a grand 101) to 237 and 262 by the Rest,
for whom Jessop played remarkable innings of 88 and 55, scoring
the last *62 of his 88 in half an hour*. In his second innings Hitch
caught him left-handed off his own bowling from a terrific
drive.

Two strokes in that game stand out in my memory—one
by Woolley, who flicked a not too short ball of Brearley's into
the topmost row of seats in the Mound Stand, and the other by
Jessop, who 'mowed' an inswinger from Foster, who was bowling at the Pavilion end, also into the Mound Stand. The match
was played throughout on a perfect wicket, and it was no mean
feat to defeat so easily a team composed of Fry, Spooner, Brearley,
A. P. Day, D. W. Carr, Mead, Strudwick, Humphreys, Dean,
and Thompson, besides Jessop. In the pavilion Lord Harris
remarked to R. D. Walker, "Russie, I believe this M.C.C. side
is just about the best team I have ever seen."

Looking back now, without any sort of prejudice, I believe
that he was right, and I rank it with the great England Eleven of
1902, Chapman's M.C.C. Australia side of 1928, and Jardine's of
1932. At all events, I would be prepared to back them against
any team of my experience, chiefly for the reasons that in Barnes
and Foster we had an almost incomparable pair of bowlers, and

that Hobbs—there has never been a greater batsman on all wickets—was in his finest form.

The season of 1912 was that of the Triangular Tournament between England, Australia, and South Africa, but, owing to the bad weather this summer, to the fact that the South African team had not yet reached the standards of the Australians or of this country, and to the unrepresentative character of the Australian team the matches did not arouse the interest anticipated.

The Australians, without Hill, Trumper, Armstrong, Cotter, Ransford, and Hordern, were heavily handicapped, but Bardsley and Macartney batted superbly, scoring 2441 runs and 2207 runs respectively, and Whitty and Hazlitt bowled well. Emery was potentially a great googly bowler, with an occasional very fast ball. On his day he was as difficult as any bowler of his style, but he was very uncertain. The fielding was brilliant, except for an occasional off day. *Wisden* wrote: "Macartney, Matthews, Bardsley, and Hazlitt were superb, and Gregory . . . was still very quick."

South Africa were no match for either England or Australia. Pegler and Faulkner did practically all the bowling, and between them sent down 2302 overs, Pegler taking 189 wickets for 15·26 each, and Faulkner 163 for 15·42 each. Pegler, a tall, finely built man with a high delivery, relied mainly on a leg-break, and varied his pace cleverly. Faulkner we knew of old, for he had made his great reputation here in 1907. This great all-round cricketer started well as a batsman, but he was far from fit, and the amount of bowling he had to do affected his run-getting. Nourse and Taylor were the best batsmen, the latter foreshadowing his subsequent greatness. As a team they were unequal, "their batting," says *Wisden*, "lacked class, and their bowling variety of pace."

England, ably led by C. B. Fry, were far the best eleven, and on the sticky wickets Barnes, Foster, Dean, and Woolley were very formidable. If we did lack one more reliable batsman, Hobbs and Rhodes were as great an opening pair, remembering the many sticky wickets, as they had been in Australia, Hobbs being magnificent. A curious feature was that Spooner could get no runs at all against the Australians, and yet made scores of 119 at Lord's, 21 and 82 at Leeds, and 26 at the Oval against the South Africans.

I do not believe that a Triangular Tournament will be repeated in future, for the two Dominion teams 'ran into each other,' so to speak.

I was invalided out of the Territorial Army some months later, but during the winter of 1912–13, when I had to go very slow, I went in for two subjects—organization and military law —in 'Q,' and managed to pass, though I only just scraped through military law. I fear I had overrated the 'learned friend' part of my make-up, but if ever there is a subject fuller of pitfalls for the unwary than military law as it then stood I have not come across it! The examination was held in one of the buildings in Exhibition Road, and those who wished to do so were allowed to smoke. The officer next to me lit a cigar with the most pungent fumes, and I came out with a splitting headache.

I was well enough to play a fair amount of cricket in 1913, but I was warned against over-fatigue. Against Warwickshire at Lord's I scored exactly 100, the last 78 in forty minutes, A. J. Webbe saying to me, "I shan't have to go and watch Jessop now!" However, I feel that after my illness in Australia, except on rare occasions, I was never the same batsman, but I still always enjoyed playing, and the exercise, so long as I did not overdo it, helped to keep me comparatively fit, if only for the time being, as it turned out; while the companionship of cricketers and the atmosphere of Lord's and the great grounds were a good tonic.

Looking through some old photographs and scores, I find the names of many who came to Caring, and among them one of the youngest, G. W. V. Hopley—"Geoff"—used to spend his Easter holidays and other vacations with us. He was at Harrow, of which he was an Exhibitioner, and eventually won a scholarship to Trinity, Cambridge. He was almost like a son to us, and was one of the nicest boys I have ever met. A great future lay before him, but he died of wounds in May 1915 while serving with the Grenadier Guards. I had known his people since my first visit to South Africa: his father was Mr Justice Hopley. His elder brother, John, the famous heavyweight boxer, won the D.S.O. in the 1914–18 War, also with the Grenadiers. He, like Geoff, was in the Cambridge Eleven, and John gained, too, a Rugger Blue. I am told he had a right like a pile-driver, as Raymond Glendenning would put it. The spring of 1914 saw the last of the "training camps."

In 1914 occurred the Centenary of the present Lord's—we go back to 1787, the M.C.C.'s first ground having been where Dorset Square now stands—and to celebrate the event a match was arranged between the M.C.C. team which, under John Douglas, had been so successful in South Africa during the winter and the Rest of England. Great was my delight when a letter arrived from Lord Hawke, President of the M.C.C., saying that he had had a talk with Lord Harris, the Chairman of the M.C.C. Selection Committee, and Lord Lichfield, both ex-Presidents and Trustees of the M.C.C., inviting me, *if chosen*—mark the words —to accept the captaincy, and suggesting, if I accepted, certain names to act with me as a Selection Committee for that particular match. Lord Lichfield also spoke most kindly to me in the pavilion at Lord's, saying that I had been so mixed up with the M.C.C. that he hoped I would accept the invitation. Imagine my surprise and disappointment when my name was not even among those who were chosen to play! But these things are part and parcel of the rough and tumble of life, and one must just grin and bear them with good humour and ready acquiescence.

What no doubt happened was that when the full M.C.C. Committee discussed the matter C. B. Fry received the larger number of votes, but most people will agree, I fancy, that unless it had been definitely decided that I should be captain Lord Hawke's letter should never have been written. He was, I know, considerably upset about the whole affair, and so was Lord Lichfield. I was in good company, however, for F. R. Foster was most unaccountably left out of the Rest of England Eleven. As it happened, Fry led his side to an innings victory, but the key man, so far as the bowling went, Barnes, was unable to play for the M.C.C. team because of lameness, and, further, the weather favoured the victors.

There was, of course, no feeling of any sort between Fry and myself. We have been lifelong friends ever since I played against him at Rugby in 1891 for W. G. Michell's Eleven against the Old Reptonians, when he drove our left-handed bowler—and a good one, too—the Rev. R. M. Samson, more than once to the screen, and he was an able captain, with a long record of success. Indeed, I doubt whether any captain has ever been more consistently successful. I enjoyed immensely playing under him, for he was always most encouraging and got the best out of his team.

Middlesex had a truly brilliant season, winning eleven out of twenty matches, drawing seven, and losing only two, but Surrey, with fifteen wins and two defeats, beat us to the post. The War, of course, which broke out on August 4, upset everything.

II

THE FIRST WORLD WAR
1914–18

*The Inns of Court—The War Office—Six Months at the Foreign Office—John
Buchan—Cricket in War-time*

A COUPLE of days after war broke out I went down to the
Headquarters of the Inns of Court in Lincoln's Inn, and
shortly afterwards was given command of the "Waiting List,"
as it was called. Men kept flocking in above the authorized
establishment, which at the time was four companies of infantry—
120 officers, N.C.O.'s, and men to a company—and a squadron
of cavalry, and, with the consent of the War Office, were allowed
to join the Waiting List.[1]

Cricketers, footballers, both Rugby and Association, rowing
men, hunting men, hockey- and lawn-tennis-players, crowded
the Orderly Room and its precincts, and Commanding Officers
cried aloud to the Inns of Court. At one time I was in command
of some 1400 men, and they were, of course, divided into companies and squads. We did a lot of drill, and many an afternoon
was spent in Regent's Park, and many an attack did we make on
the Mappin Terraces, where bears, ibex, goats, etc., were gar-
risoned. Few uniforms were at that time available, and not
enough rifles, but we borrowed everywhere, and ready assistance
was willingly given. We were very fortunate in our Commanding Officer, Colonel F. H. Errington, C.B., in our Adjutant,
Major J. Rainsford-Hannay,[2] and in the various Company
Commanders. They were busy and extremely strenuous days,
and my 'G.H.Q.' was in the chambers of the present Lord
Swinton.

I had been invalided out of the Territorial Army in 1912, but
I passed the doctor and was given a commission in the Inns of
Court, dating back to August 12, 1914, and on January 23, 1915,

---

[1] Later the establishment was greatly increased.
[2] Later Lieutenant-Colonel Rainsford-Hannay, D.S.O.

was sent to the War Office to M.T.3, shortly afterwards changed to S.D.3, with the rank of Captain attached General Staff. Our work was to find officers for Woolwich, Sandhurst, the Special Reserve, and the new Kitchener Armies. We also had to do with the O.T.C., both senior and junior. My particular work was to get officers for the infantry of the Special Reserve, and I must have interviewed literally hundreds of candidates; at any rate, 5988 went through my hands by the end of December 1915. The War Office was a hive of industry, and the work was very interesting. It was like a huge club, and everybody helped everybody else. There were also many from our Dominions and Colonies seeking commissions, and these were always sent to me. As our G.S.O.2, Major J. G. Dooner, remarked, "One had only to have bowled out Plum in some outlandish place to get a commission on one's head!"

At page 45 of General Ian Hay Beith's book *Arms and the Men*[1] are some very interesting remarks on "a perpetual struggle between the War Office and the County Territorial Associations," and many hold the opinion that it was a mistake not to use the Associations' well-established organizations to raise the officers and men who were needed, "for in that case the expansion of our military forces would have been far more expeditious."[2] Kitchener was, of course, a magic name, and "Kitchener's Army" achieved instant popularity, but both Kitchener's Armies and the Territorials suffered as a result. The great Lord Haldane's scheme was surely the one to build on, but Lord Kitchener "cherished ancient prejudice against 'Saturday-afternoon Soldiers.'" Territorials can point with considerable pride to their record in the two World Wars.

In March 1916 I was operated on, in King Edward VII Hospital for Officers, at 9 Grosvenor Gardens, by Sir William Arbuthnot Lane, the well-known surgeon. Sister Agnes Keyser, the C.-in-C. of the hospital, was a remarkable woman: her devotion to her patients was wonderful, and her kindness and sympathy were beyond words. She worked incessantly from 7 A.M. to 11 P.M., and later if necessary, and I don't believe she had a hat on twice during the War. She was a bit of a martinet, and even the War Office were afraid of her!

[1] H.M.S.O., 1950.
[2] Mr Winston Churchill, in *The World Crisis* (Eyre and Spottiswoode), expresses a similar view.

I was given six months' sick leave, at the end of which the Medical Board decided that I was not strong enough to return to the War Office, and I was told to try to find a 'light-duty' job. Providence led me to Colonel John Buchan, under whom I served in the Department of Information at the Foreign Office for six months, when I was again very ill. On March 21, 1918, appeared a notice in the *Gazette*: "Captain P. F. Warner, Inns of Court O.T.C., resigns his commission on account of ill-health and is granted the honorary rank of Captain."

I left the Foreign Office with the greatest regret. John Buchan, (afterwards Lord Tweedsmuir and Governor-General of Canada from 1935 until his death in 1940: in parts of Canada his memory has become a legend) seemed to me to possess all the virtues and great charm. He was a Scholar and Fellow of Brasenose, took a first in Classical Moderations and 'Greats,' and won almost every prize Oxford has to offer. He was also President of the Union. A more delightful personality it would be difficult to imagine. He was a fluent talker, but he brought every one else into the conversation, and to lunch or dine with him was a rare pleasure. He took me to France with him in 1917 for a few days, and at dinner at Intelligence H.Q. he remarked, "This war is not Armageddon, but Armageddes, for there are Eric and Auckland Geddes, Miss Geddes, and, don't forget, Jenny Geddes, who threw a stool in church at Bishop Lindsay!"

Driving along the Albert–Bapaume Road one day, he asked me who was the German General opposite to us, and when I confessed my ignorance he replied, "Rupprecht of Bavaria, who would be King of England to-day if the Stuart succession had remained. I was President of the Jacobite Club at Oxford, and every March we had a great dinner, and at the end of it we used to send him a telegram—'The King across the water.' He is a very good soldier and a good fellow, but I can't think why he does not shell this road." I ventured to express the hope that he would defer that pleasure! I had seen Rupprecht at Lord's in 1913: he came with Colonel Haig, Nigel Haig's father. He was a very smart and nice-looking man, with an attractive manner. John Buchan, like another famous Oxonian, F. E. Smith, Lord Birkenhead, died too young, to the detriment of English public life.

The Foreign Office was of absorbing interest. One saw many

MY WIFE WITH ELIZABETH AND ESMOND

ELIZABETH AND ESMOND AT CARING IN 1911

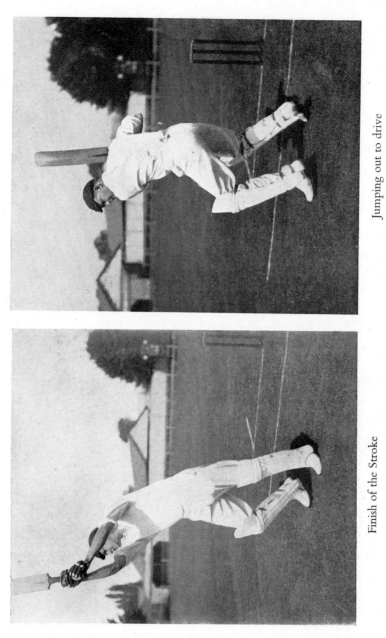

Finish of the Stroke

Jumping out to drive

P.F.W. AT THE WICKET

secret telegrams, and we had, on occasion, dealings with M.I.5. The phraseology fascinated me:

The Secretary of State for Foreign Affairs presents his compliments to the French Ambassador. . . .

His Majesty's Government would view with something akin to consternation the suggestion contained in your Excellency's dispatch of such and such a date . . .

I am Your Excellency's most humble and obedient servant,

A. J. BALFOUR[1]

It was said in those days that the Foreign Office were always most polite when they were most determined on their point of view. At one time our blockade of Holland was causing a good deal of trouble, and a representative of the Netherlands Government called at the Foreign Office, and in the course of conversation mentioned something about cricket. The official who was talking to him said, "We've got a cricketer here," and I was sent for. Blockade was not one of my subjects, and I talked cricket to our visitor for a few minutes, and then took my leave. I had mentioned the name of C. J. Posthuma, a left-handed bowler who had played in this country, and of whom W. G. had a high opinion, and next day a message came to the room in which I worked, saying, "Tell Warner, will you, that he has eased the situation!" I learned a great deal at the Foreign Office, including how to write a civil letter and how to speak on the telephone to the many people who rang up. To John Buchan and the other able and interesting men I met I owe much.

Towards the end of my time at the Foreign Office I was put in charge of the many American, Dominion, Colonial, and neutral correspondents who were in this country on visits to Dover, prisoner-of-war camps, and Aldershot. "I understand, Warner, that you have taken many cricket teams abroad, and I am now going to ask you to look after these people." There were generally some thirty or forty of them, and at Dover I sat next to Admiral Bacon[2] at lunch. These visits were, of course, full of interest, and at the end of them I was sent for and approval bestowed on my leadership. Apparently on previous visits things were rather extravagantly done, champagne and cigars being

---

[1] This is not, of course, an actual quotation, but merely indicates the phraseology used.
[2] Later Admiral Sir Reginald Bacon, K.C.B., K.C.V.O., D.S.O.

G

freely given. It never occurred to me to be so generous with the Government's money, and for this I was commended.

I had an exciting experience off Dover, when a German submarine tried to torpedo a convoy which was proceeding to France. I was in one of our destroyers which was guarding the convoy when there was a hoarse cry, "Submarine on the port bow!" The convoy scattered, and the destroyers increased speed and made for the spot, off the Varne light, near which the submarine had launched the torpedo, which missed the stern of one of the ships in the convoy by about forty yards. Within five minutes every destroyer in or near Dover was hunting the German, but whether they ever got her I never heard. She must have had a bad time, with depth-charges being dropped all over the place, but she probably sat on the bed of the Straits.

In 1916 I was 'out of action,' but in 1917 there were two matches at Lord's—the first between an English Army Eleven and an A.I.F. Eleven, in aid of St Dunstan's Hostel, and the other between the Navy and Army and the Australian and South African Forces. Both games drew large crowds, and £1400 was the happy result. Of the first match Mr Horace Hutchinson wrote the following description in the *Westminster Gazette*:

> It was on July 14th that this match was played, and on that same day Lord's presented a sight by far more reminiscent of the long-ago days of peace than any of us would have believed possible while the War lasted. The pavilion was crammed—below, above, and middle gallery—the covered stands had no sitting room vacant, and even the sun-smitten "Mound" was very tolerably crowded.
>
> The occasion was the charity match in aid of St Dunstan's Hostel for the Blind, between an Australian XI and a "Military XI." But what British XI can be other than 'military' to-day? So we had Captain Pelham Warner in supreme command, and as his subordinate for the nonce (and not for the first time) Lieutenant-Colonel J. W. H. T. Douglas. And on the other side was our old friend Mr Macartney, hero of many an Australian side. So here were some elements at least of a Test Match.
>
> Mr Macartney, disastrously for his side, was out for nought, 'l.b.w.' to Mr Douglas, his ancient enemy; and all Australia went for 130 runs. It was not enough, but England's margin of victory was not a very large one. Mr Macartney had compensations for his failure with the bat, for he bowled admirably, with good change of pace, sound length, and very few loose balls.

It must have cheered Captain Warner's heart to hear the acclamations which went with him from all round the ground when he fared out to bat. It was not only, I think, because he was such an old friend to a Middlesex, and also, in some part, to an Australian gallery, for Australia in khaki was very thick on the ground, but also because most of us knew how ill he had been, and rejoiced to see him, with the old Harlequin cap on his head, so much his old self again. It was just like his old self, too, that he batted—a fine, finished exhibition.

Never in all its peaceful life has Lord's looked so green. The ball, instead of scudding over a bare, baked soil to the boundary, lost its way in real green grass, so that runs took some getting and some running.

Encouraged by the success of these war charity matches I arranged in 1918, with the permission and the help of the M.C.C., and of the Surrey C.C.C., three games at Lord's and one at the Oval, when £4300 was obtained, all for war charities.

The King was graciously pleased to be present at one of the matches, when the two captains, E. P. Barbour and myself, had the honour of being presented to His Majesty, while H.R.H. the Duke of Connaught visited Lord's during the afternoon.

The match at the Oval was rather spoilt by the weather, but the Surrey Red Cross Society received £1000 from it. I also took teams to Bradford and Tunbridge Wells in aid of war charities, and these matches too brought in considerable sums of money.

12

MY LAST MATCH AT LORD'S
1919–20

*H.M.S. "New Zealand"—Egypt, Syria, and Palestine—A Complimentary
Sergeant-Major—The A.I.F. Team—August 31, 1920*

DURING THE winter of 1918–19 I was attached to the Appointments Department of the Ministry of Labour in Queen's Gate. There was not a great deal to do, and one evening Admiral Jellicoe rang us up and asked me to take passage with him in H.M.S. *New Zealand* to Egypt. He got into touch with the authorities, and the result was that on February 20, 1919, I was at Portsmouth. I was to work in Egypt and Palestine on behalf of the Appointments Department in connexion with questions of demobilization and of the resettlement of officers and others in civil life. I had learned something of these matters in the Ministry of Labour. *New Zealand* was a battle-cruiser, and had been in action in the Heligoland Bight, at the Dogger Bank, and at Jutland, where she formed one of the battle-cruiser squadron under Beatty.

In the Admiral's party were Lady Jellicoe; Mr and Mrs Reginald McKenna, who were travelling as far as Port Said; Flag-Commander Ramsay;[1] Captain H. H. Share;[2] Flag-Lieutenant Morgan;[3] Captain Leggett,[4] the captain of the ship; and Captain Dreyer,[5] a great gunnery expert.

We stayed a day and a night at Gibraltar, and I drove to the signal station with the McKennas. We had a magnificent view everywhere over the Neutral Ground to Linea and St Roque

[1] Later Admiral Sir Bertram Home Ramsay, Allied Naval C.-in-C. under General Eisenhower, who was killed in 1945 when the plane in which he was travelling crashed in Paris.

[2] Later Admiral Sir Hamnet Share, who died in 1937.

[3] Now Admiral Sir Vaughan Morgan, Superintendent H.M. Dockyard, Portsmouth, 1945–49.

[4] Later Admiral Oliver Elles Leggett, Naval A.D.C. to the King, 1926.

[5] Now Admiral Sir Frederic Charles Dreyer, G.B.E., K.C.B.

and to the Queen of Spain's chair, from which, during the siege of Gibraltar, she used to sit and wait for Gibraltar to surrender. The snow-capped Sierra Nevadas made a lovely background.

After leaving Gibraltar officers from the ward- and gun-rooms dined in the Admiral's quarters every night, and there was much interesting conversation. I had some talk with McKenna, ranging from war and politics to cricket and rowing—he rowed bow in the Cambridge crew—and I begged him when next he was Chancellor to bring in a simpler income-tax form!

We had a great dinner in the ward-room, McKenna and I being the guests of the evening, and for once in a way the Silent Service broke their tradition, and we had to reply to the toast of our health. An ex-Cabinet Minister was, of course, a difficult man to follow. I remarked, however, that I had a slight connexion with the Navy. Had I not played for the Second Battle Squadron at Oporto? Were not my ancestors buccaneers? Was not the Admiral godfather to my younger boy?

The gun-room, not to be outdone, also invited us to dinner, and more speeches were demanded of us. *New Zealand* had remarkably fine officers, and many, as has been seen, were later to gain the highest honours in the Navy. They were all, I believe, specially selected for this cruise, and were the very best type in every way—charm, deference, good manners, and good looks; everything, indeed, to recommend them. The gun-room officers were fine, big fellows—young Anaks most of them—with precious little of the "midshipmite" about them. They told me in confidence that they were willing to take on the ward-room at almost anything.

At Port Said I said farewell to the ship, and went up to Cairo with Jellicoe. The 'red carpet' was down everywhere, and I basked in the reflected glory of a Commander-in-Chief of the Grand Fleet! A few days later I parted from the Admiral, after a never-to-be-forgotten cruise, and I shall always remember the great compliment he paid me in inviting me to be a guest in *New Zealand*. It is seldom indeed that one meets a man capable of inspiring such absolute devotion. His officers and men worshipped him.

I saw quite a lot of Egypt, Palestine, and Syria during the next month, for I visited, at various times, Cairo, Alexandria, Haifa,

Acre, Lydda, Ramle, Jerusalem, and Kantara. At Haifa I stayed
with Brigadier-General B. T. Buckley, C.B., C.M.G., at G.H.Q.,
which was situated in a convent built about eighty years ago,
with Latin texts and "Silence" on the walls. The Turks had used
it as a barracks, and later as a hospital.

There was a lovely little *patio*, or courtyard, with trees, ferns,
and arum lilies in it, and a stone causeway connected one part
of the building with the other. The big garden was surrounded
by high walls, and on the walls were paintings of the Seven Steps
to the Cross. Through a hole in the wall one found oneself in
the Mediterranean, and I used to bathe in the sea every day, sometimes accompanied by Major Younghusband's white Italian
poodles "Mouton" and "Lulie." On the other side of the
convent we looked across a plain to Mount Carmel, and in a few
days I learned more about Elijah the Tishbite than I had ever
done at school. I saw the plain of Esdraelon and the river Kishon,
"that ancient river," and away in the distance, fifteen miles off,
lay Nazareth.

One afternoon we drove round the bay to Acre, crossing the
river Kishon by a wooden bridge on pontoons guarded by a
private in the Jewish Battalion, and most of the way one wheel
of the car was in the Mediterranean as we went along the sandy
beach, which made a first-class road. Acre was interesting, but
dirty. Everybody who is anybody has fought at Acre, from
Saladin to Allenby. One of the Turkish Governors of Acre, about
1833, killed all his harem, fifteen of them, and cut off the nose
and put out the eye of his Jewish banker from Damascus, because
he was too handsome! It is not surprising that he was called
"The Butcher."

At Haifa I dined with Major Stirling, the owner of a most
lovely dog of Arab breed—long and thin like a deerhound, the
type one sees at the foot of monuments of Crusaders in old English
churches. Stirling had fought with the Arab forces on the other
side of the Jordan with Lawrence, and among the five or six
British officers was a former Middlesex cricketer, R. V. Buxton,
a Colonel and a D.S.O., and the recipient of a gold dagger from
the King of the Hedjaz. Stirling had two rows of medals—the
bar to the D.S.O., M.C., etc., etc. He spoke Arabic perfectly,
knew the Arabs inside out, and was most interesting. He was
later Acting-Governor of the Sinai Peninsula in the Egyptian

Government and Governor of the Jaffa District in the Palestine Administration.

On the way down from Haifa to Lydda there were some West Indian troops in the train, many of them from Trinidad, and one big fellow, a sergeant, took great interest in me, and asked the officer in command of them whether I was not "Mr Pelham." "Thought I recognized him, sar," he said.

At Lydda I stayed with the 3rd (Lahore) Division (Major-General A. R. Hoskins, C.M.G., D.S.O.[1]), Major Bevington, a brother of T. A. D. Bevington, who played occasionally for Middlesex in 1900, looking after me most kindly. I was very comfortable in camp, which was prettily situated on high ground, with olive-trees all around, and through the flap of my tent I could see the Judean hills in the distance.

Bevington motored me to Jaffa one afternoon, and as we approached the town the smell of orange-blossom was lovely. Jaffa was full of every nationality—Jews, Syrians, Turks, Italians, Rumanians, French, English, etc. On another day Bevington motored me to Jerusalem, through a great part of the battlefield which led up to the capture of the Holy City.

On my last night at Lydda I dined with General Hoskins, and we talked war and cricket until it was time for me to catch my train to Kantara. Here I stayed a week at the Headquarters of the 75th Division (Major-General P. C. Palin, C.B., C.M.G.[2]). When I had last seen Kantara, in 1912, on my way home from Australia, it consisted of about four houses and half a dozen palm-trees. Now it was a huge camp, capable of accommodating 130,000 troops, and although I had been told it was "the last place on earth," I thoroughly enjoyed my week there. I had the honour of playing for, and captaining, the 75th Division against Kantara, and during my innings of 75, not out, the following conversation took place between the admirable Sergeant-Major who was umpiring and myself:

S.-M.: Well played, sir. This adds another country to the many you have already played in.

P.F.W.: Thank you, Sergeant-Major. Very nice of you to say so. But I am thinking of giving up first-class cricket. Getting too old.

---

[1] Later Major-General Sir Reginald Hoskins, K.C.B. He died in 1942.
[2] Later Major-General Sir Philip Charles Palin, K.C.M.G. He died in 1937.

S.-M.: Give it up, sir! Give it up, sir! Never heard of such a thing, sir! Don't be a fool, sir, if I may say so, sir. I have not seen as straight a bat as yours, sir, between Dan and Beersheeba!

Altogether I had a most interesting and enjoyable month, and every one was extremely good to me, especially Major R. V. Read, D.S.O., M.C.,[1] who had been in S.D.3 at the War Office with me, and who looked after me and arranged for my every comfort.

I came home on an ambulance transport. There were nearly a thousand troops on board, sick and wounded, from India, Mesopotamia, and Egypt, and at the request of the padre I gave a talk on cricket to the N.C.O.'s and men, and this was repeated, later, to the officers.

The season of 1919 will be memorable for three reasons. It was the first season of regular first-class cricket after the War; secondly, the weather, except for a short period in July, was splendid; and, finally, county matches were limited to two days.

That the game still retained, and more than retained, its hold on the affections of the public was proved by the big crowds at the principal matches. But that the two-day match was destined to be a failure was obvious early in the season, and at a meeting of the Advisory County Cricket Committee, which was held at the Oval in the middle of August, the decision was unanimous that the experiment should not be repeated. The long hours of play were laborious and inconvenient to a degree to both players and umpires. Moreover, the strain involved had a bad effect on the cricket, inferior batsmen often making large scores against bowlers and fielders who were physically exhausted, while it often proved to be a wise policy to delay the declaration of an innings rather longer than would have been the case in a three-day match, until the fielding side were thoroughly worn out.

It was not to be expected, after a lapse of four years, that the cricket would be up to the old standard, but, everything considered, the form shown was fairly good, though the bowling of many of the county elevens was deplorably weak.

The M.C.C. stuck to three-day fixtures in their own matches,

[1] Now Colonel Richard Valentine Read, C.V.O., C.B.E. He was Military Attaché, British Embassy, Washington, from 1938 to 1941

ABOARD H.M.S. "COMMONWEALTH"

A group on the quarterdeck, February 1910.

NAVAL SIGNAL FOR THE MATCH BETWEEN
H.M.S. "COMMONWEALTH" AND OPORTO

[See p. 80.]

CARING, 1911

Esmond, Miss Walker, Elizabeth, P.F.W.

A GROUP AT CARING IN 1911

E. Hendren, "Tarif," F. L. Fane, Esmond, P.F.W. and Elizabeth,
A.C.W., J. Hendren.

AUCHER, RAYMOND, AND P.F.W., ABOUT 1911

THE CHÂTEAU IN FRANCE WHERE I STAYED WITH
JOHN BUCHAN IN 1917

[See p. 96.]

(*Above*) SIR JOHN AND LADY SHAW WITH THEIR DOGS

(*Left*) COMBINED OPERATIONS IN THE SERPENTINE!

"Judy," destroyer, guarding "Peter," battleship.

P.F.W., "CAPTAIN" (ADMIRAL JELLICOE'S COLLIE), AND ESMOND AT CARING IN 1909

in the Varsity Match, in Gentlemen *v*. Players, and in the match between the Gentlemen and the A.I.F. team.

Both the Gentlemen *v*. Players matches, at Lord's and the Oval, were drawn. At Lord's the bowling of the Gentlemen was much more suited by the conditions, Douglas bowling splendidly, taking eight wickets for 49 runs in the Players' first innings, while Knight played two beautiful innings, and, like another Oxford batsman before him, R. E. Foster, made a hundred in his first Gentlemen *v*. Players match. In the Players' second innings Hobbs and Gunn showed sound defence, and it soon became apparent that a drawn game was inevitable. Hobbs played a superb innings of 113. I made 34 in the first innings, but was bowled by Woolley before I had scored in the second. An interesting feature about the match was the selection of G. T. S. Stevens, the Captain of University College School, to play for the Gentlemen, this being the only occasion on which a schoolboy has actually played in a Gentlemen *v*. Players match.[1]

Of the county teams there was, perhaps, little to choose between Yorkshire, the champions, Kent, Nottinghamshire, and Surrey. Probably Surrey, on a hard true pitch, especially at the Oval, were the best county team of the year, but on all wickets Yorkshire were superior, and they well deserved their position at the head of the list.

The long hours of two-day cricket—11.30-7.30 on the first day and 11-7.30 on the second—were too much for me, and after the middle of July I was a 'dead dog.' In the few three-day matches in which I took part—two Gentlemen *v*. Players, Middlesex *v*. A.I.F., Gentlemen of England *v*. A.I.F., and my own side *v*. Oxford University—I got on quite well, and the Surrey C.C.C. paid me a great compliment in presenting me with the ball off which I made 57 for the Gentlemen at the Oval on a sticky wicket. It was for "improvement in batting," as W. Findlay, the then Secretary of the M.C.C., put it to me. I was at the time nearly forty-six years of age.

The Australian military authorities were to be congratulated on the successful tour of the A.I.F. Eleven, and English cricketers were indebted to them for stepping into the breach when the negotiations for a representative Australian side came to nothing.

---

[1] Three of the Winchester Eleven had played in 1836, but the Gentlemen's team then numbered eighteen.

The team played twenty-eight first-class matches, won twelve, drew twelve, and lost four—to the Gentlemen of England at Lord's, to Derbyshire, to the South of England at Hastings, and to C. I. Thornton's Eleven at Scarborough. They were a really good side, not up to the standard of an Australian Test Match Eleven in batting or bowling, but the equal in fielding of any Australian side that I have ever seen. The team made friends wherever they went, and were very popular, as, indeed, they deserved to be, for they were all extremely nice men, who played the game with great enthusiasm. The outstanding players in the side were Kelleway, who played in only six matches, Collins, Willis, Pellew, Gregory, Taylor, Trennery, and Lampard. Of these Collins, Pellew, Gregory, and Taylor were, of course, members of the great Australian side two years later.

I played twice against the A.I.F.—once for Middlesex and once for the Gentlemen of England—scoring 101, retired, in the first of these games—I had severe cramp in the leg, and had to be carried off the field when I had scored 82—and 43 in the second.

One of the matches I enjoyed most this season was that at Lord's, between my eleven and the Public Schools. School cricket was very good indeed in 1919, probably better, as a whole, than it has ever been, and though I had got together a side which included R. H. Spooner, S. H. Day, R. Anson, D. J. Knight, P. W. Sherwell, and H. W. Taylor, both of whom had captained South Africa, G. A. Fairbairn, and E. R. Wilson, the Schools had none the worse of a drawn game, which was interesting from the first ball to the last.

G. T. S. Stevens captained the Schools side, and he had under him D. R. Jardine, A. P. F. Chapman, R. C. Robertson-Glasgow, C. H. Gibson, W. W. Hill-Wood, and C. T. Ashton, Captains of Eton and of Winchester in the following season.

Ever since he went to Lord's in 1898 as Secretary of the M.C.C. F. E. Lacey had done a great deal for Public School cricketers, who with one accord acknowledged that they were indebted to him for all the care and trouble he took in the selection of school sides and in the general arrangements for the matches.

At the end of the season of 1919 I sought counsel of my friend and mentor A. J. Webbe, President of the Middlesex C.C.C. I suggested that it was time that I resigned the captaincy, but he would have none of it, pointing out that if I had failed to make runs in the very tiring two-day matches I had almost invariably come off in three-day fixtures. I decided to follow his advice, and as the sequel proved the gods were to smile on my decision.

The interest in cricket in 1920 was greater than at any other previous period. Crowds flocked to the best matches, and at Lord's we had gates of 20,000, 25,000, and even 30,000.

At the beginning of the season scarcely anyone thought that Middlesex would win the Championship. There was, however, one exception, A. C. M. Croome, in the *Daily Mail*, writing that we were "the dark horse of the Championship." Croome was a very fine writer. He was a scholar, and as a master at Radley had won a great reputation as a teacher, and he brought a fine style to his description of matches and criticisms of players. He had been in the Wellington, Oxford, and Gloucestershire Elevens, and had a sound knowledge of the game and brought a right appreciation towards it. He was an equally good writer on golf and, as a beautiful hurdler, on athletics. He later adorned the pages of *The Times*.

At the end of July Middlesex were apparently out of the running for the Championship, unless we happened to win all our remaining matches, which we did—by good cricket and a bit of luck. We beat Kent at Canterbury by 5 runs and Yorkshire at Bradford by 4 runs—a match which turned my remaining hairs white!

When the final match, against Surrey at Lord's, arrived the position was that we had to win the match to gain the Championship: a draw was no use to us. And what a fight it was! In the words of the *Morning Post* of September 1, 1920: "In many a year to come we shall talk of it, for never has there been a finer battle at Lord's than that associated with 'Plum' Warner's captaincy." From the first ball the air was charged with electricity. But I will not attempt to describe the whole of the match—it has been done so often—but will come to ten minutes to four on the afternoon of the third day, August 31, when for the last time I led the Middlesex Eleven on to the field.[1] Actually three hours and seven minutes remained for play, for stumps were to be drawn at 7 o'clock—not at 6.30, as *Wisden*, nodding for once, erroneously states!

[1] Middlesex, a few days later, played the Rest of England at the Oval, but this was the last occasion on which I captained them at Lord's.

I should be less than human should I ever forget it. Indeed, I can, even after more than thirty years, recall every phase, every ball, every moment, of it, and the wonderful reception the crowd gave me is one of the most treasured memories of my cricketing life. I was carried into the pavilion, as I had been as a Rugby boy thirty years before, and was called on to make a speech from the balcony of the dressing-room, surrounded by the rest of the eleven, to a cheering and emotional crowd. This was my last match at Lord's. Thirty-one years had passed since my first appearance.

Here is the score of the match:

MIDDLESEX v. SURREY

Played at Lord's, August 28, 30, and 31, 1920

Result: Middlesex won by 55 runs

MIDDLESEX

First Innings		Second Innings	
C. H. L. Skeet, c. Ducat, b. Rushby..	2	c. Fender, b. Hitch	106
H. W. Lee, c. Hitch, b. Fender	12	b. Hitch	108
J. W. Hearne, c. and b. Hitch	15	l.b.w., b. Rushby	26
E. Hendren, b. Reay	41	c. Sandham, b. Rushby	5
P. F. Warner (Capt.), b. Rushby	79	not out	14
F. T. Mann, c. and b. Fender	12	c. Peach, b. Fender	22
N. Haig, b. Reay	18	b. Rushby	1
G. T. S. Stevens, b. Fender	53	not out	21
H. K. Longman, b. Fender	0		
H. R. Murrell, c. Ducat, b. Hitch	9	b. Reay	0
T. J. Durston, not out	0		
Byes 12, leg-byes 12, no-balls 3	27	Byes 8, leg-byes 4, wide 1	13
Total	268	Total (7 wkts., dec.)	316

SURREY

J. B. Hobbs, c. Mann, b. Hearne	24	c. Lee, b. Haig	10
A. Sandham, not out	167	c. and b. Hearne	68
M. Howell, c. Murrell, b. Durston	7	st. Murrell, b. Stevens	25
T. F. Shepherd, c. Murrell, b. Durston	0	c. Hendren, b. Stevens	26
H. A. Peach, hit wkt., b. Stevens	18	b. Stevens	11
A. Ducat, st. Murrell, b. Lee	49	l.b.w., b. Hearne	7
P. G. H. Fender (Capt.), c. Haig, b. Durston	30	b. Durston	1
J. W. Hitch, b. Durston	1	b. Stevens	6
G. M. Reay, c. Haig, b. Lee	6	b. Hearne	5
H. Strudwick, b. Hearne	9	b. Stevens	10
T. Rushby, not out	6	not out	7
Byes 17, leg-byes 5, no-balls 2	24	Byes 11, leg-bye 1	12
Total (9 wkts., dec.)	341	Total	188

BOWLING ANALYSIS
SURREY

First Innings	O.	M.	R.	W.	Second Innings	O.	M.	R.	W.
Hitch	32.1	10	66	2	Hitch	20	5	71	2
Rushby	23	9	48	2	Rushby	22	7	73	3
Fender	28	4	76	4	Fender	16.5	2	70	1
Reay	26	17	31	2	Reay	18	1	61	1
Ducat	3	1	10	0	Ducat	3	0	12	0
Shepherd	6	3	10	0	Shepherd	4	0	16	0

MIDDLESEX

	O.	M.	R.	W.		O.	M.	R.	W.
Durston	30	9	97	4	Durston	14	1	42	1
Haig	10	4	25	0	Haig	8	0	19	1
Stevens	16	0	72	1	Stevens	13.4	0	61	5
Hearne	24	8	57	2	Hearne	11	0	37	3
Lee	15	2	66	2	Lee	4	0	17	0

Umpires: J. Blake and G. P. Harrison

On the following day *The Times*, the *Morning Post*, the *Daily Express*, the *Westminster Gazette*, and the *Evening Standard* had leading articles on the match, and I received scores of letters, some of which I quote below:

From A. J. WEBBE

MY DEAR PLUM,

As I told you last night, I could hardly bear to leave you.

What a glorious triumph for the county, at which I rejoice, but believe me *more still* because of your personal triumph. No one has ever had such a one, and certainly no one has *ever* deserved one more —indeed, as much as you have. I would not have missed being present for anything in the world.

I am glad to see you have a leading article in *The Times*. I don't believe any other cricketer has ever had this. I am repenting now that I ever said I would not press you to continue to hold the captaincy. Your retirement is a great disaster to Middlesex.

What a match it was! There never has been such a one. How splendidly you managed the bowling!!! You have besides the wonderful gift of getting the best out of the side, earning the affection of every one, and the great virtue of *moral courage*. You took the whole responsibility of the declaration, and were rewarded as you deserve.

To me personally your giving up is a great blow; you are really the last and only link that I have with the county side. I have valued more than I can say the affection you have always shown to me. Thank you a thousand times, and for all the kind things you have said about me over and over again. I am thinking of you to-day, indeed, we all are here, resting and dreaming of the great triumph.

Every cricketer in England, and no doubt in Australia too, is rejoicing in your glory.

Your affectionate old friend

From the RIGHT HON. W. H. LONG, M.P., *First Lord of the Admiralty*
H.M.S. "ENCHANTRESS,"
AT CHRISTIENSSAND,
NORWAY

MY DEAR PLUM WARNER,

Excuse the familiarity; this is the name by which thousands of us talk of you, tho' they are not among the privileged ones who can claim so to address you.

We have followed the contest for the County Championship with profound interest. We rejoice, and all drank your health and that of your gallant team to-night.

What a match it must have been! And what a scene at Lord's! I rejoice especially. I love cricket, I have followed it as closely as my engagements have permitted; just now and then I have been haunted by the fear that the old high standard might be lowered, but never by you; you have nobly maintained those great traditions which have given to the world that biting condemnation: "It is not cricket."

May the old spirit ever prevail; and may you live many years to teach others how to play the game and to reflect upon the glories of a triumphant and unstained record.

From C. B. FRY

MY DEAR PELHAM,

Avoiding the crowd of congratulations which I was sure would be showered on your very brilliant finale in Middlesex cricket, nevertheless one cannot omit to offer you pronounced felicitation on your well-merited success.

Having shone as a star of the first magnitude in the firmament of the game—all stars being suns, you have achieved a glorious sunset of which the unfading colours will illuminate the great quantity of cricket that remains to you in a less exacting world of the game.

Your good feeling for the great game and your unremitting enthusiasm have I am sure done a lot of good to county cricket. The way you kept up your success when at times much handicapped by physical difficulties I shall always regard as an eminent example of what grit and resolution can do.

Vixere fortes ante Agamemnona
Sed non fortiores; nec vivent.

But the reference in your case should be to Ulysses.
Well, bless you, excellent warrior.

From P. G. H. FENDER, *the Surrey Captain*

DEAR PLUM,

I feel that I should like to write you to tell you how much I congratulate you on being champions. I speak for the whole of our side when I say that with ourselves out of it, there is no one we should prefer to see on top.

We were out to beat you to-day if we could, but after such a sporting match there is not a regret on our side at the result.

Personally I feel that it has been my greatest match so far, in being associated, to no matter how small a degree, with you in our respective positions as skipper.

A few people have been good enough to say nice things about me as skipper of the Surrey side at times this year, and I want you to know one thing in that connection. Whatever I have been able to do, I learnt all I know about skippering from you—I hope you won't consider this a doubtful compliment—but it is a true one, for when I have failed it has been due to my faulty interpretations of your methods.

We are all delighted to have you bring the Championship south again, and if it really means your retirement from first-class cricket, it is a fitting one.

13

THE EARLY TWENTIES
1921–24

The "Morning Post" and "The Cricketer"—The Australian Tour of 1921—Douglas and Tennyson—Middlesex again Champions—The Channel Islands—An Operation—C. M. Wells—Sandhurst

WITH THE close of the 1920 season my career in first-class cricket came to an end, but my interest in the game by no means ceased, for from time to time I played in a less strenuous sphere, and extended my experience of tours abroad with visits to South America, to Holland, and, shortly before the Second World War broke out, to Denmark, though not as an active member of the side.

From the beginning of 1921 and for thirteen years subsequently I was the cricket correspondent of the *Morning Post*, and in the same year I undertook the editorship of *The Cricketer*. I was also busy with *Cricket Reminiscences*, articles which appeared originally in *The Times*, and were subsequently published in book form by Grant Richards, Ltd. I was also editor of, and a contributor to, the 1920 edition of the Badminton Library on cricket.

At various periods I was a member of the Committee and the Cricket Sub-committee of the M.C.C., and acted as Chairman of the Selection Committee for Test Matches in the years 1926, 1931–32, and 1935–38. These activities kept me in touch with almost every phase of the game, and with the younger generation, an experience which I enjoyed, for it helped one to maintain one's youth and to hold on to one's enthusiasm.

The *Morning Post* were delightful people to work for. They gave me a free hand and every facility and encouragement. Starting a new cricket paper demanded, and entailed, a great deal of work and thought. Many people pointed out that no such paper had lasted more than a few years, but to-day, thirty years later, *The Cricketer*, after some anxious financial years, is going strong, and is, I believe, firmly established. This is due very

P.F.W. IN 1920

This is the portrait by Miss Katherine Lloyd which hangs in the
Long Room at Lord's.

[*See p.* 152.]

THE M.C.C. FLAG FLYING AT LORD'S IN 1926 DURING THE
ENGLAND *v*. AUSTRALIA MATCH

[*See p.* 123.]

Photo Sport and General

largely to A. W. T. Langford, who came to us in 1926, and has been ever since the life and soul of the paper. His energy and enthusiasm are tremendous, and without him I do not care to think what would have happened. At first we were housed in Fleet Street, and then in Wine Office Court, in rooms overlooking the Cheshire Cheese, but the German bombers damaged us badly, and we were forced to move, and now carry on our efforts in Mr Langford's house in Surbiton, no little inconvenience, I fear, to him, a fact which does not, however, diminish in any way his zeal and activities.

At the end of 1920 my wife and I took a house at Datchet, which had a garden on the banks of the river, in view of Windsor Castle and the Home Park. In the garden I made—it almost goes without saying!—a wicket, and as Sir Walter Allen (father of G. O. Allen), who lived close by, also had one in his garden, we had many good practices, in which a number of well-known cricketers took part. Both gardens also boasted tennis-courts, and I remember A. P. F. Chapman playing so finely that had he devoted his attention seriously to lawn tennis he would assuredly have been a big figure on the Centre Court.

Wilfrid Bowring, another near neighbour, had given my daughter a lovely springer spaniel, Peter. He was a wonderful swimmer, was always in the river, and, incidentally, enjoyed some rat-hunting on the banks. He could also catch a tennis-ball as well as Little Jim. He was a most lovable dog, and a bit of a 'churchman,' for did he not seat himself in a pew in Datchet Church, and before that at Holy Trinity, Sloane Street, both of which he was, of course, asked to vacate? At Holy Trinity, as he was led out, I heard the remark, "What a pity! Why can't he stay? In Scotland they allow the shepherds to bring their dogs into church." In due course he was gathered to his fathers, but all of us had certainly "given our hearts to him to tear."

The Australian Team of 1921, under the captaincy of W. W. Armstrong, a slim enough youth in my playing days, but now almost Falstaffian in figure—indeed, I fancy he and W. G. are the only two men nearing eighteen stone who have played in Test Matches—won the rubber easily (three victories and two drawn games), but England had not recovered from the First World War, and, moreover, Hobbs was out of action because of an injury and, later, an operation for appendicitis. He took the

H

field in the third Test, at Leeds, but never batted, being suddenly taken ill and hurried off to hospital. He could not, of course, be replaced, but amid all our disappointments and failures I saw a gleam of hope for the near future; and in 1922 there was some fine cricket in Gentlemen *v.* Players at Lord's.

Douglas captained England in the first two Test Matches, at Trent Bridge and Lord's, but after the Lord's game Tennyson was elected captain, the selectors (H. K. Foster, R. H. Spooner, and J. Daniell) thinking, no doubt, that a change of captaincy might, perhaps, change the luck, for we had lost five matches in Australia under Douglas's leadership during the previous winter and two here—no fault of his, for the Australians were far the stronger side. Douglas, as every one who knew him anticipated, took a natural disappointment with dignity and good temper, and gave, as always, loyal support to the new leader. Tennyson played two fine innings of 63 and 36 at Leeds, in spite of a very badly injured hand, the sort of innings on which his grandfather would have written an ode. He was a very good player of fast bowlers like Gregory and Macdonald, and at the Oval he scored 51. "Tennyson has never played better.... When 21 he received a dreadful crack over the heart, and was nearly knocked out, but after a few minutes' delay he went on batting as if nothing had happened," says *Wisden*. The next ball, indeed, from Macdonald, he on-drove into the far corner of the Oval.

Lionel was stoutly built, and nowhere more so than in the region of the heart. The first time I met him was in 1903 in Australia. The M.C.C. team had been lunching with his father, who was then Governor-General of Australia, and he asked us to "come and have a look at my young Trumper." A few months later Lionel departed for Eton, and eventually got into the eleven as a bowler, but his contemporaries do not speak with any fervour of his skill in that sphere of the game.

Middlesex again won the Championship in 1921, under the captaincy of F. T. Mann. As in 1920, the Championship hinged on the result of the last match with Surrey, at Lord's, but with this difference, that nothing short of an actual victory would have given Surrey first place. At one time Surrey looked like winning, but some fine bowling by Haig in their second innings brought about a collapse. None the less Middlesex had to make 322 runs in order to win—a heavy task in a fourth innings. Splendid

batting by Twining (135) and Hearne (106) put on 277 runs for
the second partnership, and victory was gained by six wickets.
Many years later, in 1949, Mann's elder son, F. G. Mann,[1] led
Middlesex to the joint Championship with Yorkshire, and this is
the only instance of father and son achieving this distinction.
A. N. Hornby and A. H. Hornby were Captains of Lancashire,
and though the father led Lancashire to the top of the competition, A. H. never had the good fortune to do so, though he
captained some very good elevens. Mann, father, was a magnificent driver, and Mann, son, hits a cricket-ball almost as far as his
sire. Frank, in 1924, hit Rhodes for four sixes, two, off successive balls, on to the top of the pavilion at Lord's—he was unlucky
not to clear it—and George hit a ball over the pavilion at Leeds
in the Test Match against New Zealand in 1949.

I spent some three or four weeks in Guernsey in 1922, and
played quite a lot of cricket. We won our matches, and Alderney,
hearing of this, threw down the gauntlet. We sailed through the
dreaded Swinge, where, it is alleged, seven currents meet, and
formed up in battle array on the Butte. We made 75, which
some thought was enough to ensure victory, but we were easily
beaten. The wicket was matting on grass, and the outfield one
of the roughest I have ever known. Point was hit on the forehead, cover had his right ear severely cut, and our deep third
man disappeared into the sort of sunken road into which Napoleon's cavalry fell at Waterloo, and returned covered with dirt,
dust, and leaves. But the climax came when our wicket-keeper,
a man of great strength, was hit over the right eye by a ball from
our cover-point, a slow medium bowler, which leapt from the
matting. He went down like a felled ox, and we gathered round
with set and anxious faces. The inimitable Gerry Weigall, however, eased the situation with "He's all right, Pelham; the bruise
is coming out!" And what a bruise it was! Yellow, green, and
black, and about half the size of a cricket-ball! We bore the vic-
tim to the ringside, and he did not recover consciousness for some
time. That outfield on the Butte would have tested to the uttermost the greatest of fielding sides.

During the winter of 1922–23 I was seriously ill, and on April 5
I was operated on by the great James Sherren. He did his work
so skilfully that since then I have never experienced any pain at

---

[1] F. G. Mann, D.S.O., M.C., Scots Guards.

all from my duodenum. Except for an occasional few days, I had never really been free of pain for thirty years. I missed seeing any cricket until the middle of June, but Datchet was a pleasant place in which to recover, and I spent ten days at Scarborough, thanks to the kindness of Leveson Gower, who invited me to share in the happy surroundings of the Festival there. It was here that the West Indies came near to defeating Leveson Gower's powerful eleven, who had to make but 28 runs in the last innings. Francis and John, both fine fast bowlers, had six men out for 19. A piece of fielding by Constantine remains in my memory: stopping a hard hit at cover-point, he threw the wicket down at the bowler's end, and, racing across the pitch, backed up the ball, which had ricocheted off the stumps! In those days the West Indies had a very strong battery of fast bowlers in Constantine, John, and Francis, with Browne, medium right, and Pascall, an uncle of Constantine, slow left, in support. George Challenor was their great batsman. As *Wisden* wrote: "He had everything —style, hitting power, and strength of defence." He, like many another West Indies cricketer, was at Harrison College, Barbados.

On October 2 I was fifty, and C. M. Wells came over from Eton with several beautifully bound volumes of *Scores and Biographies* as a birthday present. We had first met at Sidmouth in 1890,[1] when he defeated me with a beautiful leg-break, and for many years we played together for Middlesex. He was a fine all-round cricketer, a Rugby international, and a great scholar, and, indeed, a very versatile man, learned in many things. He was eighty on March 21, 1951, and looks at least ten years younger! He is my closest link with the Middlesex Eleven of what must now be called "the old days."

There was a spell of fine weather for a month in June and July, otherwise the summer of 1924 was one of the wettest on record. Our cricket continued to improve, for Tate was now a great bowler, and we had many formidable batsmen—Hobbs, Sutcliffe, Woolley, Hendren, E. Tyldesley, Chapman. The South Africans were no match for us, and the M.C.C. team, under the captaincy of A. E. R. Gilligan, departed for Australia full of confidence. However, they did not win the rubber, but Australian opinion was almost unanimous that there was little difference between the sides.

---

[1] Actually we had had a previous meeting in the autumn of 1889, when he came to Rugby to play football, and dined in Whitelaw's.

Early in this year I played in a remarkable match at Datchet, for my eleven got the village out for 7, 2 of which were extras, in their second innings, and though we had been led on the first innings by 17 runs, we won by ten wickets. Wells took three wickets for 1 run, and Calthorpe seven for 2 runs.

For some years after the First World War I used to take teams to play at Sandhurst, where it was my good fortune to stay with the Commandant. I never missed watching the parade of the Cadets, with all its perfect drill and discipline, and on one occasion I heard a most interesting lecture on the battle of the Marne, to a civilian, and, I dare say, to some others, a most complicated battle. I enjoyed these visits to Sandhurst immensely, and was sorry indeed when the fixtures were cancelled. I nearly always succeeded in getting together good sides, and the Cadets on more than one occasion ran us hard.

14

SELECTION COMMITTEES
1925–27

Hobbs's Year—S. H. Pardon—Chairman of the Selection Committee—England win the Ashes—H. A. Gwynne—Tour in South America

THE SEASON of 1925 was "Hobbs's Year." He headed the batting averages with an aggregate of 3024 runs and an average of 70·32, and scored sixteen centuries. On August 17 he equalled W. G.'s record of 126 hundreds, and the next day surpassed it, in the match between Somerset and Surrey at Taunton. Taking him all in all, he was the best of the many great English batsmen on every type of wicket and against every type of bowling. Some may claim Hammond as his equal, and I should be loath to dispute this, but he was not greater than Hobbs, though his innings of 240 for England against Australia at Lord's in 1938 was as fine an innings as any batsman has ever played. But comparisons of the really great are of little or no value. I should give them all an Alpha Plus.

Cricket suffered a severe loss by the death, on November 20, 1925, of S. H. Pardon, for thirty-five years the famous editor of *Wisden*. He had a very sound outlook on cricket matters, and wrote with a charm peculiar to himself. He was a most interesting man to talk to, for, besides cricket, he knew a great deal about racing, music, and the drama. Had he lived I do not think he would have approved of some of the cricket criticisms of to-day, and if the wireless or television comments on cricket had been in vogue in his time he would never have been guilty of some of the expressions used—for instance, 'speed merchant,' as I have heard a fast bowler described. He would have shunned it with absolute horror. Nor would he, I feel sure, have approved of the use of Christian names and nicknames in the Press and on the air.

In February 1926 I was appointed Chairman of the Board of Control Selection Committee for the Test Matches against

Australia, my colleagues being P. Perrin and A. E. R. Gilligan. At the time I was the cricket correspondent of the *Morning Post*, and I was told that there was a long and animated discussion as to whether, because of this, I should be a member of the Selection Committee. However, I was elected, and I do not think I 'dropped any bricks' in my descriptions of the various matches; at least, so I was informed by a high authority at Lord's at the end of the season. This, of course, was a great satisfaction to me.

At the time I am writing of there was a strong prejudice against cricketers writing on the game, and I remember causing a certain amount of astonishment when I chanced to remark that some of our greatest men had been closely connected with the Press— Prime Ministers, for example, and other eminent people—and that cricket might well be recorded in a fitting manner. And in this connexion it is pertinent to recall that many well-known cricketers have written books and articles on the game. Having said this, and the world being what it is to-day, with so much publicity and a certain lack of grace and manner, I am certain that it is wise not to allow a cricketer to write on any match, or to give interviews in the Press, or to speak on the wireless or on television, while he is a member of an England team, either here or abroad.

The selectors in 1926 were kept very busy, but the work was of absorbing interest, and Perrin and Gilligan were staunch colleagues. In addition to the five Test Matches, there were three trial games—South of England *v.* the Australians, at Bristol; North of England *v.* the Australians, at Birmingham; and England *v.* the Rest, at Lord's. On the first day of the Lord's match 26,623 paid gate-money. Of the previous fifteen matches against Australia only one had resulted in a victory for England, but we were full of hope that after the good fight Gilligan's team had made in Australia fortune would at last smile on us. And so it proved, for, after every one of the first four games had been drawn, we won the last, at the Oval, by 289 runs. Here is the England Eleven in the order of going in, which after many long years of waiting and disappointment restored the prestige of English cricket: Hobbs, Sutcliffe, Woolley, Hendren, Chapman (Capt.), Stevens, Rhodes, Geary, Tate, Larwood, and Strudwick. Carr, the Captain of Nottinghamshire, had led England in the first four matches, but was taken ill with a severe attack of tonsillitis. on July 26, during the Old Trafford match, and when we met on Sunday, August 8, the situation was not easy.

Hobbs and Rhodes had been co-opted on the Committee, and we had a long meeting. After the most careful thought and deliberation we came to the conclusion that Carr should be asked to stand down. It was a distasteful task, but it was essential that the best eleven on the form of the moment should be chosen, and Carr was not fit enough to take part in a match of such vital importance. He had our deepest sympathy, and, indeed, the sympathy of all cricketing England, but we had to think of England first, and not of the individual. I fear that he was bitterly disappointed, but other Captains of England had before this undergone such an unhappy experience. We recalled Rhodes to the colours: he was within two months of his forty-ninth birthday, and had first played for England in 1899, before Chapman, Stevens, and Larwood were born. The score-sheet shows what an influence his inclusion in the team had on the result.

The match will ever be memorable for many things, but none more so than for the superb batting of Hobbs and Sutcliffe on a very difficult wicket for at least a couple of hours. Never has there been more skilful batsmanship on false turf. Has England ever had a better opening pair? I doubt it.

At five minutes past six on August 18 Geary bowled Mailey, and England had at last beaten Australia. The large crowd swarmed in front of the pavilion and acclaimed Chapman, the young captain, who had led the side so ably, and the rest of the England team. Then the crowd yelled for Collins, the Australian captain, and his men, and, amid a crescendo of shouting and hand-clapping, people gradually began to leave the ground. Had Hammond been able to play this England Eleven would have been a great side—as it was, it was a very good one—but a severe illness contracted on tour in the West Indies kept him out of cricket for the whole of the season.

Here is the score of the match:

ENGLAND v. AUSTRALIA

Played at the Oval, August 14, 16, 17, and 18, 1926

Result: England won by 289 runs

ENGLAND

First Innings		Second Innings	
J. B. Hobbs, b. Mailey	37	b. Gregory	100
H. Sutcliffe, b. Mailey	76	b. Mailey	161
F. E. Woolley, b. Mailey	18	l.b.w., b. Richardson	27
E. Hendren, b. Gregory	8	c. Oldfield, b. Grimmett	15
A. P. F. Chapman (Capt.), st. Oldfield, b. Mailey	49	b. Richardson	19
G. T. S. Stevens, c. Andrews, b. Mailey	17	c. Mailey, b. Grimmett	22
W. Rhodes, c. Oldfield, b. Mailey	28	l.b.w., b. Grimmett	14
G. Geary, run out	9	c. Oldfield, b. Gregory	1
M. W. Tate, b. Grimmett	23	not out	33
H. Larwood, c. Andrews, b. Grimmett	0	b. Mailey	5
H. Strudwick, not out	4	c. Andrews, b. Mailey	2
Byes 6, leg-byes 5	11	Byes 19, leg-byes 18	37
Total	280	Total	436

AUSTRALIA

W. M. Woodfull, b. Rhodes	35	c. Geary, b. Larwood	0
W. Bardsley, c. Strudwick, b. Larwood	2	c. Woolley, b. Rhodes	21
C. G. Macartney, b. Stevens	25	c. Geary, b. Larwood	16
W. H. Ponsford, run out	2	c. Larwood, b. Rhodes	12
T. J. E. Andrews, b. Larwood	3	c. Tate, b. Larwood	15
H. L. Collins (Capt.), c. Stevens, b. Larwood	61	c. Woolley, b. Rhodes	4
A. J. Richardson, c. Geary, b. Rhodes	16	b. Rhodes	4
J. M. Gregory, c. Stevens, b. Tate	73	c. Sutcliffe, b. Tate	9
W. A. Oldfield, not out	33	b. Stevens	23
C. V. Grimmett, b. Tate	35	not out	8
A. A. Mailey, c. Strudwick, b. Tate	0	b. Geary	6
Byes 5, leg-byes 12	17	Leg-byes	7
Total	302	Total	125

BOWLING ANALYSIS

AUSTRALIA

First Innings	O.	M.	R.	W.	Second Innings	O.	M.	R.	W.
Gregory	15	4	31	1	Gregory	18	1	58	2
Grimmett	33	12	74	2	Grimmett	55	17	108	3
Mailey	33.5	3	138	6	Mailey	42.5	6	128	3
Macartney	6	3	16	0	Macartney	26	16	24	0
Richardson	7	2	10	0	Richardson	41	21	81	2

ENGLAND

	O.	M.	R.	W.		O.	M.	R.	W.
Tate	37.1	17	40	3	Tate	9	4	12	1
Larwood	34	11	82	3	Larwood	14	3	34	3
Geary	27	8	43	0	Geary	6.3	2	15	1
Stevens	29	3	85	1	Stevens	3	1	13	1
Rhodes	25	15	35	2	Rhodes	20	9	44	4

Umpires: H. Young and F. Chester

Before the season, at a luncheon to the Australians, Sir James Barrie, in a speech, remarked that he had no doubt that we should win. "You talk of your fast bowler, J. M. Gregory. Wait until you see ours. We keep him in a dungeon. His name is *P. K. Thunder.*"

I was sitting next to H. A. Gwynne, the Editor of the *Morning Post*, during the final moments of the match, and he said to me, "Now, Plum, go to the Club, have a whisky-and-soda, and write a description of the match worthy of the occasion!" I replied, "Why the whisky-and-soda?" and his answer was, "Years ago no self-respecting leader-writer ever sat down to write without first having a drink of some sort. It stimulates and gives one ideas." I took his advice, and next day I received letters of congratulation both from him and Guy Pollock, the *Morning Post's* Managing Editor. I do not think that my worst enemy would describe me as a wine-bibber or a two-bottle man, but I find that a small amount of alcohol is a definite help to writing, and certainly it is if one has to make a speech; but it must be wine that cheers and does not inebriate!

At dinner one night at Gwynne's house in London Lord Darling was present, and, among others, Sir Stanley Jackson. During the conversation the Judge remarked that it was a Yorkshireman who had invented the guillotine, and our host said, "You say that to flatter Jackson!" Is there any basis for this very original theory?

I played cricket at Morden for the *Morning Post* against the Lords and Commons, and Sir Thomas Inskip (later Lord Caldecote, Lord Chancellor) on-drove me for six, a mighty blow over a far-distant tree. However, I bowled him presently with a slow one, for, endeavouring to hit another six, the bat slipped out of his hands and nearly cut off the head of the square-leg umpire. When Sir Thomas was appointed Minister of Co-ordination of Defence in 1936 I ventured to write a letter to *The Times* recalling this match, and it was published under the heading "Sir Thomas Inskip at Bat." This led to other letters from people who had taken part in the game.

On December 3, 1926, I started on yet another tour abroad, to South America, in the *Andes* of the Royal Mail Line. I was fifty-three, and there was another veteran in the side, G. J. V. Weigall, who was three years older, but we had a good lot of younger, excellent cricketers to carry us—Captain T. O. Jameson, Captain R. T. Stanyforth, Captain L. C. R. Isherwood, M. F. S. Jewell, G. O. Allen, G. R. Jackson, Lord Dunglass, J. C. White, H. P. Miles, and T. A. Pilkington, the son of my old Oxford colleague, C. C. Pilkington, with Captain C. Levick as Honorary Manager, who not only did everything for our comfort, but also acted as banker. A more unselfish man I never met.

We had a delightful voyage, stopping at Vigo, Rio de Janeiro, Santos, and Montevideo, where we disembarked. As we steamed into the harbour Captain Parker paid us the unique honour of flying the M.C.C. flag at the yardarm, a compliment subsequently repeated at Callao, the port of Lima, by Captain Splatt, of the *Orbita*. Never before had a cricket flag been flown on any ship in any sea. This flag had been given to me by the M.C.C. after the 1903–4 tour in Australia, and has since then been flown on many cricket-grounds—at Lord's and the Oval, in this country; in Australia in 1911–12 and 1932–33; in South Africa with Colonel Stanyforth's team in 1927–28; and in Holland in 1928. It has never been hauled down in a rubber of Test Matches, and by some cricketers, including Hobbs and, of course, myself, it was regarded with superstitious reverence. Once, for a few awful hours at Sydney in 1933, it was lost, but it is still in being, tattered and torn, for it has braved the battle and the breeze in many quarters of the globe. It is now at Lord's, and I have left it to the M.C.C. in my will.

We played seven matches in the Argentine, and one at Montevideo, and then, crossing the mighty Andes, we played at Valparaiso and Lima. The tour was unique in that not a single game was played within the British Empire—another proof that cricket has set a girdle round the earth, and that it has become the interest not only of the British race, but of half the world. It was remarked by Sir Hilary Leng in his speech at the dinner given to the team at the Jockey Club at Buenos Aires that we were ambassadors not only of cricket, but of Empire. Never have I travelled with a more charming lot of men, and I, who have sailed in many seas, consider myself very fortunate to have been given the opportunity of seeing so much of the world with such delightful companions.

In Buenos Aires we were received by Dr Alvear, President of the Argentine Republic, and at Lima by Señor Leguia, President of the Republic of Peru, who arrived on the ground heavily guarded.

The Trans-Andean Railway and the Panama Canal might, possibly, be included in the wonders of the world, and I would add the guano birds off the Peruvian coast. There were literally thousands of them: one of the ship's officers said there were 50,000 'on parade' manœuvring about under apparently absolute control. They made a weird and fascinating picture. As we came through the Panama Canal we noticed a cricket-match in progress between teams of West Indian natives, who waved their caps and cheered us. At Colón we found a deputation of them awaiting us on the wharf, and we had a talk with them. They told us that there were seven cricket clubs in Panama, and nine in Colón, all West Indians who were working in the Canal Zone. I presented them with a bat, and congratulated them on the splendid way in which they were keeping the flag of cricket flying.

And so across the Caribbean, where many of our greatest sailors have fought—did not Froude call the Caribbean "the cradle of the naval Empire of Great Britain"?—to Havana, a city set in delightful surroundings. Corunna—it was at Corunna that the Armada finally assembled, and on July 12, 1588, sailed to its doom—Santander, and La Rochelle were our next stopping-places, and on March 5, 1927, we arrived at Plymouth, and a memorable tour was over. We had played ten matches, won six, drawn three, and lost one. There were four games against the Argentine: the first was drawn, the second we won by 127 runs, we lost the third by 29 runs, and the fourth we won by an innings and 12 runs, White taking the last wicket, clean bowled, with the third ball of the last over of the match. White, Allen, Jameson, and Jackson were the best men on the side, and Stanyforth kept wicket admirably. The two 'veterans' did fairly well, and Weigall had no hesitation whatever in proclaiming loudly that we were the best batsmen on sticky wickets!

The Argentine were a pretty good side, captained by C. H. Gibson, of Eton and Cambridge fame. H. Dorning, a bit of a veteran, was a very fine left-handed bowler, slow medium, with flight and accuracy. Their fielding was splendid.

When we returned home each member of the team was presented by the M.C.C. with a pair of sleeve-links in the M.C.C.

colours, bearing monograms. It appears that the then British Minister to the Argentine, Sir Malcolm Robertson, had written saying that "we were worth all the ambassadors in the world"— a graceful compliment indeed from one who, among many others, had helped to make the tour a delightful experience.

15

TOURING TEAMS
1927–29

Visit of the New Zealanders—G. A. Faulkner—Oxford v. Cambridge Centenary—
R.N. and R.M. v. the M.C.C.—Tour in Holland—Choosing a Side for Australia
—The Tour of 1928–29

IN THE following season (1927) the Board of Control threw overboard the selectors of 1926. Many people thought that this was "ingratitude, more strong than traitors' arms," but the new selectors—Leveson Gower, Douglas, and Carr—were sound choices, and helped to build up the splendid team that was to achieve such a great triumph in Australia during the winter of 1928–29. Judging, however, by the many letters I received, the view seemed prevalent that we had had something of a raw deal; but so far as I was concerned, I had no hurt feelings.

There were no Test Matches this year, the New Zealanders, who visited us for the first time as cricketers under the captaincy of T. C. Lowry, not having been given Test Match status, but there were three Trial Matches, and it was clear that we were stronger all round. For one thing, Hammond was in harness again, having completely recovered from his illness, and he had a splendid season, while Jardine was, on figures, even more successful, though he played far fewer innings. Duleepsinhji, after starting the season with scores of 101 against Yorkshire, and 254, not out, against Middlesex, caught a chill on a bitterly cold day at Fenner's, and, pneumonia following, at one time his life was despaired of. Prayers were offered for his recovery in his college (Clare) chapel, and his uncle, Ranjitsinhji, wrote a beautiful and touching letter in appreciation of this to the college authorities. Duleep was a great batsman, and Ranji was very proud of him. Whether he was as great as his uncle is questionable, but he may certainly be numbered among the best batsmen. No one ever played googly bowling better than he did—he simply 'murdered' it—but whether he was quite so secure against fast bowling at the

start of an innings as Ranji is questionable. He owed much to the
coaching of G. A. Faulkner, the famous South African all-
rounder, whom I recollect saying to me in the spring of this year,
"It isn't a question of how to get Duleep out: the question is, how
to stop him scoring."

Faulkner had considerable influence at this period on our cricket,
and, besides Duleep, Jardine, Robins, Peebles, and Killick, who
all eventually played for England, came under his guidance. He
was a great coach, who encouraged his pupils and was neither
too rigid nor too theoretical. He encouraged and did not crab,
imparted a pleasant atmosphere, and made the practices great
fun. He knew everything there is to know of the various depart-
ments of the game, and his book *Cricket: Can it be taught?* now
unfortunately out of print, was a masterpiece. I recall his telling
me that there was a small red-headed boy at St Piran's Private
School, in Maidenhead, which he visited occasionally. "You
watch him. He will make a name for himself." The boy's name
was F. R. Brown.

The Centenary of the Oxford *v.* Cambridge match was celebrated by a dinner at the Savoy Hotel, and there was a notable
gathering of Old Blues of every generation from 1871 to 1927.
Lord Harris made an admirable speech, and said he regarded
himself "as the connecting-link in University cricket, as he had
known one or more of the players in every match from the first
in 1827." Unfortunately the other orators never got farther than
the middle seventies, which naturally annoyed the younger
generations. But it was none the less a happy evening, during
which friendships were renewed and battles refought.

There was another occasion in the autumn when Sir Rowland
Blades, Lord Mayor of London (now Lord Ebbisham), gave a
dinner at the Mansion House "In Honour of Cricket." Lord
Ebbisham and Sir Edward Campbell were the Bedser and Bailey
of the Lords and Commons cricket team shortly after this period,
and there was a wonderful match at Lord's, a few years later,
which ended in a tie, between the M.C.C. and Lords and Commons, when a fast yorker from G. O. Allen sent Lord Ebbisham's
middle stump flying in a cloud of dust. I should like to see a
revival of Parliamentary cricket—Lords *v.* Commons and Government *v.* Opposition—but in these strenuous and anxious days
both Houses are tied to Westminster more than they used to be.

There are many good cricketers in both Lords and Commons, a large proportion of them on the Labour side, and, indeed, I have seldom met a keener cricketer than the Minister of Education, the Right Hon. George Tomlinson, M.P., a Red Rose if ever there was one, spoiling for the blood of the Yorkists!

One of my most pleasant memories of the summer of 1928 is a match at Portsmouth between the Royal Navy and Royal Marines and the M.C.C. It was the first occasion the M.C.C. had played at Portsmouth, and a splendid game ended in a draw. The scores were: R.N. and R.M. 439 for nine wickets—Lieutenant-Commander T. E. Halsey 124, Major R. A. D. Brooks[1] 78, Sub-Lieutenant R. H. Stephenson 80, Lieutenant R. J. Shaw 50, Lieutenant-Commander S. V. Jephson 55—and 148 for four wickets, declared—Stephenson 63, not out—and M.C.C. 295—S. Brown 111, Captain L. C. R. Isherwood 64—and 286 for eight wickets—B. H. Lyon 135, Hubble 52. We went for the runs, but just failed to win. It was a three-day match, and on the second evening there was a big dinner at the Naval Barracks at which Vice-Admiral Sir Hugh Watson[2] presided, and the C.-in-C. at Portsmouth, Admiral de Beauvoir Brock,[3] Admiral Sir Montague Browning, Admiral Cecil Hickley, General Halliday,[4] Lord Harris, Captain G. H. D'Oyly Lyon,[5] the famous England Rugby full-back, Major E. G. Wynyard, and many other distinguished officers were present. It was a great occasion; the lovely band, the beautiful room, with the portrait of the immortal Nelson and the frescoes on the walls of Trafalgar, the Nile, Copenhagen, the glorious First of June, and Sir Richard Grenville's fight off the Azores, were inspiring to a degree, for there on the walls was the history of England. The Loyal Toast, "Mr Vice, the King—Gentlemen, the King," made my blood tingle, as it always has done and always will do. It was an evening which none of us will ever forget, and in after-years it was often said to me, "If you are taking a side to Portsmouth again, please don't forget me."

After dinner in the anteroom there was a great wrestling-match between Sub-Lieutenant K. A. Sellar[6] and Midshipman J. F.

[1] Now General Sir Dallas Brooks, K.C.B., C.M.G., D.S.O., Governor of Victoria.
[2] Now Admiral Sir Hugh Watson, K.C.B., C.V.O., C.B.E.
[3] Later Admiral of the Fleet Sir Osmond de Beauvoir Brock, G.C.B., K.C.M.G., K.C.V.O.
[4] Now General Sir Lewis Halliday, V.C., K.C.B.
[5] Later Admiral Sir George Hamilton D'Oyly Lyon, K.C.B., C.-in-C., The Nore.
[6] Now Captain K. A. Sellar, D.S.O., D.S.C.—like Lyon, a great England full-back.

ON THE VOYAGE TO SOUTH AMERICA IN 1926

Left to right—Back row: L. C. R. Isherwood, G. O. Allen, H. P. Miles, J. C. White, G. R. Jackson, M. F. S. Jewell, R. T. Stanyforth. *Middle row*: T. O. Jameson, P. F. W., G. J. V. Weigall. *Front row*: T. A. Pilkington, C. Levick, Lord Dunglass.

R. H. TWINING AND G. T. S. STEVENS GOING OUT TO BAT AT THE HAGUE IN 1928

Cochrane—"Cockroach" to his friends. They rolled all over the
floor like a couple of Hackenschmidts, amid shouting and laughter,
urged on by their respective partisans.

At the end of July I was asked by the M.C.C. to captain a side
in Holland. It was their Jubilee, for they have been playing
cricket at The Hague since 1878, and I was the bearer of a letter
of congratulation and good wishes from Lord Lucan, the President of the M.C.C. We won our three matches, the last, at
Harlem, by five wickets off the last ball of the day. We had a
good side—G. T. S. Stevens, E. R. T. Holmes, R. H. Twining,
G. D. Kemp-Welch, N. G. Wykes, M. A. McCanlis, M. J. C.
Allom, H. P. Hunloke, my son E. P. Warner, and E. H.
Tattersall, D.S.O., a fine wicket-keeper and a very gallant man,
who was recommended for the V.C. in the 1914–18 War. It
was a delightful week. We were put up in private houses, and
my host was so keen a cricketer that he invariably spent a few
weeks in England during the summer to watch some of the
big matches. He was a great admirer of England, though he
did not approve of capital punishment. I had the good fortune,
too, to meet C. J. Posthuma at his lovely house, and he showed
me his rose-garden, which was a sight indeed. Hunloke knew
quite a lot about pictures, and we explored the famous galleries.

Our opponents were a good side, and they knew our strokes
and placed the field cleverly. This was the last M.C.C. side
abroad which I was privileged to captain. I had been so honoured
on five occasions—1903–4 and 1911–12 in Australia, 1905–6 in
South Africa, 1926–27 in South America, and now in Holland.

I was one of the Selection Committee appointed by the M.C.C.
to choose the side for Australia. Lord Harris was Chairman, and
no one could have desired a better. There were six or seven of
us, and at a later date Harris brought Hobbs into our deliberations. It was in a way an easy task, except that we suffered from
an *embarras de richesses* so far as batting was concerned, and in
the end we left out Woolley! This nearly drove Weigall mad,
and, looking back across the years, I think that we made a mistake.
But competition was severe, with three left-handed batsmen—
Woolley himself, Mead, and Leyland. They were all in tremendous form that season, and eventually Mead and Leyland were
given preference. Woolley rubbed it in with a vengeance when
in the concluding days of the season he made three centuries. The

I

anger of Kentish men and women was shattering, and I hesitated to go to the Folkestone Festival, where I knew I should encounter Weigall. Outwardly we were friendly and courteous, but in private he let go some of his most stinging phrases, which crumpled me up. Woolley was "a god," Leyland "a cross-batted village-greener," and Mead "a leaden-footed cart-horse"! In the sequel, Leyland, playing in only one Test Match, the last, scored 137 and 53, not out. Mead also played in only one Test, the first, and did not do anything like so well, though he made 73 in the second innings, and I think Woolley had good cause for his natural disappointment.

The tour was a tremendous success, England winning four of the five Tests under Chapman's splendid captaincy. His catch in the slips in the first Test, at Brisbane, off Larwood, which got out Woodfull, is one of the greatest catches in cricket history. As I have said before, this side of Chapman's was one of the finest that has ever represented England. I place it second to none. This tour saw the first appearance of Bradman in Test Matches. No bigger than a cloud the size of a man's hand when he first appeared, he was destined to plague and dominate our bowlers for nearly a quarter of a century, and to write his name in very big letters in the chronicles of the game.

16

A VOYAGE TO SOUTH AFRICA
1929–31

*The South Africans in England—Woodfull's Team—Bradman—Illness and a Trip
to South Africa*

BEARSTED WAS once again the scene of an interesting match,
for before their tour began the South Africans were good
enough to play a game there, but it was a bitterly cold day, and
it ended in a draw. We had a pretty good side, with such notables
as Woolley, Ashdown, Stevens, Hendren, B. H. Lyon, Tennyson,
Enthoven, Peebles, A. J. Evans, and Stanyforth. This 1929 South
African side did not win one of the five Test Matches. They lost
at Leeds after a good fight, and ran us hard in the other four
games, which were all drawn. H. G. Deane was a most able
captain, and other good men were H. B. Cameron, H. W.
Taylor, B. Mitchell, D. P. B. Morkel, and H. G. Owen-Smith,
eventually as famous on the Rugger-field as on the cricket-field.
They were a great fielding side, and confirmed the reports which
Stanyforth's team which toured South Africa during the winter
of 1927–28 had brought back: that they were a difficult side to
defeat. Who that saw it will forget Owen-Smith's catch in the
deep field at Leeds, when he ran some fifteen yards at full speed
and held a hard, low drive of Tate's? And Cameron may be
ranked with any wicket-keeper of any age, and a glorious driver
of a cricket-ball, who, against Yorkshire at Sheffield in 1935, hit
Verity for 30—4, 4, 4, 6, 6, 6—in one over. Cameron died at the
age of thirty from enteric fever, on November 2, in the same year,
to the grief of all who knew him. As *Wisden* for 1936 wrote:
"Cameron was a very fine personality, one who enriched the
game." Whether they come to challenge us at cricket, Rugby
football, or any other game, the South Africans are always very
welcome, for they invariably play in the finest possible manner
and spirit.

When the Australians, under the captaincy of W. M. Woodfull, arrived in 1930 there was an unusual amount of confidence expressed that England would retain the Ashes; but close observers had not forgotten that Chapman's splendid side had been hard pressed in the last three Tests, and I recall Hobbs uttering a word of caution. Woodfull and Ponsford were more reliable batsmen than ever; Oldfield was the best wicket-keeper in the world; and there were several young batsmen, headed by Bradman. In the end we lost the rubber to a fine side which always seemed to be on top of us after the first Test, at Trent Bridge, which we won by 93 runs. At the end of the tour Bradman wrote *Don Bradman's Book*,[1] and he paid me the compliment of asking me to write an introduction. I venture to mention that my prophecy as to his future career as a batsman turned out to be pretty accurate!

Just before they left for home Sir Kynaston Studd, President of the M.C.C. that year, gave a dinner in honour of the Australians in the beautiful hall of the Merchant Taylors' Company, at which Dame Clara Butt sang *Land of Hope and Glory*, which no one who was there will ever fail to recall. And there were fine speeches too, by Lord Harris, Ranjitsinhji, and Sir James Barrie —Ranji's a masterly oration.

In the autumn of 1930 I suddenly became very ill with a form of virulent poisoning. In three weeks I lost two stone, and as I am no Falstaff I could not afford to do so. A voyage to South Africa in company with my daughter followed, and the sea-breezes, plus Jack Rennert's[2] daily glass of champagne, quickly restored me to health. Before the end of the voyage I was strong enough to take part in a game of deck cricket, and when I was batting a passenger asked, "Who is that young fellow? He shapes uncommonly well!" As my head was hidden in a Panama, he had not, from the back of the net, discerned the ravages of time. The voyage to South Africa is probably the most health-giving in the world, and the time passed very pleasantly. Sir Abe Bailey was a passenger, and he had brought with him a library of books, to which he kindly gave me access, and many a talk did I have with that most interesting and able man.

At our table were Mr and Mrs Graham, a charming couple from Natal, who told us tales of the black mamba which used

[1] Hutchinson, 1930.
[2] J. Rennert, Harrow Eleven, 1904–5. In the latter year he scored 20 and 94 against Eton.

it, but that the first volume took him only to the age of nineteen! We suggested that it did not matter in the least how many
volumes he wrote, for he had touched life at many points. People
will recall later how he was to lose both his legs, and how cheer-
fully and pluckily he took his misfortune, saying that he had one
leg in England and the other in South Africa, and that no one
could pull his leg now! For South African cricket he did much,
as he put his hand deeply into his pocket to further its interests
and development, as did the great Rhodes, of whom he was a
fervent admirer, and who died in a cottage next door to Rusten-
Vrede.

Those happy days in South Africa seem like a dream. Bathing
in the sea at Muizenberg, fishing from Sir Abe Bailey's motor-
launch, tennis at the Van der Bijls', and the race-meetings, at one
of which we met Captain Bonham-Carter, one of the heroes of
Zeebrugge, and a very popular personality—so popular, indeed,
that a cocktail was named "The Bonham" in honour of him.[1]
He invited us to lunch in his ship, H.M.S. *Carlisle*, and there I
renewed my friendship with R. B. Cunliffe and K. A. Sellar, who
had played in the Navy *v*. M.C.C. match at Portsmouth. But
just before I was due to return to England this pleasant tour was
marred by the news of Douglas's death, of which I read in an
evening newspaper on the stoep of the McCarthys' house. He
had died trying to save the life of his father when the ship in
which they were sailing from Norway on the voyage home was
sunk in collision with another vessel. For a second or two my
heart stopped beating. John had served me so well in Australia
in 1911–12, when I was laid aside by illness, and it was hard to
realize that so vital and strong a life had gone. Father and son
were devoted to each other—their relationship was a beautiful
one—and if John had to die I imagine that he would have sought
no finer end.

On Boxing Day I sailed for England, thoroughly restored to
health, and with unforgettable memories of South Africa and its
people. Southampton on a January morning was a bit of a
contrast to the glorious skies of the Cape Peninsula. Shall I ever
see the Lion's Head again? Like Kipling's soldier, I think I
shall, if I live, trek there once more, before Father Time gives
me out.

[1] Now Admiral Sir Stuart Bonham-Carter, K.C.B., C.V.O., D.S.O.

17

THE AUSTRALIAN TOUR OF 1932-33

1931–33

Chairman of the Board of Control Selectors—The New Zealanders Again—The Scottish Public Schools—Death of Lord Harris—The Tour of 1932-33

I WAS back as Chairman of the Board of Control Selectors in 1931, the other two members being P. A. Perrin and T. A. Higson. We were to hold office for two years in order to build up a team for the M.C.C. Australian tour of 1932-33. The rule prohibiting any member of the Committee from writing in the Press was still in force, but Gwynne, hearing of this, intimated that he would forgo my writing on the Test and Trial games. I greatly appreciated, and welcomed, his generous attitude, for serving on these Committees was, to me, at any rate, of absorbing interest. We chose Jardine as captain. He was as good in the committee-room as he was on the field of play, for he was versed in cricket lore and history, and took enormous pains. This Committee was the best on which I have ever served, and W. Findlay, the then Secretary of the M.C.C., who was very near to us and very helpful, maintains to this day that we were "the best of all the Selection Committees."

The New Zealanders were here this year, under the captaincy of T. C. Lowry. Originally only one Test Match was arranged, but after their fine cricket at Lord's two more were given them, at the Oval and Old Trafford. England won at the Oval, the games at Lord's and Old Trafford being drawn. It was a very wet and cheerless summer.

By the end of the season we were full of optimism, for we felt that we had a team in being. Our chief problems were a partner for Sutcliffe to open the innings, the right type of bowlers, and the batting order—"concrete in the middle," as I called it, a phrase which Jardine liked. Finally we were determined to have a side that would put cricket first, second, and all the time. We knew that we should have to put finishing touches, as it were, to

the team during the next season, but we felt confident that w
should eventually produce a sound combination.

The New Zealanders had a great batsman in C. S. Dempster,
and were a very good fielding side. Lowry was a most able
captain, who invariably insisted on a strict adherence to the two-
minute law between the fall of wickets. They were an attractive
and popular side, and in the latter part of their tour we were glad
to welcome A. T. Donnelly,[1] Chairman of the New Zealand
Cricket Council.

I greatly enjoyed the University Match, and some of the best
cricket of the season was shown when Pataudi and Owen-Smith
were batting to the bowling of Brown, Farnes, and Hazlerigg.[2]
This was the game in which Ratcliffe scored 201 in Cambridge's
first innings, a record score in the University Match, which he
was destined to hold for only twenty-four hours, for next day
Pataudi beat it. Ratcliffe was a last choice, and gained his Blue
only because J. G. W. Davies had sprained his ankle a few days
before. How often has a last choice proved an outstanding
success! Oxford won by eight wickets. The Oxford Captain,
D. N. Moore, was unable to play because of illness, but before
this he had been very successful as a batsman, and had built up a
splendid side. In his absence A. Melville, who was later to lead
Sussex and South Africa, captained Oxford, and did so un-
commonly well.

I captained an M.C.C. team in Scotland, playing against Fettes,
Loretto, Merchiston Castle, Edinburgh Academy, and the Grange
Club. There were three veterans in the side—George Challenor,
the great West Indies batsman, K. G. Macleod, and myself—supported by a complement of excellent and energetic youth.
Macleod's hair was now grey, but he was still a magnificent
fielder. I had never before seen the great Scottish schools, and it
was a very happy experience for me. I am glad to think that
before I ceased to take the field I had the pleasure of seeing these
famous schools. Did not Mr Churchill say, "I have only one
criticism to make of the Scots: there are not enough of them"?
It was delightful for me to meet, after a lapse of many years,
James Rhoades, who was at Rugby with me, and a good fast-
medium left-handed bowler, now a master at Fettes. I stayed
with him, and after making some 40-odd runs I was very stiff

indeed. So he put me in a hot bath with some unstiffening ingredient in it, and I remember feeling good after it, and even better when, later, the oldest cask was opened, and we spent a delightful evening and were boys again and back at Rugby.

What splendid Rugger players these Scottish schools have turned out, and none greater than Kenneth Macleod, who was asked to play for Scotland when a boy at Fettes, but the Head-master wisely said no. To this day I can hear the shouts of "Feet, Scotland, feet!" at the internationals at Twickenham, which is apt to turn the hearts of Englishmen to water, as does *Land of My Fathers* sung as only Welshmen can sing it.

About this time my younger boy was at Mr Gilbert Ashton's preparatory school, Abberley Hall, in the most beautiful part of Worcestershire. Did not Lord Baldwin of Bewdley say, "Men of Kent and Kentish men call their county the Garden of England. We do not argue with them. We know that Worcestershire is that garden"? In two successive years I captained the Fathers *v.* the Sons. On the second occasion my son, John, was the School Captain, and, as the school magazine put it, "when the rival cap-tains went out to toss they were faced by a battery of cameras." General Sir Reginald Pinney, with his lobs, was one of our bowlers, and assured me that, had he been put on earlier, he would have run through them.

Lord Harris died on March 24, 1932. In him the M.C.C. lost their greatest and most devoted son. To him Lord's was as the breath of his nostrils: he loved every nook and corner of it.

It was on the Finance and Cricket Committee of the M.C.C. that my old friend was the guiding star. No one could have watched over expenditure with a more eagle-like eye, and yet, when it came to spending money or buying property to benefit the Club, no one could have advised me more earnestly than he did, to go ahead.[1]

And Findlay said, "Cricket and M.C.C. have lost their best friend."[2]

Perhaps Harris was a bit of a dictator, but he was eminently just and fair. I played only twice with him—at Eton for the M.C.C., captained by C. M. Wells, and at Vincent Square against Westminster School, to play whom I had got up a side. On both occasions he made a few runs in a fine upstanding style, and no one could have been nicer or more pleasant, though I have heard

[1] Lord Hawke, in *Wisden*, 1934.   [2] *Wisden*.

it said that some people did not always enjoy playing with him. That, however, was certainly not my experience. The beautiful Memorial to him at Lord's, with its garden—it was suggested during the Second World War that we should grow potatoes on it! I by-passed the idea, and I think I may claim some credit for the lovely garden we have to-day, which has become a trysting-place during Eton *v.* Harrow and Oxford *v.* Cambridge. Lord Harris and W. G. are the only men who have permanent Memorials at Lord's.

The Indians were here this year (1932), and were given a Test Match at Lord's, which in the end we won fairly easily, but it was a stern fight for a long time. C. K. Nayudu and Amar Singh were very fine all-round cricketers, the latter, indeed, good enough to be considered for a World Eleven in his day.

The selectors were kept pretty busy, for, in addition to the Test Match, we were concerned with two Test Trials—at Old Trafford and at Cardiff—and we also had a big say in Gentlemen *v.* Players. Duleepsinhji was taken seriously ill early in August —an illness which was to close his brilliant cricket career—and Robins had informed us that because of the claims of business he was not a candidate for Australia. These were heavy losses, but in spite of them we believed that we had at hand a strong side. Those responsible for the final choice of the team were Lord Hawke, as Chairman of the M.C.C. Cricket Committee, Jardine, Perrin, Higson, and myself. Never was there an easier Selection Committee meeting. There were, of course, the usual number of critics who considered that we had not a chance of victory—one of them Neville Cardus, of all people—who thought me a con-firmed optimist. I had ventured to suggest that we should win the rubber unless Fleetwood-Smith, a left-handed googly bowler, who had been tremendously 'boosted' in the Australian Press, turned out to be a superman.

Anyhow, Hammond, stimulated by the entreaties of his com-panions to 'put him right,' did so with such marked effect in the first match, against Victoria at Melbourne, with a glorious innings of 203, that Fleetwood-Smith was not chosen for a single Test Match, at which we all rejoiced, for he certainly bowled a very difficult ball, if not always having control of length.

Before the season began Lord Hawke sounded me as to whether I would go to Australia as Manager of the team. I asked for time to consider the matter. I knew Australia well, of course, and had always got on with the Australians. I had many friends there, but I hesitated long and spent some sleepless nights. I had read Rolf Boldrewood's (his real name was Browne, and we had met in the Melbourne Club) *Robbery under Arms* and *A Sydney-side Saxon*, and I knew by heart many of Adam Lindsay Gordon's and "Banjo" Paterson's verses. I loved the climate and the mysterious-looking gum-trees, and I had a nostalgia to see again Sydney Harbour, Mount Lofty, and the Adelaide ground, and to hear the hum of the great crowds at a Test Match. And so, in the end, I went, and with me came R. C. N. Palairet, whom I had known since my Oriel days. A cruel fate had decided that he should break his knee-cap playing Association football, which, of course, greatly handicapped his cricket—at Repton he was said to be as good a batsman as his brother, Lionel—but I never heard him utter one word of complaint. W. Ferguson, the most-travelled man in the world, came with us as scorer and baggage-manager —a genius at both.

We returned, having won four of the five Test Matches, but "Body Line," as the Australians called it, cast a shadow over the tour. The Australians objected to it strenuously, and not always tactfully—but thousands of words on the subject have already been written, some of them by myself, and I do not propose to discuss it here. It would serve no good purpose, and let us hope that it is now buried in the dust-heap of oblivion. The curious and ironical sequence was that in 1948 in this country we saw a recurrence of it by, of all people, the Australians themselves— Bradman's famous team—who had been so bitterly antagonistic to it. At Trent Bridge, in the first Test, Miller, as *The Times* put it, "with a toss of his mane and a petulant mien, gave the impression that intimidation was at least part of his object," and at Old Trafford in the third Test there was a good deal of unpleasantness. Private conversation between the authorities subsequently put matters on a calmer basis, and we hope we shall see no recurrence of it, for, whatever may be said, it is not in the best interests of the game, for it destroys its harmony, to say the least of it, and is against the spirit of cricket.

Body Line was first seen in England as far back as 1910, when W. B. Burns, an extremely fast bowler, of Worcestershire, bowled it against Middlesex at Lord's. I objected to it then, as I did later when Macdonald, the great fast bowler of Armstrong's 1921 eleven, and later of Lancashire, adopted these tactics, and also when Bowes did so in the Surrey *v.* Yorkshire match at the Oval in 1932, just before we sailed for Australia. My objection to it, therefore, goes back to a period when Jardine was a boy of ten at a preparatory school.

Jardine bore much harsh treatment and barracking in Australia with dignity and courage. He considered that this type of bowling was within the law, but I fancy that he would admit that it was a stern policy. However, let sleeping dogs lie, and congratulate him on his splendid captaincy of a great side. As for Larwood, a great bowler and a very nice man, he was more sinned against than sinning, and when he returned to England a section of the Press exploited him in a most unworthy manner. He might well have said, "Save me from my friends," but that he was personally admired by the Australians is certain, and this has been emphasized by the great welcome and widespread kindness shown to him on his recent arrival in Australia, where he has now made his home.

In another part of this book I have suggested that this M.C.C. team, so ably led by Jardine, was one of the best we have ever had. It was a splendid fielding side, only one catch, in the slips, being dropped until the last Test, and that a very difficult one, and Ames was a most reliable wicket-keeper. We were never quite happy about a partner for Sutcliffe, Jardine, Wyatt, and Leyland filling the rôle at various times, but the bowling was very good indeed in the hands of Larwood, Allen, Voce, Verity, and Hammond, and, collectively, it has seldom been surpassed on the fast wickets on which all the Test Matches were played. Paynter's great innings of 83 in the fourth Test at Brisbane, when he rose from a sick-bed with his throat bandaged after an attack of tonsillitis, was a monument of grit and courage, and I am not sure that this match will not be known as "Paynter's Match" by future historians. At one time it was very doubtful if he would be able to bat: he was taken ill on the first day, and when I told Jardine this he said, "What about those fellows who marched to Kandahar with fever on them?"—a remark which delighted me, and was typical of our captain's grit and determination.

The beautiful young batsman Archie Jackson, whose style was a blend of that of Trumper and Kippax, died during this match, and at his Memorial Service in Sydney I was asked to speak, and for the first and only time in my life ascended a pulpit. The church was packed, and there was a large crowd outside listening to the loud-speakers. It was indeed a compliment, and a gesture which showed that amid all the trouble there was still much good feeling.

During the tour we met many of the famous old Australian cricketers, and many a happy evening did we spend in the Union Club at Sydney, the Melbourne Club, the Adelaide Club, and the Weld Club at Perth. We also went to Canberra, where Jardine, Palairet, Allen, Pataudi, and I stayed two or three days with the Governor-General, Sir Isaac and Lady Isaacs. Sir Isaac was one of the most interesting men I have ever met. A distinguished jurist, he knew innumerable languages, and our stay at Canberra was made very pleasant. Lord and Lady Gowrie—he was then Governor of South Australia—were also delightful hosts, and all over Australia we met with great hospitality.

From Australia we sailed for New Zealand, where Hammond played magnificent innings of 227 and 336, not out, in the Test Matches, and it was remarked that "the coming generation of New Zealand cricketers should be batsmen. They have certainly been shown how to do it." The sequel has proved that the speaker was not far wrong. We spent a few days at Rotorua, and were welcomed by the Maori Chief. Through an interpreter he made a most eloquent speech, beginning with "Distinguished strangers from beyond the far horizon," and referred to King George V in terms of great loyalty, and to "that country beyond the seas of which they were so proud to be a part, if a distant part." I had to reply, and I felt that I could not open in conventional style, but I bethought me of *King Solomon's Mines*, and began with "Great Chief, Incomparable One," which went down well, as did a reference to the Maoris' skill at Rugby football. I was told afterwards that I could not have made a happier remark, "as it is still the ambition of every Maori wife to have a Rugby-playing son." We came home via Fiji, Honolulu, Victoria, Vancouver Island, and over the Rockies to Toronto.

18

THE PROBLEMS OF SELECTION

1933–37

The West Indies Tour of 1933—The "Morning Post" and the "Daily Telegraph"—
The Australian Tour of 1934—A Trip to Gibraltar—The South African Team of
1935—Selection Committees

THE WEST INDIES were here in 1933. They were a good side,
but not a great one, and they lost two of the three Test
Matches, that at Old Trafford being drawn. They were well
captained by G. C. Grant, an old Cambridge Blue, a magnificent
fieldsman at backward point or short leg, and a useful batsman.
He was brimful of zest and enthusiasm. In G. Headley, "the
Bradman of the Caribbean," as he was called, they had a great
batsman, who scored 2320 runs, with an average of 66·28, and
in E. A. Martindale, a really fast bowler, with a loose, free swing
of the arm, who at his best was probably the equal of any of the
great West Indies fast bowlers. The team left behind them an
impression of keenness, combined with modesty and good
humour.

It was not, however, a happy season, for the Body Line controversy was still simmering, and cables continued to pass between the M.C.C. and the Australian Board of Control. A special
committee was appointed, with Lord Hailsham, the President of
the M.C.C., as Chairman, before which I gave evidence. Some
people thought that I had got the wrong perspective, but that I
was correct in opposing this type of bowling was proved by subsequent happenings. The cricket world for the moment was upside-
down, and nerves were frayed. Even in the University Match
Body Line was used by Farnes, and one Oxford batsman was
bowled off his jaw, while another hit his wicket after being struck
on the neck. Constantine and Martindale also employed it in the
Test Match at Old Trafford, and Hammond had his chin laid
open. *Wisden* had strong comment on all this, and people began
to realize that even if Body Line was within the law it was not in

the best interests of cricket. At Old Trafford Jardine played a magnificent innings of 127, but one ball from Constantine missed his jaw by a fraction of an inch. England were without Larwood, but were none the less a powerful all-round team, and Jardine was as able a captain as he had shown himself in Australia. I was asked to be a member of the Board of Control Selection Committee for these Test Matches, but I declined. I had had enough of controversy for the time being, and Lord Hawke took my place as Chairman.

At the beginning of this season my connexion with the *Morning Post* came to an end. Just before leaving New Zealand I had sent a cablegram to the Editor suggesting that I should write less on the actual matches, and once a week give a general appreciation, as had been the case in some previous years, and which, apparently, people had liked. Cables are not always the best way of expressing oneself, for they are expensive and tend to be cryptic or vague, and the Editor regarded my cablegram as an ultimatum, rather than a suggestion, which was very far from being my intention. On my return to England I hastened to see Gwynne. No question of money came into the matter. Apparently he thought that I had some other newspaper in view, against which I protested strongly, and asked whether he really thought that I would behave like that after our long and happy association. He said, "No; but the season was approaching and I was afraid that I might be left without a cricket correspondent." We parted, and remained, the best of friends, until his death a year or so ago, but I fancy that he acted rather on the impulse of the moment, and I know that this view was held by some of his closest associates. But I learned a lesson. Cables are often an unsatisfactory method of communication. Now, with an air-mail service, matters such as this can be dealt with without a chance of misinterpretation or lack of clarity. My loss was the *Morning Post's* gain, for R. C. Robertson-Glasgow succeeded me, and the paper gained an able writer, and one who knew his cricket. I do not hesitate to say, however, that I felt deeply the break in a very happy relationship.

Some weeks later the *Daily Telegraph* invited me to write for them, and the invitation was renewed in 1934, but I was not altogether so happy in my relationship with them as I had been with the *Morning Post*. We did not always entirely agree as to how cricket should be written.

ETON *v.* HARROW, 1936

My great-nephew, aged seven. Regardez le chapeau!

Photo Sport and General

FIELD–MARSHAL VISCOUNT MONTGOMERY ARRIVING AT LORD'S. IN 1945

Photo Sport and General

The season of 1934 was an Australian one, but Body Line was still simmering, and, indeed, began to seethe. As in the previous year, there was considerable unpleasantness. Larwood "put himself beyond the pale of being selected for England" (*Wisden*) by a statement in the Press, and 'the trouble' also deprived England of the services of Jardine and Voce. We were, therefore, greatly handicapped. We lost the rubber by two matches to one, two games being drawn, one of them much in favour of the Australians. In the second Test, at Lord's, Verity caught them on a sticky wicket, and took fifteen wickets for 104 runs, thus beating Rhodes's feat at Melbourne in 1904 of fifteen wickets for 124 runs; but Verity had far better support in the field than Rhodes had had. The Selection Committee (Sir Stanley Jackson, P. Perrin, and T. A. Higson) had a very difficult task, for they were robbed of three indispensable cricketers. They had every one's sympathy.

My wife had gone to Gibraltar in October for her health, and my younger boy and I joined her for a month at Christmas, in the course of which we visited Algeciras, Cadiz, Malaga, Jerez, and Tangier. At Jerez we lunched with the Marqués and Marquesa de Torresoto, the head of the Gonzalez family, at their lovely place, El Cuco. We were a large party. Our hostess told me that she had forty-nine grandchildren: a few years later she got her 50! A memorable day, graced by the courtesy of a very charming family, and I felt my Spanish blood asserting itself. New Year's Eve was a festive occasion at the Rock Hotel. Some of the younger officers of the Gordon Highlanders gave a superb imitation of a bull-fight. The 'bull' was magnificent, and at the end of the fight was dragged out of the ballroom amid tremendous applause. The Royal Navy were always in and out of Gibraltar, and as the ship in which I was returning to England was about to sail the gun-room officers of H.M.S. *Shropshire* made a farewell signal to me. The Governor of Gibraltar and Commander-in-Chief, General Sir Charles Harington, and Lady Harington were very good to us, and he persuaded me to give a talk on cricket before a considerable company, which included admirals, generals, bluejackets, and privates, and I was cross-examined about Body Line by a keen cricketing bluejacket.

One word more on the season of 1934. Bradman, after, for him, a modest start, finished with an aggregate of 2020 runs, and an average of 84·16. He played many glorious innings, as did

K

Ponsford, a very great player indeed, who dealt out heavy punishment with a bat weighing nearly three pounds, and McCabe. As great an innings as any Bradman played on this tour was his 160, out of 225, in just over two hours against Middlesex at Lord's—without a chance. Robert Lyttelton told me next day that his absolute limit was one glass of port after dinner, but "last night I had to have another in honour of that innings." Truly another champion had arisen!

The South Africans visited us in 1935, and for the first time in their history won a Test Match in this country, defeating England at Lord's by 157 runs, and a great crowd gathered in front of the pavilion and cheered them loud and long. It has been said that more than one match has been lost in the Committee Room. In my view two rubbers have been lost by faulty selection. The first on this occasion, and the second in the choice of Allen's M.C.C. side to Australia in 1936–37. The choice of the England Eleven for the Lord's match involved the longest Selection Committee meeting in my experience. It began at eleven o'clock in the morning, and did not end until seven, with intervals for lunch and tea, during which we continued to argue. The point at issue was whether Robins or Mitchell, of Derbyshire, should play. The selectors (Perrin, Higson, and myself) were unanimously in favour of Robins, while Wyatt, the England captain, was equally emphatic in supporting Mitchell. No argument, no comparison of previous performances, could convince him, and in the end, physically and mentally exhausted, we gave way. To this day I curse myself. But we were in this difficulty: the captain has a casting vote, and obviously great weight must be given to his views, for he has to run the side in the field and work out strategy and tactics. I have come to the conclusion that the rule has its weakness, and I believe a better method would be to decide by a majority vote, after weighing most carefully, as we did, all the captain has to say. There are few cricketers I admire more than Wyatt. Apart from his skill as a player, he is a man of great courage, who has been hit in almost every part of his body, from the jaw to the ankle, and has never turned a hair and never flinched from any bowler, however fast, or however bumpy the wicket. Moreover, he is a great companion on a tour, always 100 per cent. fit, and an asset to captain and manager.

In 1935 the leather-jackets descended on Lord's, and caused it to look like "the sand on the seashore," as Perrin put it, and Wyatt was cast-iron in his opinion that Mitchell would win the match for us. But his determined resistance to the views of his colleagues—an experienced body of men, if I may say so—ended in disaster, for Mitchell, in a comparatively small-scoring match —South Africa 228 and 278 for seven wickets, declared; England 198 and 151—took but three wickets for 164 runs, and he was not, of course, in anything like the same class as—indeed, a very long way below—Robins as a batsman and a fielder. It was a case of theory run wild, and, trying to prove that he was right in his theory, Wyatt overbowled Mitchell. It was a sad affair.

On the second occasion there was the same Selection Committee, and on this occasion Sir Stanley Jackson, Chairman, Lord Cobham, and H. D. G. Leveson Gower, as representing the M.C.C., and, of course, Allen, the captain, joined us in our deliberations. Jackson, Cobham, and Leveson Gower had seen little first-class cricket that season, and Perrin, Higson, and myself had added another year to our experience. We felt that Paynter should be included. We needed an opening partner for Barnett, for Sutcliffe had "experienced his worst season since his early association with the county [Yorkshire]"[1] and was also suffering from some shoulder-trouble. Wyatt and Fagg were also candidates for this position, but Wyatt was not the batsman he had been, and because of his honourable wounds had become very brittle. Paynter seemed to Perrin, Higson, and myself the obvious choice. He had had a very successful season —2016 runs, with an average of 45·81—and we stressed his splendid record with Jardine's team in Australia, of which Allen was fully cognisant, for he was there. Moreover, Paynter was a left-hander, and a counter to the leg-break, googly bowling of O'Reilly, the bowler we had most to fear. He could bat anywhere in the order of going in—No. 1, 3, 5, or 6—and was a superb fielder. I expressed my apprehension of Wyatt's fitness, and, as fate decreed, he fractured a bone in his hand during the third match of the tour, and missed the first three Tests. The opening pair were changed from Test to Test—Barnett and Worthington in the first, Barnett and Fagg in the second, Barnett and Worthington in the third, Barnett and Verity in the fourth, and Barnett and Worthington in the fifth, Wyatt going in No. 5

[1] *Wisden.*

in the fourth and No. 6 in the fifth Test Match. It is freely admitted that Allen had very bad luck, for "seldom has a touring side been so persistently dogged by injuries and illness as this one was," as *Wisden* put it, but surely it was a mistake to leave Paynter behind? We argued for hours, but Jackson held that as Allen insisted on Wyatt, instead of Paynter, he, as captain, must have the final decision. And so it was, but how Allen was so forgetful of Paynter's qualities seemed difficult to understand. I hasten to add that these discussions were carried on with courtesy and good temper on both sides.

When the Australians came here in 1938 Paynter, under Hammond's captaincy, was chosen for all the five Tests—the third, at Old Trafford, was abandoned without a ball being bowled—and made scores of 216 not out, 99 and 43, run out, 28 and 21, not out, in a small-scoring match at Leeds, and 0, with an average of 101·75. In South Africa, during the winter of 1938–39, Paynter scored 1072 runs with an average of 76·57, including one double century and two centuries in Test Matches, for the M.C.C. team under Hammond's captaincy. It seems to me that both Wyatt in 1935 and Allen in 1936 were rather like the Soviet(!): they kept on stressing their own views, and did not give sufficient weight to the arguments of the other side. They appeared to set little store by facts. Now, I readily admit that it may well be said that Perrin, Higson, and I were, for our part, equally insistent on our own views, but I claim that those views were based on recent performances, and the sequel showed that we were right.

This team of Allen's was rather haphazardly chosen: it contained four fast bowlers—Allen himself, Farnes, Voce, and Copson, the last of whom never played in a Test Match—and two leg-break bowlers—Robins and Sims—and none of our bowlers of this last type have ever had much success in Australia—for example, J. W. Hearne, Freeman, and Wright, though the critics in Australia aver that Wright deserved much more than came his way. I regretted the absence of Captain J. W. A. Stephenson, a steady, untiring fast-medium bowler, a truly magnificent fieldsman, and a plucky determined batsman at No. 8 or 9 in the order; and not enough credit was given to him for his superb bowling in Gentlemen *v.* Players, when he took ten wickets in a row—nine in the first innings, followed by the dismissal of one of the opening batsmen, Barnett, in the second.

So much for the worries of selectors. My own preference, for what it is worth, is for a Selection Committee of four, including the captain, with, perhaps, one other, all of whom should be thoroughly conversant with past and current form, and not be carried away by theory. Also temperament is often quoted against a candidate: "Oh, he is too temperamental." I have known some cricketers who might be so described, men who were nervous and fidgety in the dressing-room, but lions in the middle. Some of the greatest were among them.

Allen, a most hard-working and able captain, won the commendation of the critics. "Allen must be congratulated on the way he handled his side. He made the most of his limited material. He fought manfully to mould a combination in face of great difficulties, working himself like a tiger," said Macartney. "His popularity is something which must be seen to be appreciated," said another; and "Third Man" paid a tribute to his "tactical ability." There was little or no barracking, and Allen restored the good feeling between honourable opponents which had been ruptured by the Body Line controversy. So if he did lose the rubber after winning the first two Tests he has the great satisfaction of knowing that he restored the old amity.

On July 15, 1937, the one hundred and fiftieth anniversary of the M.C.C. was celebrated by a dinner at the Savoy, at which Colonel the Hon. J. J. Astor, President of the Club, presided. H.R.H. the Duke of Gloucester was present, and read a message which His Majesty the King was graciously pleased to send. It was a great event in the history of the M.C.C., but the speeches were not worthy of the occasion, and a fearful *faux pas* was committed when the names of Lord Harris and W. G. Grace were not even mentioned. I do not know whether the speakers were badly briefed—if they were briefed at all—but if I had been a scion of either the house of Harris or of Grace I must confess that I should have been greatly hurt. No two men have played a greater part in the history of the M.C.C. than these two.

19

MEN OF LAW

1937–38

*The New Zealanders in 1937—The New Pavilion at Rugby—Frank Woolley—
The Australian Tour of 1938—Inns of Court, Inner Temple, Middle Temple, and
Lincoln's Inn Dinners*

THERE WAS a setting of the field in the Test Match at Lord's
against the New Zealanders in 1937 which interested me,
and, I believe, made others of my generation stare. Gover, of
Surrey, had only two men in front of the wicket, the farthest
from the batsmen being forward short leg. This form of attack
meant that he had perforce to bowl on the short side, and to
deprive the batsmen of any sort of forward or driving stroke,
which was dull to watch and negative. We had, of course, seen
this method of bowling with Body Line in Australia, but in this
case it was not dangerous to the batsmen, for Gover did not make
the ball rise head-high as Larwood, with his extra pace and complete control of length, was able to do on the very fast Australian
wickets. With the new ball, Gover was a very good bowler,
and to the end of his career always looked to me, from the
pavilion, very difficult to play at the start of an innings. He was,
I think, unlucky not to represent England more frequently.

The New Zealanders were a good side, and ran us hard, but
England, under Robins, won the rubber of three matches—one
win to two drawn games. Robins was a dynamic captain, and
his glorious fielding was a great inspiration to his side, but he
gave me the impression that he was somewhat inclined to under-
rate his opponents, though I may well be wrong. The New
Zealanders could bat down to No. 11, they had a fine and most
persevering bowler in Cowie, fast-medium right, and an able
captain in Page, but far too many catches were dropped in the
slips. A very young player, M. P. Donnelly, who was destined
to achieve great fame, made his first appearance in Test Matches.
He was later to score centuries at Lord's in the Varsity Match,

for Oxford, for Gentlemen *v.* Players, and for New Zealand against England.

In June 1936 I had received the following letter from Sir John Maffey,[1] then President of the Old Rugbeian Society:

COLONIAL OFFICE,
DOWNING STREET, S.W.I
24th June, 1936

DEAR WARNER,

It is the pleasant prerogative of the President of the Old Rugbeian Society to nominate a new Vice-President who, after a year's service in that office, normally succeeds to the office of President in the second year. That is to say, my nominee will be Vice-President for 36–37 and President for 37–38. Of all the names which have been suggested to me yours is outstanding today as indeed it always has been in the past. As you know, the duties are not arduous and I am sure you realise that some time or other this is an office which the fates will insist on your filling. Since with a new Cricket Pavilion cricket interests at Rugby are likely to receive a stimulus it would indeed be most appropriate for you to accept nomination now, and I write to you in the firm hope that you will be able to say 'Yes.' I shall be very grateful for an early reply as I must put the matter up early in July.

Yours sincerely,

J. L. MAFFEY

The new pavilion at Rugby was opened in 1937. Mr Kenneth Swan, K.C.,[2] who succeeded Lord Rugby as President of the Old Rugbeian Society, was in charge of the proceedings, and I was asked to speak, and from the top of the pavilion addressed a large gathering. I confess that it was not without a considerable lump in my throat that I did so. Memories came surging back beyond the far horizon of memory—of my first appearance on New Bigside at the age of fourteen, of many good friends among both masters and boys, and of that moment when I came back to the old pavilion between cheering lines of boys, after making 177, not out, against the Free Foresters, forty-seven years earlier. It was a perfect summer's day, and, looking across the Close and remembering the many happy hours I had spent there, I should have been less than human if I had not spoken with some

[1] Lord Rugby, G.C.M.G., K.C.B., K.C.V.O., C.S.I., C.I.E., Governor-General of the Sudan, 1925–33, Permanent Under-Secretary of State for the Colonies, 1933–37.
[2] Now Lieutenant-Commander Sir Kenneth Raydon Swan, O.B.E., K.C.

emotion. I am very proud to think that a copy of the portrait of me, by Miss Katherine Lloyd,[1] which is in the Long Room at Lord's, hangs in the pavilion at Rugby during the summer, but goes into winter quarters in another place. The Headmaster, H. Lyon, was there, himself an old Rugbeian, as well as Lord Hankey,[2] to whom I gave his XXII, and who, no mean wicket-keeper, would probably have got into the Eleven but for a badly injured finger, and Lord Rugby (what a lovely and romantic title!), who bowled me neck and crop when I was well set with a ball I remember to this day. He was in the Rugby Eleven of 1896, one of the best school sides of that year, and I have heard it suggested that that particular ball gained him his colours! *Wisden* records that he took only four wickets for 19·1 runs each, and, judging by the ball which confounded me, he was, perhaps, not bowled enough, but the school had three un-commonly good bowlers that year in E. R. Wilson, H. V. Spencer, and N. Fletcher. Hankey sat next to me in Fifth form. He was some three or four years younger than I was, and possessed of considerably more grey matter than I could boast. I recall him as a very slightly built boy with a large head.

At the end of the season Frank Woolley retired, and at the Folkestone Festival Mr G. R. Wood, Chairman of the Committee, presented to him a radio-gramophone "in appreciation of a great cricketer, from the Folkestone Festival Committee." I was asked to speak, and this is what I said:

We are here to-day to say good-bye to a great cricketer, Frank Woolley, but there is no sadness of farewell in his retirement, for time cannot dim the memory of his glorious batting. He has set a standard of batsmanship which the coming generation will not fail to note and profit by. His method of play is an almost unique combination of ease, grace, style, and power, and, above all, of correct-ness, the foundation of the art of batting, which the present England Captain, W. R. Hammond, so exactly typifies. But to Kentish men and women, and to men of Kent and their ladies, I need not dwell on these points. From Gravesend to Dover and from Canterbury to Tonbridge you know Woolley well, and you regard him with a

[1] Miss Lloyd's father, the late E. W. M. Lloyd, was in the Rugby Eleven, and in 1864 scored 95 against the M.C.C. at Lord's, and 139, not out, against Marlborough on the old Middlesex ground at Islington. All his sons were at Rugby, in Whitelaw's House.

[2] Lord Hankey, P.C., G.C.B., G.C.M.G., G.C.V.O., the famous Secretary of the Imperial Defence Committee, 1912-38.

very proper affection, for is he not the Pride of Kent—and may we not also say of England?

The career of any cricketer is comparatively short, but it is not only the runs you make and the wickets you obtain which count. It is the friends you make because of and owing to cricket and the manner in which you play the game which really matter; and Frank Woolley has thousands of admirers and friends the British Empire over. His fame will never die. He is one of the immortals. And you must remember, too, what a fine bowler he was. The cricketers of my time feared him on a sticky wicket almost as they did his great *vis-à-vis*, Blythe. And you have seen him only recently pick up catches at short slip like a young man, and I can assure you that in his prime he was one of the finest slips in England. This is, perhaps, no time to dwell on figures, but I may remind you that in first-class cricket he has scored 58,969 runs, taken 2068 wickets, and made over 900 catches.

The years pass, but Woolley remains a star of the first magnitude. He has adorned this splendid game, for he has not only been great on the field of play, but a good and loyal companion and a charming man off it, as I know only too well, having travelled with him to the other side of the world on a not forgotten tour.

In your retirement, Frank Woolley, we wish you every happiness and good fortune. What delightful memories you will have! And when you listen in to this wireless-set may the commentator on cricket one day be able to say, "I think I saw to-day a batsman who reminds me of Frank Woolley." If that can be said it will be a happy day indeed for English cricket, in which we are all interested, and which, indeed, we love so well.

In the spring of the following year (1938) the Board of Control chose Perrin, A. B. Sellers, the Yorkshire Captain, M. J. Turnbull, Captain of Glamorgan, and myself as Chairman of the Selection Committee, which meant four members, instead of three as hitherto. Higson was omitted. He felt it deeply, and Perrin and I both regretted his exclusion. We three had worked well together, but it may be that there was some rivalry between the Red and White Roses.

The Australians under Bradman were a fine side, even if they had made the mistake of not bringing Grimmett, and thereby splitting the famous O'Reilly-Grimmett combination. Our chief concern was the selection of a captain, for Allen had played only two or three matches during the previous season, and, though he did appear for Middlesex against Nottinghamshire and against

Worcestershire at Lord's, his old strain bothered him. He also did not see his way to playing for the M.C.C. and for Middlesex against the Australians, or in the Test Trial Match, England *v.* the Rest, at Lord's. It was impossible, therefore, to judge his form and his fitness. And so we chose Hammond. As every one knows, the rubber of Test Matches ended all square. The Australians won at Leeds and England at the Oval, the other games producing no result, that at Old Trafford, where it rained without ceasing from Thursday afternoon to Tuesday night, being abandoned. We were, I think, the stronger of two fine teams, but where we lost the rubber was at Leeds, where illness and accidents deprived us of Hutton, Leyland, and Ames, all key men, with the result that we had a fearful tail, which began at No. 7. Compton and Hutton, who had made their first appearance for England *v.* New Zealand during the previous summer, came to the front with a vengeance, and ever since have been the mainstay of our batting, while Farnes, Bowes, who was not available because of injuries until the fourth Test, at Leeds, Verity, and Wright were bowlers of no mean ability. Bradman, McCabe, and Brown were great batsmen, and O'Reilly the best bowler in the world at this period, and the Australians' fielding, with Fingleton outstanding, was very fine indeed.

This was the last year of my service as a member of the Selection Committee. I had first served in 1905, then, after twenty-one years, in 1926, again in 1931 and 1932, and, finally, four consecutive years, 1935–38, seven times as Chairman. I enjoyed it all immensely, but, as I have said earlier, I prefer a Committee of not more than four, including the Captain of the England Eleven. One can always co-opt others, if it is thought wise, as Rhodes and Hobbs were co-opted in 1926, and as E. R. T. Holmes was in 1937.

About this period of my life I was more than once asked to dine at the various Inns of Court, Inner Temple, Middle Temple, and Lincoln's Inn, and delightful occasions they were, when one met all the great men of law and others who had made their mark in various spheres of life. It is the custom for a guest to be taken into dinner by his host and given his arm. On one occasion when I was present the Archbishop of Canterbury, Lord Lang, was, of course, taken in to dinner by Lord Simon, the Treasurer of Inner Temple, one of whose guests I was, but I was

fortunate enough to be given the arm of "Master Mellor." After
dinner we moved into another room for dessert, and sat next to
a different Bencher of the Inn, and later we repaired to the Library
for coffee. Barristers are always the best of company, and the
Bar is one of the professions which likes talking 'shop,' and there
is no more interesting 'shop' than the law, which deals so often
with many of the faults and frailties of mankind, and has to give
decisions on vital points of procedure. Crime has a great fascina-
tion for many, and the biographies of such eminent jurists as,
for example, Lord Carson and Sir Edward Marshall Hall, both
by Edward Marjoribanks, command a large public. Personally,
I read and re-read them, and never tire of doing so, and I go now
and again to the Law Courts and listen to cases and trials.

I used to enjoy, too, lunching in the Inner Temple Hall—alas!
now a shell—and hearing about the latest cases. They talk a lot
of cricket too, but I try to turn the conversation to their own
profession, often with little success, for many barristers are keen
cricketers. Are there not matches between the Bar and the
Clerks—in which I took part years ago—and between the Bar
and the Police, at the Oval? And is not Sir Norman Birkett one
of the finest of after-dinner speakers on cricket?

I once sat next to the Vinerian Professor of Law at Oxford,
Sir William Holdsworth, when I was the guest at Lincoln's Inn
of Colonel F. H. L. Errington, my old Commanding Officer in
the Inns of Court O.T.C., and I felt bound to warn Sir William
that I had taken only a Third in law; but as his son had rowed in
the Oxford boat, we were soon in smooth water. On these occasions men, however famous in their learned profession, recapture
very readily the days of their youth. In the Garrick Club too, of
which I am fortunate enough to be a member, thanks very largely
to Bernard Darwin, who, though an Etonian, is prepared to bet
any Rugbeian he would defeat him in an examination on Tom
Brown, one often meets Judges, eminent K.C.'s, and Junior
Counsel, and I delight in their conversation.

20

THE OUTBREAK OF WAR
1939

The West Indies—Eton v. Harrow—Denmark—Deputy Assistant Secretary of the M.C.C.—John Curtin—House of Commons Debates—Cricket Talks at H.M. Prisons—Yesterday and To-day

DURING THE summer of 1939, in the words of John Bright at the time of the Crimean War, "The angel of Death has been abroad throughout the land; you may almost hear the beating of his wings." The West Indies were a good side, under the captaincy of R. S. Grant, with J. M Kidney as Manager, and their tour went well, with large crowds to watch these able and attractive cricketers; but because of the situation their last six matches were cancelled, their final appearance being against England at the Oval on August 19, 21, and 22. England won at Lord's by eight wickets, the games at Old Trafford and the Oval being drawn. Headley had his crowning triumph at Lord's, with two centuries (106 and 107), and this great batsman scored 1745 runs, with an average of 72·70, for the whole season. He carried the side on his shoulders, so far as batting went, and C. B. Fry suggested that he should have been christened Atlas, and not George. He had good support from K. H. Weekes, left-hand, J. B. Stollmeyer, and L. Constantine. The last also bowled well, changing his pace from a cleverly flighted slow to an occasional fast ball, and his fielding still remained that of the best fielder in the world. England had four great batsmen in Hammond, Compton, Hutton, and Hardstaff, and Bowes, Copson, Verity, and Wright (in the Lord's match) made up a strong and varied attack.

Harrow had not defeated Eton since 1908, and their victory by eight wickets evoked tremendous enthusiasm. *Forty Years On* was sung, while the crowd roared and a few top-hats were broken. Those who have not heard these Harrow songs have missed a great deal. We know what Mr Churchill feels about them,[1] and they are, indeed, most moving. I was to hear them on Speech Day, 1949, and though I am a neutral, I confess that they brought tears to my eyes. *Forty Years On* and *Five Hundred Faces* must surely rank among our famous songs, but I do not wish to get into trouble with Etonians, and they may well claim that the *Eton Boating Song* also makes your heart-strings crack. Perhaps I have a bit of sentiment in my make-up—which is a different thing from sentimentality—but is anyone the worse for that?

In July I went to Denmark—not as a player, of course, but as 'Father' to an M.C.C. side, ably led, both on and off the field, by G. C. Newman. We played two matches, at Aalborg and at Copenhagen. The year 1939 was the Jubilee of cricket in Denmark, and we had a great welcome and enjoyed the hospitality of a charming people. Baron Rosencrantz, a direct descendant of the family whose name Shakespeare used in *Hamlet*, was our guide and friend. His staff-work touched perfection, and he was a good umpire. We lunched at the British Embassy, and the Minister and his staff watched our match at Copenhagen. The team was the tallest cricket team I have ever seen. The two Fords, Neville and Christopher, almost hit the sky, and there were others only little less in stature. At a fun fair in Copenhagen I killed sixteen 'birds' and grievously wounded two, urged on by shouts of "Go it, Grandpa!" Aird was astonished at my accuracy of aim, and how he laughed! "That's nothing," I replied. "All the cricketers of my time threw like that!" Not, perhaps, quite accurate, but I thought it proper to stick up for the men of my generation.

When, on September 3, 1939, the Second World War broke out Colonel R. S. Rait Kerr and R. Aird, the Secretary and Assistant Secretary of the M.C.C., left Lord's to take up military duties, and I was appointed Deputy Assistant Secretary, with Findlay coming up once a week to guide my footsteps. At a later

---

[1] "I do beg you to regard these precious songs and words and ideas and themes as a great inspiration in later years, and as a bond of contact and unity between you when you meet far away across the world, and to keep alive in your hearts the great themes of duty and honour for which this school has ever stood, and for which its sons have been willing to make every sacrifice in life at any time they are called upon. These songs are an inspiration; they are a companion; they are a comfort. The more you sing them and the better you know them by heart and remember them, the more glad you will be to have them with you in the browner evenings of life."—MR CHURCHILL at Harrow. From *The Harrovian* of November 29, 1950.

date the R.A.F. requisitioned the practice ground and the build-ings, but we had the use of the match ground and the pavilion and the stands for cricket. And here I should like to pay tribute to the R.A.F. for their consideration, courtesy, and help. They often used the Long Room for lectures, sometimes to within half an hour of the start of a match, but before play began the room had been completely cleared.

It was realized by the Government and the Services that cricket provided a restful antidote to war strain, and each summer we had a good programme of matches, generally lasting one day, which grew to three days in 1945. All branches of the Services sent teams to Lord's, as did the Universities, except in 1940, and the Public Schools. And we had a very welcome new match, the Dartmouth Cadets playing the R.A.F. Cadets. Cabinet Ministers, prominent sailors, soldiers, and airmen, together with dis-tinguished Allied Generals, including a Russian General, at different times watched the matches, and Mr Curtin, Australia's Prime Minister, the Prime Minister of Queensland, who gave me a beautiful walking-stick of Queensland wood as light as a feather, and the High Commissioners of our Dominions were frequent visitors. It was Mr Curtin who in a speech in London said, "Australians will always fight for those twenty-two yards. Lord's and its traditions belong to Australia just as much as to England."[1]

I have always been interested in the debates in the House of Lords and the House of Commons. My memory of the House of Commons goes back to 1898, when I recall Lord Curzon (then the Hon. George Curzon), who was Under-Secretary of State for Foreign Affairs, saying, "The British Empire, under Provi-dence, is the greatest instrument for good the world has ever seen." I can almost see him now, in a frock-coat, with his square shoulders and Roman face, uttering the words with rare pride and fervour. I never met Lord Curzon, but I saw him once or twice in the pavilion at Lord's, and his career has always interested and fascinated me. Many wonder whether the history of this country, and of the world, would not have been very different had he been made Prime Minister on Bonar Law's retirement in May 1923. For a wonderfully graphic and sympa-

[1] The Right Hon. John Curtin died at Canberra on July 5, 1945.

thetic history of his career Harold Nicolson's *Curzon: the Last Phase*[1] is indeed worth reading.

My second visit to the House of Commons was in April 1904, just after I had returned from Australia, and on the Front Bench was A. J. Balfour, with Alfred Lyttelton by his side. In subsequent years I was almost a frequent visitor, and nearly always heard the introduction of the Navy Estimates. The Estimates for 1939 were to be introduced on March 15, and John Simon had kindly given me a seat within the precincts of the House, but early that morning Hitler had marched into Prague, and a general debate took place. I sat glued to my seat from half-past two until nearly eight o'clock. The tension in the House was extreme.

In a previous year I heard Mr Churchill crossing swords with Sir Samuel Hoare (now Lord Templewood) over the India Bill, and another memorable occasion to me was when the Conservative Government were urging that the Treaty of Versailles was too severe and ought to be amended, and Lloyd George intervened, saying that he was one of the authors of that Treaty, and recalling that at the time he had received strong protests from many Conservatives saying that the Treaty was not severe enough. And then, pointing to the Government Bench, he mentioned several names—Sir Samuel Hoare, etc., etc., and Mr Wood, "now in another place": he had become Lord Halifax. "They have grown mellower since then. We have all grown mellower." A good many Members seemed to shuffle in their seats!

I recall, too, Lloyd George introducing the Conscription Bill during the First World War, and adding, "This measure will also apply to Ireland," whereupon an Irish priest sitting next to me in the Gallery jumped up and made the most vehement protests in no uncertain voice. He was promptly tapped on the shoulder by an attendant and asked to leave. I also heard Churchill pleading for rearmament on more than one occasion, and I recall the occasion when, after Sir Thomas Inskip (later Lord Caldecote) was appointed Minister for the Co-ordination of Defence, while most people were hoping that Churchill would fill the position, an M.P. is said to have remarked, "Since the Emperor Caligula made his horse a Consul there has been no more extraordinary appointment."

I was in the House when the Prime Minister, Mr Chamberlain,

[1] Constable, 1934.

in 1939, referring to Mr Churchill, said, "The Right Hon. and gallant Member for Epping has many good qualities, but judgment is, I fear, not one of them." In a subsequent speech in the House Mr Churchill made a reference to this: "I use the word 'judgment' with some temerity, because my Right Hon. Friend twitted me some time ago about that notorious defect which I have in my composition."

Since the end of the Second World War the late Lord Lucan often asked me to the House of Lords to lunch and to listen to the debates afterwards. Indeed, I went so often that when I was coming out one bitterly cold evening a policeman remarked to me, "Wrap up well, my lord; a very nasty night, my lord." I was indeed so wrapped up that I was completely disguised! The House of Lords' debates are invariably conducted with great dignity and courtesy. There are none of the interruptions of the House of Commons. It is indeed a Council of State, in which the speakers are experts in their own particular line. You can obtain a considered opinion on almost any subject on earth, and the Lord Chancellor (Viscount Jowitt) looks the part, if anyone ever did, with his uncommon good looks, wonderfully melodious and attractive voice, and his easy and conciliatory manner.

About this period and at other times I have given talks on cricket at several of H.M. prisons—Wormwood Scrubs, Wandsworth, and Broadmoor. I must admit that I go with a feeling of sympathy, and, indeed, sadness, but the moment one enters the room in which one is to speak the atmosphere is not at all sad. To begin with, one is given a warm welcome, and after a few minutes one feels that one is addressing any ordinary assembly of cricket-lovers. My method is not to deliver a lecture, but, after five or six minutes of giving a review of what cricket means and what it stands for in the life of the British people, to ask them to question me and 'try to bowl me out.' It is really surprising what good questions are asked, and in a few minutes, as it seems, the whole scene changes. The majority of the prisoners were very much up-to-date, and cross-examined me about the misdeeds of Selection Committees—why didn't So-and-so play for England, and why was X left out of this or that tour abroad? All this play of debate is conducted quietly and with courtesy. At Broadmoor there were five or six women among the inmates, and I remember one of them—a gentle-looking woman—asking,

"ALL OUT OF STEP EXCEPT MICHAEL!"

Three generations—J.P.F.W., Michael John Pelham, and P.F.W.—at the Eton v. Harrow match in 1946.

Photo Sport and General

UNVEILING THE W. G. GRACE MEMORIAL AT BRISTOL IN 1948

The Lord Mayor of Bristol, the Duke of Beaufort, and P.F.W.

[See pp. 183–184.]

Photo "*Western Daily Press*" *and* "*Bristol Observer*"

"Tell me about the Ashes, will you? What exactly do they mean?" There was, too, a Lancastrian who tried to draw me into an argument as to whether Red or White Rose were the better cricketers. I answered that I liked both on my side, and that calmed him. "You're a sport, anyway," he said.

At the end of these talks one invariably received what really amounted to an ovation, which continued as one walked out of the room. A prison is of necessity a grim place, and if one has brought even a ray of happiness into the lives of its inmates, maybe a good mark or two will go down in the book which the Recording Angel is said to keep.

Speaking of the courtesy with which I was received in these places, I am reminded that it is often said that manners, generally speaking, have deteriorated since the days when I first came to London,[1] but this I believe to be passing, though men do not always give up their seats to women in the Tubes and buses, as they invariably used to do. My own view is that the courtesy received depends very much on the courtesy shown. I do not find ticket-collectors on trains or buses rude, and I do not recall a taxi-driver being impertinent, though I doubt very much whether one could be found to-day, in these hard times, who would drive one to Lord's for 'love,' as once happened to W. G. "It's an honour to drive you, Doctor, so long as you have not knocked the bottom out of the hansom." The Champion then weighed some seventeen stone! But then there was only one W. G., who was as well-known by sight as anyone in England, and a national figure.

---

[1] I remember a story of these days concerning C. N. Day, of the Rugby Eleven of 1890. On arrival at Baker Street on his way to Lord's he caught sight of a poster with the words *A Pair of Spectacles*, a play which was running in London in which the famous actor John Hare was appearing. It upset him greatly, for he took it as an evil omen. He had made quite a lot of runs that summer, but that poster destroyed his confidence completely, and he did get 'a pair' at Lord's.

L

21

WAR-TIME CRICKET
1939—45

One-day Matches—England v. The Dominions—A Question of Captaincy—Dinner in the Tavern—I relinquish my Duties at Lord's—The " Tom Brown" Match

ONE OF the features of war-time cricket at Lord's was the success of the one-day matches, which, particularly on Saturdays, attracted large crowds. These games frequently provided an exciting finish, for it was rare for the side batting first not to leave their opponents sufficient time to force a victory if enterprising cricket was played, and this was seldom wanting. This determination to secure, if possible, a finish was very welcome to the spectators, who were able to indulge in pleasant and varying views as to when a closure would be applied.

The peak was reached when five unofficial Test Matches with the Australians, mainly those serving in the Royal Australian Air Force, were arranged, two of these fixtures being at Lord's. These games excited such enthusiasm that the gates were frequently closed before midday, and in the second match a record attendance of 85,033 was reached.

Yet, these matches apart, the greatest of all the games played at Lord's was England v. The Dominions on the 25th, 27th, and 28th of August, 1945. This was truly a great game, which gripped the imagination as it moved from phase to phase. A brilliant century by Donnelly in the opening innings of the Dominions side set a tempo to the match which, with gathering momentum, reached a crescendo in an inspiring finish. In its course Hammond scored a century in each of England's innings, and Miller, with 185 in the Dominions' second innings, played, perhaps, the greatest of his innings in England. Off one of his strokes the ball hit the awning above the English dressing-room, the most spectacular of no fewer than sixteen sixes hit in the course of the game, which is surely a record number for Lord's.[1]

[1] In the first innings Donnelly hit two sixes and Hammond three, while Miller, in the Dominions' second innings, hit no fewer than seven sixes.

In the end England lost by 45 runs when set 357 to win. The climax came when Phillipson was run out, that great fielder Constantine making one of his lightning returns from wide mid-on which hit the wicket.

Before this match started a difficulty arose when Hassett, who was to have captained the Dominions side, was taken ill and unable to play. His place as captain was filled by Constantine, the great West Indian player, who was the senior international cricketer on the sides. In this country, certainly on the cricket-field, colour does not excite the feeling and prejudice that exists in some other parts of the Empire. It was, however, necessary to secure both the consent and co-operation of the rest of the Dominions side, and I went to their dressing-room. I chose my words with care, referring to his seniority and position in the cricket world. I think I sensed that for a moment there was some slight hesitation, but after a very prominent member of the side had agreed that it was a proper choice one and all fell into line. On leading his side into the field Constantine had a great reception.

There is some misunderstanding in many quarters that the M.C.C. rule the cricket world and govern it by their own *ipse dixits*. That is not the position. The M.C.C. presides over the destinies of cricket by common consent, but there is no alteration of the laws without consultation with the Dominions and other cricketing bodies like the Board of Control, the Advisory C.C.C., and the Imperial Cricket Conference, and no regulations except such as concern the Club itself are under the sole jurisdiction of the M.C.C.

It is also not the M.C.C., but the Board of Control Selection Committee, that chooses the sides for the Test Matches in England. The M.C.C., however, undertake the management and handle the finances, and have their own representative on the Selection Committee for tours abroad.

The M.C.C. is the adviser, counsellor, and friend, not, as some may suppose, the autocratic ruler, of the cricket world.[1]

In August 1943 I was honoured by an invitation to dine by some friends at Lord's, and just over a hundred people were present. The dinner was held in the Tavern, when Mr Portman,

[1] Mr Arthur Bryant, in an article in the *Sunday Times* of April 29, 1951, wrote of "The only unchallenged authority in the world, the Marylebone Cricket Club."

that modern Lucullus, who recently retired after forty-eight years' great work as Manager of the Refreshment Department of the M.C.C., contrived a dinner which just did not cross the boundary of war-time stringency. It was a rare compliment, and I returned it by speaking for, perhaps, five minutes too long, but as I referred to Chaka, the Black Napoleon, Cetewayo, and J. Cannon, who served Lord's loyally for over sixty years, besides many of my cricketing friends, and also to "the clink of the roller, the scent of new-mown grass, and the smell of asphalt," there was, I claim, some variety in my remarks! Anyway, James Agate, who proposed my health, used some complimentary words in his *Ego 6*. The late Mr C. Hill and Mr H. E. Brown, now a member of the committee of the Middlesex C.C.C., were the prime movers in this dinner, at the end of which I was presented with a silver rose-bowl.

I left Lord's in September 1945, and I venture to give an extract from *The Times* a few weeks before my departure:

SIR PELHAM WARNER
From our Cricket Correspondent

The announcement that Sir Pelham Warner will next month relinquish his duties as Deputy Secretary of the Marylebone Cricket Club on the return of Colonel R. S. Rait Kerr from his military duties deserves far more notice than the few formal words can imply.

It can surely be said without fear of contradiction that no man has ever devoted his life to any one branch of sport more faithfully than Sir Pelham Warner. From Rugby, and then on to Oxford, Middlesex, and England, he has been a familiar and respected figure —"Plum" always equally to those who knew him personally and to those who watched him play or read of him. But possibly nothing he achieved on the field, none of the books and articles which he has written on the game, surpasses the work which he has done during the recent years of war to keep alive the game he loves so much. His difficulties in gleaning teams, in nursing a scanty staff at Lord's, and in many another respect must have been enormous, and yet all through those seasons cricket of quality and interest was provided, and the debt which the game owes to him is incalculable.

Laudatory as these remarks are to me, I should like to emphasize that I could have done little, or nothing, without the support I received from the President, S. Christopherson, the Treasurer,

Lord Cobham, and the Committee, and also from every member of the Staff. Colonel H. A. Henson, the Secretary of the Gloucestershire C.C., was at Lord's during the last eighteen months of the War. He was a master at finding additional accommodation for the large crowds, and in every way was a great prop to me. I can hear him now—"Mrs Belsham, come on, come on; get under cover"—when the V.1 was about, and her arriving with unhurried step, cool and calm, showing the courage which was characteristic of every woman in England. Mrs Belsham, too, was a great help; she knew everything about Lord's. But are not all these things written in my book on Lord's, and I would, therefore, end merely by saying that my six years at Lord's was an extraordinarily interesting and happy experience. I was proud and delighted to serve, to the best of my ability, the great Club which has been so much a part of my life.

There was one match played away from Lord's which I must mention, and that was on Tuesday, June 17, 1941, when I took a strong M.C.C. team to Rugby to celebrate the Centenary of the famous "Tom Brown Match." I endeavoured to follow precedent as much as possible, and Colonel Rait Kerr was persuaded to get himself leave to captain the M.C.C., as Benjamin Aislabie, "old Mr Aislebie," had done a hundred years earlier. Such excellent cricketers as R. H. Twining, R. E. S. Wyatt, E. R. T. Holmes, G. O. Allen, and the giant J. Smith, of Middlesex, were in the Club side, and it was not surprising, therefore, that "the Lord's men were declared the winners." Two of those present— R. B. C. Currie, a nephew of "Currie Major," and P. A. Landon, a great-grandson of Benjamin Aislabie, formed a direct link with Tom Brown's team. As in 1841, we lunched in Old Big School, but no one sang comic songs after lunch to amuse us, in the manner of "the cover-point hitter." Some fine catches were made by the boys, but we did not notice anyone standing on his head to express his delight, as Jack Raggles had done in 1841. The Headmaster entertained us most hospitably, and *The Times* wrote a leader on the match, and sent a special correspondent and a photographer to describe and illustrate it.

22

INDIANS, SOUTH AFRICANS, AND AUSTRALIANS
1946–48

The Indian Tour of 1946—The Tour in Australia, 1946–47—"Lord's, 1787–1945"
—Cruise to Gibraltar—South African Tour, 1947—Tour in the West Indies,
1947–48—The Australian Tour of 1948—Great Australian Teams—Centenary of
the birth of W. G. Grace

FIRST-CLASS cricket was in full swing again in 1946, but after the strains and stresses of the War the standard of play suffered, and one of the wettest of summers did not help matters. None the less this cricket season will go down in history as one of the most successful: seldom has the game received more enthusiastic support.

The Nawab of Pataudi captained the Indian team; he played some beautiful innings, but his health was not of the best. England won at Lord's, the games at Old Trafford and the Oval being drawn, that at Old Trafford being greatly in our favour, for the last two Indian batsmen were at the wickets with 126 runs needed to win. Indians are, perhaps, the most *natural* cricketers in the world, though here I think the West Indians are close rivals, and it would be difficult to recall a side whose batting possessed more style and charm. The art of batting was seen in its most attractive form. Merchant was their best batsman—and a great one at that, who excelled on all wickets—and Hazare, Mankad, Modi, and Mushtaq Ali were of high class. In Mankad and Amarnath the Indians had two good bowlers, and their fielding was brilliant.

Pataudi was a witty and fluent speaker, and his pleasant manner made for a happy atmosphere, but he was too prone to alter the batting order. Indeed, the order was often changed after it had been written out, and this led to a lack of confidence and uncertainty. I had known Pataudi well in Australia in 1932–33, and a more pleasant companion it would be difficult to imagine, and it would be equally hard to imagine a better-mannered team than his: their grace on the field was equalled by their manners off it.

After a great deal of discussion the M.C.C., on the urgent pleading of the Australians, decided to send a team to Australia during the winter. Many good judges disagreed with this decision, but the Australians stressed that the game from the Imperial aspect would profit by a resumption of Test Matches with them, and, taking a long view, I think that they were right. We knew full well that the War had hit us hard, for our pre-War great players were older, and the younger generation had had little opportunity of showing their skill. We had two fine, and young, bowlers in A. Bedser and Wright, but there was little else in the way of bowling, and some of the batsmen selected were past their best. There was a great gap to be filled. Every one knows that we did not win a single Test Match, losing three and drawing two, but my own view is that the game as a whole benefited. Yardley, Hutton, Compton, Edrich, Washbrook, A. Bedser, Evans, and Wright all gained greatly by the experience. They were to form the strong core of our future England Eleven. The great Hammond's highest score in Test Matches was only 37, but he suffered much from fibrositis and had other worries to contend with. An Army Corps of cricket correspondents from this country accompanied our team, and, to put it mildly, some of them were not helpful.

I spent a good part of the years 1945-46 writing *Lord's, 1787-1945*, which was eventually published by Messrs Harrap in December 1946. There are, to my mind, two trying periods for an author—the beginning and the end. One falters and hesitates at the start, and then, suddenly, one gets going—it is rather like that moment at cricket when one feels 'set'—and one cannot stop. Towards the end one becomes tired and stale, and the only thing to do then is to forget all about the book and take a complete rest for ten days or a fortnight. I believe that most writers have fixed hours for work, but I could not bring myself to a rigid time-table. I wrote when the spirit moved me. The typewritten copies of one's manuscript—I cannot type—were a stimulus, but I confess to a dislike of reading proofs.

Some people may imagine that most of my reading has been confined to *Wisden*, *Lillywhite*, and other books on cricket, but this is very far from the fact, for I possess a fairly well-stocked library of books on history, biographies, autobiographies, and reminiscences, and I have derived great profit from reading the works of Churchill, Bryant, Trevelyan, and others. I knew something about the history of Lord's—but not half enough—and that meant a good deal of research and perusing again the descriptions of great matches. It was hard toil, if pleasantly laborious toil, and I was thankful when I had come to the end and could sit back for the day of publication, on which I departed for a few weeks to Gibraltar, for I had taken a good deal out of myself and needed a change and a rest.

When I lunched one day with my son-in-law, Captain Harold Henderson, D.S.O., R.N., there were present other naval officers I knew, and they agreed that what I wanted was a cruise. A few days later the telephone rang, and I was informed that a passage had been given me to Gibraltar in H.M.S. *Manxman*, and that she would leave Plymouth on such and such a date. I lunched with Captain Leggett at Admiralty House, and afterwards was driven to the Hoe by a very nice Wren in great state (!), and thence by picket-boat to the ship. *Manxman*, a very fast mine-laying cruiser of 2560 tons, with a complement of some 240 officers and men, had won great renown during the War, and her captain, Captain G. H. Oswald, was indeed worthy of his ship. He was the kindest of hosts, and insisted on giving up his cabin to me. When I protested he replied that it was really no inconvenience to him, for while at sea he always slept in his sea-cabin on the bridge. In a few days we were at Gibraltar, and lay alongside the Mole, just ahead of H.M.S. *Vanguard*, which was on a 'shaking-up cruise' prior to taking the King and Queen to South Africa. It was December 14, the King's Birthday, and the great battleship was dressed all over—a most impressive sight. *Manxman* stayed but a day or two at Gibraltar on her way to Hong Kong. I enjoyed every moment of my visit to Gibraltar, and I owe much to Dr Douglas Valentine and his wife, who, with their two boys, had been prisoners-of-war in Hong Kong. They used to motor me into Spain, as did Mr Cann, the manager of the Rock Hotel, and we were often at the Christina Hotel at Algeciras. I saw the famous Bull Ring at La Linea, and made them laugh when, as we approached it, I took off my hat to what I called "the local Lord's"! Famous cricketers in these days are much in the limelight, but it is nothing to the halo of romance and adulation which surrounds a bull-fighter. He is indeed a hero, who commands a vast salary, and to whom all bow the knee. I have never seen a bull-fight—and have no wish to—but full marks for bravery must be awarded to those who tackle *el toro*,

His Excellency the Governor, Sir Ralph Eastwood,[1] honoured me with invitations to lunch on two occasions, and others who helped to make my stay pleasant were Dr and Mrs Heraldi, Mr and Mrs Harry Smith (my old friends on my previous visit), and Colonel and Mrs Smith-Bingham, our Military Attaché in Madrid and his wife, who passed through on their way home after we had withdrawn our Ambassador. At the Rock Hotel too was A. E. W. Mason, the famous novelist, who told me that he was busy on a book on the Tenth Legion, which is supposed to have disappeared when the Romans were in occupation of Britain, but he was clearly in bad health, and a year or two later he died. There, too, on occasions, were Colonel and Mrs Brinton, and he talked to me one lovely afternoon on the veranda of the Rock, and told me of the varied and interesting life which had been his.

A day at Tangier is another happy memory. We rose at cockcrow and went aboard a destroyer (Captain J. H. Ruck-Keene, C.B.E., D.S.C.), saw as much as we could of that very interesting and romantic town, lunched well, and bought a few nylon stockings and other presents at the Magasin du Louvre. The Flag Officer, Gibraltar, was Admiral Sir Victor Crutchley, V.C., who not only wined me and dined me, but made me a temporary member of the Yacht Club. There were five men at dinner, and three of them—naval officers—were bearded. The Admiral seemed very fond of his Flag Lieutenant, Lionel Abel-Smith, a charming young man who is now a barrister, I believe, and finally there was Captain George Philip, D.S.O., Chief of Staff, with whom and his family I made great friends. He arranged my passage home in the aircraft-carrier H.M.S. *Formidable* (Captain G. C. P. Menzies, D.S.O.), and after a smooth trip we arrived at Devonport with England feet deep in snow in one of the most severe winters—a contrast indeed to the pleasant climate of the Rock.

I find it very hard to understand why the Royal Navy have been so good to me on so many occasions. Their kindness goes

---

[1] Lieutenant-General Sir Ralph Eastwood, K.C.B., D.S.O., M.C. He retired in 1947.

back to my earliest days in the West Indies, when I was given a ribbon with H.M.S. *Flamingo* on it, and has continued through the years. Maybe the fact that I played for the Second Battle Squadron at Oporto, as already mentioned, may have had something to do with this, and it has been my great pleasure and delight on various occasions at Lord's to endeavour to show in some small way my deep appreciation of, and thanks for, the many opportunities given me of seeing the world under the most interesting conditions.

Last summer I saw that most thrilling and moving of all sights —Trooping the Colour—from the Admiralty at the invitation of Viscount Hall, the First Lord, a keen cricketer himself, and in his youth no mean Rugger-player. Sometimes I feel half a sailor! Indeed, I can claim to have sailed most of the Seven Seas, some thousands of miles of them, amid the incomparable history, tradition, and glamour of the Royal Navy.

Abundant sunshine and the visit of the South African team in 1947 again drew crowds to our cricket-grounds, and the result of the Test Matches, three victories to England and two drawn games, led many people to hope that, in spite of our disappointments in Australia, English cricket was once again on the upgrade. H. S. Altham, however, in the *Daily Telegraph*, struck a warning note. "Our cricket in much that passes for first class is little short of lamentable, and this is at least reflected at the highest level."

In the Test Matches Edrich and Compton had the almost fantastic averages of 110·40 and 94·12, while Washbrook averaged 49·50, Hutton 43·00, Evans 41·80, and Yardley 39·00, but our bowling, generally speaking, was found wanting. The South Africans, captained by Melville, backed up some accurate bowling by beautiful fielding, and had the better of a drawn match at Trent Bridge, while honours were even at the Oval. They were an attractive side both on and off the field. Melville was an admirable leader, and his graceful figure and charm of manner created a pleasant atmosphere. Watching many of their matches, I could not but recall that tremendous game on the Wanderers' ground at Johannesburg, when on January 4, 1906, South Africa won their first Test Match. And here to sharpen my memory was A. D. Nourse, son of the man who had played such a prominent part in that victory, himself a most powerful right-handed batsman—unlike his father, who was left-handed—of many strokes.

A day or two before Christmas 1947 I left Liverpool in the S.S. *Tetela*, of the Elders and Fyffes Line, bound for the West Indies with the M.C.C. team under the captaincy of G. O. Allen. It was a rough voyage, with the wind almost dead ahead most of the way. The captain, a very handsome man, and his officers looked after us well. All the cricketers were first-class fellows, and there was only one woman on board, the stewardess, whose grandfather was murdered during the Gordon Riots in Jamaica in the middle of the last century. Reading and bridge—at which Hardstaff made the most daring declarations—doubles and re-doubles—which caused Butler, his colleague in the Nottingham-shire Eleven, to raise his eyebrows—helped to pass the time away, and early in the morning of December 6 we arrived at Barbados. Sir Hilary Blood's Private Secretary took me in the Governor's launch to the wharf, where Mrs George Challenor and her brother-in-law, Robert Challenor, were there to meet me. Sir Hilary had invited me to stay at Government House—a Georgian house of large rooms with high ceilings and nice furniture, and pictures, photographs, and engravings of Kings, Queens, and Governors. I had a large room, and three to look after me—two boys and a girl—all black, and so nice and quiet and efficient. The gardens are huge, with many shrubs and flowers, and if the sun is hot, from ten o'clock to five o'clock there is always the cool trade wind, which makes the palms rustle with a fascinating noise. There is no twilight, and the sun sets before six o'clock, while the nights are cool. A glorious climate, but at that time they had had no rain for weeks, and the sugar crop was one-third short. I quote from a letter I wrote to my wife:

> There are dinners and luncheons, and on Wednesday night we dined with Sir Allan Collymore, the Chief Justice, and Lady Colly-more—a party of twelve. Here is the dinner: Hors d'œuvres, pumpkin soup—a West Indian delicacy—flying fish, with a glorious sauce, turkey, a Guava ice made in Heaven (!), and a wonderful savoury. I gobbled up the lot like a turkey, and the turkeys near "Obbie's"[1] hotel gobbled so much that they kept him awake, and those already destined for the pot met their fate some days earlier than had originally been intended.

[1] "Obbie," one of G. O. Allen's nicknames, though "Gubby" is the best-known.

On Tuesday night a dinner here of twelve, and I met several of the old names—Challenors, Austins, Skeetes, Evelyns, Piles, etc., all at Harrison's with me. On Wednesday I opened the George Challenor Memorial Stand on the cricket ground—a wonderfully well-organized affair, and over two thousand people. H.E., the Bishop in his robes, the Chief Justice, Allen, and myself spoke; there was a band, *God Save the King*, and a short prayer of dedication. The whole thing lasted twenty-seven minutes, and I spoke for ten. Every word broadcast—amplifiers, etc. Never in so small a community has there been such love of, and enthusiasm for, cricket. I cannot tell you how good every one is to me. They regard me as "One of us, Sir Pelham."

I had the most wonderful and affectionate welcome any man could possibly have had at Harrison College yesterday. Some 150 old boys, Headmaster, H. N. Haskell, H.E., a band (with a quite lovely little fox-terrier pup as their mascot), and speeches by the Headmaster, and Robert Challenor. I walked over the famous old ground: no school of its size has produced so many fine cricketers in so short a time (since 1871). In my day there were only about 180 boys, some thirty of them boarders. Now it is a day school of 500 boys, the whole place greatly altered and extended, with a very good cricket-ground on what was in my day a cane-field.

I am enjoying it all very much indeed, and the climate is perfect. I leave Government House on the 16th, and go to the Challenors' until the 23rd, and then to Lady Austin's for a week-end, and then back to Government House until I leave for Trinidad by ship— *Lady Rodney*—on January the 30th, arriving there on February the 1st, after stopping for a few hours at St Vincent and Grenada. I had a message from Sir John Shaw, the Governor of Trinidad, asking me to stay at Government House, and I go there immediately on my arrival.

The crowds at cricket are splendidly behaved. There are about 7000 each day, and the ground literally hums with interest and excitement. Walcott and Weekes are splendid batsmen. Both young —Walcott, only twenty-two, a big, tall fellow, and Weekes, quick as lightning—and both glorious stroke-players. A terrible wicket to bowl on: the ball never gets up more than half-stump high.

That we were going to meet a very good side in the Test Matches was clear, but the M.C.C. team suffered a succession of accidents and illnesses which has only been equalled—and, indeed, surpassed—by our team in Australia during the past winter. Later, when in Trinidad, Allen had to cable for reinforcements, which arrived speedily by air in the person of the great

Hutton, who at once proceeded to show the art of batting at its best and most stylish.

To return to my own doings. The Chief Justice admitted me within the Barbados Bar, and so, in wig and gown, I appeared in court, and for the first and only time in my life found myself on my feet addressing a Chief Justice, and endeavouring to express my appreciation of the great compliment paid me.

As I write it is bitterly cold and raining heavily, but I forget that in my memories of days in the sunshine and warmth of Barbados. Mrs Challenor had me to stay for a week in her delightful house, Valery, where I bowled a few balls every day to her boy, George, who was soon to depart for Harrow. We were at the cricket every day before play began, returned to lunch, and then, after a short siesta, back to the cricket, George meanwhile coming up to my room every now and again to tell me the latest scores, which had come over the wireless. Uncle "Laddie," Robert Challenor, was there too, and we were a happy party.

I stayed for a week-end at Enmore, with Lady Austin, the widow of Sir Harold Austin, a distinguished figure in the island, for he was Speaker of the House of Assembly, captained the West Indies not only in Barbados, but in England, and was a fine lawn-tennis-player.

And so back to Government House for the last few days, and thence by sea to Trinidad, stopping on the way at St Vincent and Grenada, which I had known as a small boy on my way to and fro between Trinidad and Barbados, and as one of Lord Hawke's team.

One duty remained to me before I left Barbados, and that was to call on Sir George Pile at his beautiful place, Bulkeley, in the country. He was a very old man and in bad health, but he was good enough to see me, and when I reminded him that I had watched him play cricket for Barbados, of which he was captain, in 1884, he produced some old score-books and cuttings, and insisted on my paying him another visit, which I was only too delighted to do. He was a very good-looking man, with the courteous manners of his generation. A few months later he passed away, but he was one of those people one does not forget. The Piles are a notable West Indies family, and in him they had a distinguished representative.

I was up early to see the ship pass through the second *boca*—Spanish for 'mouth'—one of the entrances to the Gulf of Paria, past Chaguaramas Bay and the Five Islands, where as a small boy I had enjoyed delightful week-ends. When I was in Trinidad fifty years before ships had to lie a mile and a half from the shore because of the shallowness of the water, but now we steamed through a buoyed channel, and came alongside the quay, where many ships were berthed, including the 9800-ton training cruiser, H.M.S. *Devonshire*. So far as this part of it was concerned, Port of Spain had changed almost out of recognition.

Sir John Shaw had sent one of his A.D.C.'s, Commander Goddard, R.N.V.R., to meet me, and at Government House I stayed for the whole of my visit, and the memory of this happy time and the hospitality of my charming host and hostess, in that lovely house, will remain with me to the end. In a few days I felt as if I had known them for years. Sir John is a most impressive man, standing 6 ft. 5 in., with a charming smile and a twinkle in his eye. Lady Shaw is as fond of dogs as I am, and never have I seen better-trained dogs than Nobby and Toots, who, sent for a run in the gardens, on the sound of a whistle came to heel at once.

The weather was much hotter than in Barbados. It was fairly cool from sunset until about 8 A.M., then it stoked up, with little or no breeze to lessen the rays of the sun. The view from Government House across the Savannah over the town, with the sea in the distance, is not easily forgotten, and the whole island is full of beauty.

Of course, we hastened to the cricket-ground, where I met with an almost embarrassing reception, with many a "Mr Pelham, I see you, sir, make a hundred here when you come with 'De Lord' [Lord Hawke]." The ground itself is one of the most beautiful in the world, and at the setting of the sun the Maraval hills turn all sorts of entrancing colours as the shadows chase each other. At Maraval I spent the evening with Mr and Mrs Charles Child, he a prominent K.C., formerly in my brother Aucher's chambers, of which he was still in occupation, and many whom I had known as a boy took notice of me.

At Government House one met many people, including officers of the United States Navy, very smart in their white uniforms, with uncommon good manners, and interesting indeed to talk to. It was carnival-time, and the whole town was given up to this, and at the Prince's Building there was a great evening when Sir John presented the prizes to the best teams and individuals in a really beautifully put-on masquerade.

The M.C.C. team were invited by Captain Evans to dine in *Devonshire*; I was included in the party, and some forty or fifty of us dined on the quarterdeck beneath the 8-inch guns. Personally, I never go aboard a British warship without a thrill, and one or two of the cricketers who had never before seen a warship were greatly impressed, as well they might be. On a previous occasion in Barbados I had lunched with Captain Evans in *Devonshire*, and before lunch he assembled the cadets on deck and asked me to give them a talk on cricket, and I did not forget to remind them that they were sailing in classic waters, for the great Battle of the Saints, the battle of April 12, 1782, when Rodney defeated De Grasse, was fought around Dominica and Martinique—a battle which changed the history of England. But you may read about that epic fight in the history-books, or ask me about it! I will here say only this—that Rodney split the French line in the centre and Hood the rear of it.

But away from the sea to dry land again, and to the Queen's Park Oval, where England, in spite of fearful casualties, put up a splendid fight in the Test Match, and succeeded in making a draw of it, Robertson playing a great second innings of 133, and Griffith, in his first innings in a Test Match, going in first, scoring 140, and making some off-drives in the Hutton manner. There, too, Worrell played glorious innings of 97 and 28, not out, and it was easy to see that here was a superb batsman, polished to a degree, with exceptional quickness of foot and eye, and with supple wrists.

In the late seventies of the last century my father had bought some twenty-two acres of land at Belmont—within a quarter of a mile of Government House—and he left four acres of these on which to build a church. The Rev. Canon John D. Ramkeesoon, Canon of St Chad Holy Trinity Cathedral, Port of Spain, and Rector of St Margaret's, Belmont, hearing that I was in the island, asked me to attend a service, and there on a Sunday morning I went with Sir John and Lady Shaw, and heard a prayer said for the repose of my father's soul, and his memory and generosity eulogized.

As mentioned in an earlier chapter, I was given what amounted to the freedom of Port of Spain in the City Hall, which had been our house during the last year of my father's life. Some time later it was burned to the ground. I went, of course, to see our old house, in which I was born and lived until I was twelve years old. The front of it remained almost the same, but the rest of it had been greatly altered. Gone was the gallery in which I took my first footsteps in cricket, the pond in which I sailed my boats, and the swimming-bath, and the stables were now classrooms, for the Hall is now half a private hotel and half a school. Much of the delightful garden remains, and as I walked about memories came crowding back "quick like a shot through the brain."

Sir John drove us in his car to the cocoa district on a Sunday afternoon, through lovely country, and Freya Stark, who was spending a day or two at Government House, was one of the party. She fascinated us all with her personality and gentle charm. The result, so far as I was concerned, was that I have read most of her books.

Trinidad cannot be an easy place to govern, and Sir John was in his office every morning at eight o'clock, and seemed to work most of the day, though he found time to pay occasional visits to the cricket-ground. A West Indian Governor who did not take an interest in cricket would not go down well!

Members of the M.C.C. team often came to dinner, and one evening there was a cocktail party, which ended up with dancing in the beautiful and large ballroom. And so the days went by, and the time arrived for me to leave for British Guiana, whither I went by air, my first experience of flying.

To Sir John and Lady Shaw my sincere gratitude is due, for they gave me a wonderfully happy time, and I would add my thanks to the A.D.C.'s, Major Bolus and Commander Goddard, and the quiet, well-mannered, and most efficient servants.

I was met at the airport in Demerara by Mr J. St F. Dare, who had sent me a cordial letter asking me to stay with him in Georgetown, the capital of British Guiana. The lower portion of the town is below the level of the sea at high tide, and is protected by a sea-wall. A stone house is rarely to be seen, owing to the difficulty of obtaining a sound foundation, and the houses are usually built on heavy balks of greenheart timber. Many of the streets

GOVERNMENT HOUSE, TRINIDAD

SIR JOHN AND LADY SHAW, WITH THEIR A.D.C.'S,
COMMANDER GODDARD AND MAJOR BOLUS

QUEEN'S PARK, TRINIDAD, IN 1897

are intersected by canals, in which the lily Victoria Regis grows to perfection.

My host and hostess gave me a warm welcome, and during my long stay showered on me the same kindness and hospitality as I had received in Barbados and Trinidad. John Dare had represented Demerara in the inter-island matches, and it was only natural, therefore, that we should see much of the cricket, though he was a busy man. The ground, if on the small side, is one of the best in the West Indies, and since I had last been there a new and comfortable pavilion had been built. The first of the games against British Guiana was drawn, Hutton, within three days of a long and tiring journey by air, playing superb innings of 138 and 62, not out, but the second was washed out by torrential rain.

We lost the Test Match, having the worst of the wicket. Allen began at his best and fastest, but after bowling Goddard, the West Indies captain, pulled a muscle in his leg and was compelled to leave the field, Cranston taking over the captaincy. At the end of the first day the West Indies had scored 284 for five wickets (Worrell 127, not out). It rained in the night, Goddard soon declared, and the M.C.C. had to bat on a sticky wicket. We failed to save the follow-on, Allen putting himself in last, which I would suggest was a mistake, for he was a batsman of experience and determination, and, lame as he was—he had to have a runner —he might well have stayed there. In the second innings he went in earlier, and scored an invaluable 20. Had we saved the follow-on we should have got the West Indies on a still sticky, if gradually improving, wicket, and anything might have happened. Hardstaff played a beautiful innings of 63, and the West Indies were set 78 to win. Three were out for 28, but a dropped catch upset any chance of victory, and the West Indies won by seven wickets. Allen made a graceful speech of congratulation, and the applauding crowd gradually dispersed. The West Indies owed a great deal to Goddard, who captained extremely well, bowled finely on the false turf in the first innings, and made two good catches in the slips in the second innings. Sir Hilary Blood came down from Barbados to see the last two days of the match, combining affairs of State with cricket.

So much for the cricket. Meanwhile the days passed very happily. A dance at Government House was an occasion. Sir

M

Charles and Lady Woolley enjoy their own parties; consequently everything went with a rare swing. The ladies, the best-dressed in the West Indies, if I may say so without bringing down coals of fire on my head(!), were as pretty as their frocks. Fifty years ago I had danced at Government House, and there was a good deal of persuasion that I should do so once again, and at the end of the evening I was bold enough to tread a measure. I hope, and believe, that I did not put my feet altogether in the wrong place, but I felt that I had been unduly brave. I would, however, plead extenuating circumstances!

The Dares had three children, two boys and a girl. The eldest, Michael, was at school in England, but I often bowled a few down to Simon under the house, while his little sister was a bundle of energy and activity, and a rare dancer. Both the boys are now at school in England, and look to me like being cricketers. I was to see a good deal of the Dares in England subsequently. They will know how much I appreciated all they did for me, and especially their care and kindness when I slipped on the highly polished floor, which one so often finds in the West Indies; I took an extremely heavy toss on my left shoulder and was pretty badly shaken. It is not wise to fall when one is over threescore years and ten.

I returned to Trinidad by flying-boat, said farewell to Sir John and Lady Shaw, and in the evening went aboard an American pleasure steamer, which stopped at La Guaira on the voyage to Jamaica. La Guaira was sweltering in terrific heat, and I did not go ashore, but the port was a hive of industry—Venezuela is bubbling over with oil—and a great deal of dock extension and general building were going on. I should have liked to have seen Caracas, but there was no time for that, and so away across the Caribbean to Kingston, in delightful weather, in a most comfortable ship full of interesting Americans. I was lucky too in my cabin companion, who used to help me to dress, for my shoulder was still painful. I was met at the docks by R. K. Nunes, captain of the West Indies team in England in 1928, President of the West Indies Board of Cricket Control, and a big influence in West Indies cricket. I stayed for two or three days at the most comfortable, if very expensive, hotel in Kingston, then to Government House for the inside of a week with Sir John and Lady Huggins, and later to Mr and Mrs Nunes, who put me up for a fortnight and more. King's House, as Government House is called, is a large house set in delightful surroundings. Lady Huggins was very much a personality. On a recent lecture tour in the United States she earned fame, and, I believe, she has been asked to repeat her visit. She worked unceasingly in Jamaica to further any good cause. I met Mr Bustamente, a picturesque figure with his snow-white hair, for the first time at a cocktail party in H.M.S. *Liverpool* (Captain Tennant[1]), where the tattoo was beaten at sunset, and though I did not meet his cousin, and political rival, Mr Manley, I was told by an eminent judge that he was a great advocate. Indeed, he said it would be difficult to imagine a greater.

The tattoo in H.M.S. *Liverpool* was most stirring, and I suggested to Karl Nunes that he might venture to approach Captain Tennant and ask if the Royal Marines might repeat the performance on the cricket-ground, as that sort of thing stirs the blood, like Trooping the Colour, and does good. Captain Tennant consented, and a few days later at the close of play a space was roped off, the crowd gathered round, and amid tremendous cheering the Marines went into action. This caused emulation in the hearts of the Gloucestershire Regiment, the famous "Fore and Aft," and in the Police, with the result that they too appeared on the ground. The Police were as smart as either of the other two: born dancers and graceful movers, they marched and counter-marched in superb style.

The Jamaican crowds were as keen and enthusiastic as those in Barbados, Trinidad, and Demerara, and as the last over of the day was being sent down one could see them rising and preparing for a rush to the pavilion, almost like the charge of the Dervishes at Omdurman!

One night I witnessed an Homeric cat-fight in the Nunes' garden: the rivals woke me up, and I sat at the window encouraging them. The snarls of approaching battle of the two gallants suddenly broke into a terrific roar as they joined in close combat, and I laughed as I have seldom laughed in my life. Hackenschmidt and Madrali, "the Terrible Turk," never engaged in such a wrestle, nor did Dempsey and Firpo, "the Wild Bull of the Pampas," ever fight each other with such terrible rage, hate, and venom. What 'the young lady' for whose favours they were contending thought of them I do not know, but had I

---

[1] Now Admiral Sir William Tennant, K.C.B., C.B.E.

been she I would have given both of them a wide berth: they were really far too tough!

The Nunes had a small house in the Blue Mountains, and we often spent the day there on Sundays. Jamaica has been described by Mr Beverley Baxter as a paradise, and many there are who will agree with him. It is indeed a most beautiful island, with a vast variety of scenery, and I was fortunate enough to motor across it with the M.C.C. team to Port Antonio, whither we sailed for England, arriving at Avonmouth at the end of April. I have but one regret: I had hoped to visit St Kitts and, like the Chinese, worship at the tomb of my ancestor, Sir Thomas, but it was not possible to do so.

Before we left I spent three or four days at Montego Bay, where we almost lived in the sea, and were entertained in the most lavish fashion. And so four delightful months came to an end. I hope I have paid tribute to the quite exceptional kindness I received on every side, and I would like here to thank Allen and his team for many acts of kindness and consideration. Except for the last week of the tour, I was never in the same hotel with them, but they were good enough to regard me as almost one of themselves, and it was a moment of great satisfaction to me when, travelling up in the train from Avonmouth to London, several of them, headed by Evans, came into my compartment and said what a pleasure it had been to have me with them.

One word more about the cricket. We lost the fourth, and last, Test Match at Sabina Park, Kingston, by ten wickets, the West Indies playing very fine cricket. Johnson, ten wickets for 96 runs, bowled splendidly, and Weekes played a great innings of 141, but, as I have already said, the M.C.C. were heavily handicapped throughout the tour by illness and accidents. The West Indies were to show two years later in England that they were now on a par with any Dominions side, and I believe that, if they can get together their best side, they will make the Australians go all the way during the coming winter.

Following the tour as Cricket Correspondents were E. W. Swanton, of the *Daily Telegraph*, Crawford White, of the *News Chronicle*, and C. T. Bray, of the *Daily Herald*, all of whom wrote excellent descriptions of the various matches. They were good friends with the team, and almost invariably took part with them at golf on the off days. Mr and Mrs Bray were skilful bridge-players, but I claim no skill at the game. We left that to the Captain. To Mrs Bray I am indebted for many excellent snapshots of our various doings.

Whether the team of 1948 was the best Australia has ever had is, of course, a matter of opinion, and is likely to remain so, for it is difficult indeed to compare teams of different generations, taking into consideration the varying factors of weather and wicket. Some aver that Armstrong's side of 1921 was the strongest, and others go back farther and claim precedence for Darling's 1899 and 1902 elevens, while a third body of critics cast their votes for the 1930 and 1934 teams. In an article in *The Cricketer* Annual of 1948 H. S. Altham, summing up, ended with these words: "Shall we find consolation in the belief that we lost to the greatest Australian cricketers who have ever come to England?"

I have heard it suggested that Armstrong's team of 1921 would have "swallowed" Bradman's. This comes from some perhaps quite properly over-patriotic members of Armstrong's side, and they were undoubtedly a very fine eleven, with two great, and very fast, bowlers in Gregory and Macdonald, a splendid googly bowler in Mailey, a most accurate leg-break bowler in Armstrong, and reserves in Macartney and Hendry. The batting order too is impressive, while the team fielded beautifully, and Carter was a great wicket-keeper.

One could go on arguing in favour of each one of these teams, but my own view is that Bradman's 'had everything'—batting, bowling, fielding, and wicket-keeping in the highest degree of skill, and all this outstanding talent blended together, and led on the field with great ability.

Bradman's eleven won four of the five Test Matches, that at Old Trafford being drawn. We were overwhelmed at Lord's and the Oval, but we made a good fight at Trent Bridge, after being 344 runs behind on the first innings. Victory looked within our grasp at Old Trafford, and at Leeds some thought that we should have won, and a large number that we should, at any rate, not have lost. We had four fine batsmen in Compton, Hutton, Washbrook, and Edrich, but we could not find the bowlers to dismiss the Australians at a reasonable cost. The omission of Hutton from the third Test at Old Trafford "aroused intense pre-match discussion" (*Wisden*). His record over a series of years, before and since, stamps him as the finest batsman in England on all wickets, and to-day he is, in Australian opinion, the greatest batsman in the world.

It is interesting, I think, to give the names of these sides under discussion. Here they are, in the order of batting:

1899 *At Lord's*	1902 *At Old Trafford*	1921 *At Lord's*
J. Worrall	V. T. Trumper	W. Bardsley
J. Darling (Capt.)	R. A. Duff	T. J. E. Andrews
C. Hill	C. Hill	C. G. Macartney
S. E. Gregory	M. A. Noble	C. E. Pellew
M. A. Noble	S. E. Gregory	J. M. Taylor
V. T. Trumper	J. Darling (Capt.)	W. W. Armstrong
J. J. Kelly (w.k.)	A. J. Hopkins	(Capt.)
H. Trumble	W. W. Armstrong	J. M. Gregory
F. Laver	J. J. Kelly (w.k.)	H. L. Hendry
E. Jones	H. Trumble	H. Carter (w.k.)
W. P. Howell	J. V. Saunders	A. A. Mailey
		E. A. Macdonald

1930 *At the Oval*	1934 *At Trent Bridge*	1948 *At Lord's*[1]
W. M. Woodfull	W. M. Woodfull	S. G. Barnes
(Capt.)	(Capt.)	A. R. Morris
W. H. Ponsford	W. H. Ponsford	D. G. Bradman
D. G. Bradman	W. A. Brown	(Capt.)
A. F. Kippax	D. G. Bradman	A. L. Hassett
A. Jackson	S. J. McCabe	K. R. Miller
S. J. McCabe	L. S. Darling	W. A. Brown
A. G. Fairfax	A. G. Chipperfield	I. W. Johnson
W. A. Oldfield (w.k.)	W. A. Oldfield (w.k.)	D. Tallon (w.k.)
C. V. Grimmett	C. V. Grimmett	R. R. Lindwall
T. W. Wall	W. J. O'Reilly	W. A. Johnston
P. M. Hornibrook	T. W. Wall	E. R. H. Toshack

July 18, 1948, was the centenary of the birth of W. G. Grace, and Gentlemen *v.* Players at Lord's, on July 15 and 16, had, therefore, a special significance, the Memorial at the Mem-

---

[1] At Leeds S. J. Loxton, a great fielder and hitter, whose innings of 93 included five sixes, took the place of Barnes, who was injured. His position in the batting order was No. 6, Hassett going in first with Morris.

bers' Entrance—the Grace Gates—being adorned with laurels. I missed the first day's play, as I had been paid the compliment by the Gloucestershire C.C.C. of being invited to Bristol to take part in the celebrations on the county ground, where a plaque was unveiled in memory of the Champion. The Duke of Beaufort, President of the Gloucestershire C.C.C., presided, and among those present was C. L. Townsend, who had played in the Gentlemen *v.* Players match at Lord's fifty years earlier. Townsend, himself a famous Gloucestershire cricketer, Kortright, and J. R. Mason are the only survivors of the two elevens of that famous match. The *Western Daily Press*, reporting the celebrations, said:

> One of the most interesting ceremonies in the history of the County Cricket Ground, Bristol, took place yesterday—the celebration commemorating the centenary of the birth of Dr W. G. Grace, described as "Greatest of all Cricketers. . . ."
>
> The events included a speech by Sir Pelham Warner . . . the unveiling of a plaque on the Nevil Road gate—now known as the Grace Gate—and a luncheon at which, in addition to civic representatives and those of the Grace family, the guests included Gloucestershire cricketers who played with W. G. back in the nineties.
>
> The first event was Sir Pelham's speech, and the crowd assembled at the luncheon interval around the special enclosure, decorated with red-and-white canvas, from which the visitors watch the game.
>
> Sir Pelham related many reminiscences of his association with W. G., and assured the younger generation that W. G. was a really wonderful batsman, even at the age of forty-eight
>
> "He was a most lovable, charming and kindly personality, and do not believe those little inferences that he was not. He played cricket keenly and energetically as it should be played. He was a man of tremendous stature, and he was one of the best-known men by sight in the country."

The writer then added:

> "The immortal memory of William Gilbert Grace" was again given by Sir Pelham Warner . . . and, following this, Mr John Daniel (Old Cliftonian Captain of Somerset cricket and England at Rugby) and Captain G. R. Jackson (former Captain of Derbyshire) responded to the toast of "The Visitors."
>
> An interesting incident was the presentation of a bat to the

County Club by Commander E. Grace. It was the bat with which his grandfather, Dr W. G. Grace, made his 1000 runs in May 1895, and in the Champion's own handwriting was every score he made to complete his record total.

On many occasions during recent years I have been a guest of Lord and Lady Belper at Kingston Hall, about a dozen miles from Nottingham, where it is their custom to entertain a large party for the Test Match at Trent Bridge. No more charming hosts could be imagined. On Sundays the England Eleven, the Selection Committee, the Dominions teams and their ladies, and any prominent Dominions personalities who may chance to be in England spend the afternoon there. The great Australian Prime Minister, Mr Menzies, has been there—and who will forget his delightful speech, followed by some very witty verses, made up as it seemed on the spur of the moment, in proposing the health of our hostess, who is herself a most accomplished speaker? Should she ever stand for Parliament no constituency could resist her, not only because of her eloquence, but also because of her charm and a sense of humour which she possesses in a marked degree. Kingston is a lovely place, and I am sure that Lord and Lady Belper have made an important contribution to the happy relations and good feeling between ourselves and our kinsmen the world over.

23

MORE EMPIRE VISITORS
1949–51

The New Zealand Tour of 1949—"Gentlemen v. Players, 1806–1949"—West Indians' Tour of 1950—House of Commons Dinner—Whitelaw's Old Boys' Dinner—The Crimes Club—M.C.C. Tour in Australia, 1950–51—The "Cricket Brains Trust"

THE New Zealand team of 1949 made a great advance on any previous form they had shown in this country. Four Test Matches of three days each were given them, all of which were drawn, the batting of both sides being far superior to the bowling. They had two outstanding batsmen in Donnelly and Sutcliffe, with Wallace, Reid, Scott, and Hadlee giving strong support, their bowling was very accurate, and they were backed up by splendid and well-placed fielders. Donnelly we knew well, of course, and Hammond's M.C.C. team brought back flattering reports of Sutcliffe. Both were left-handers, and at the end of the tour ranked among the best batsmen in the world. They were very ably captained by Hadlee, and in J. H. Phillips they had the ideal manager. The scoring in the Test Matches was very high indeed, Compton (2), Hutton (2), Edrich, Robertson, Simpson, and Washbrook making eight centuries between them, and Donnelly and Sutcliffe one each.

The great advance cricket has made in our Dominions in recent years is worth noting. One need only instance the West Indies and New Zealand, both with comparatively small populations producing most able cricketers. We may say with some pride that we originally taught them cricket, and, as events have proved, the pupil is now as good as his master, and this is for the general benefit of the game. Gone for ever are the days when we and Australia thought that we were the only people who could really play cricket!

On October 11, 1949, I was invited to the Jubilee Dinner of the North Staffordshire and District League at King's Hall, Stoke-on-Trent. Never have I seen a better-organized dinner. There were over five hundred people present, and the galleries were crowded with those who had been unable to obtain places at the dinner. Sir Ernest Johnson, an old Rugbeian, President of the League, presided, and on my left was S. F. Barnes, the great bowler, my trusty and faithful colleague in Australia in 1911–12. There were speeches by the President, the Lord Mayor of Stoke-on-Trent, Alderman A. P. Spark, and Sir Francis Joseph, my most hospitable host. I returned with a beautiful blue Coalport bowl and an equally beautiful dinner-service.

I was busy during the winter of 1949–50 writing *Gentlemen v. Players, 1806–1949*. The book, with a truly wonderful index, which I had nothing to do with, covered over five hundred pages, and was indeed a labour of love, for it meant reproducing the full scores of all the matches and writing descriptions of them, as well as giving scores and descriptions of the matches between the Gentlemen and the Australians and the Players and the Australians. I had, however, several 'devils' to help me in collecting, and, indeed, often copying out, the scores. This saved me much work, but it was a far greater tax on my energy than the writing of *Lord's* had been. I am happy, however, to have attempted some sort of history of an historic match, which began long before Test Matches were dreamed of, and which, I hope and believe, will never die out. In these days some may suggest a different title for this match, but, in the words of Craig, "the Surrey Poet": "All the Players are Gentlemen, and all the Gentlemen Players." We may leave it at that, and I happen to know that many of the most distinguished professional cricketers do not favour an alteration in the title. "It is a classic match," as not by any means the least distinguished of them put it; and he added, "Don't you let them alter it!"

There were great doings at the Grand Hotel, Sheffield, when the Centenary of the Red and White Roses match was celebrated. There was gathered together a large company of great cricketers, and the two famous counties sat down in mutual respect and admiration. What, indeed, would England have done without the representatives of Yorkshire and Lancashire? As one peruses the pages of cricket history a long list of tremendous names catches the eye. If one has lived in a less rigorous climate one does not, in old age, if one is wise, venture during the winter into the "murky stronghold of Tykedom" (C. B. Fry), but I sent a telegram in which I tried to express my admiration for all that Yorkshire and Lancashire had done for English cricket. May they continue to produce men as skilful and as courageous as they have in the past to do battle for England.

Those who had seen the West Indies in their own islands realized that we should be meeting "foemen worthy of our steel." As *The Cricketer* put it: "Make no mistake; we have formidable opponents. They will test us to the uttermost." That they did so, and a good deal more, was proved to the hilt, for though they lost the first Test, at Old Trafford, they won the next three by such huge margins as 326 runs, ten wickets, and an innings and 56 runs. We had the usual run of accidents and illness which since the War have been so prevalent, but the West Indies were clearly the stronger side.

When they were defeated by the M.C.C., at Lord's on May 23, by 118 runs some people expressed the opinion that they had little chance of winning the rubber, but it is a mistake to judge a touring team until they have been in England at least a month and played six or seven matches. The Australian tour of 1909 is a case in point, and there have been other instances. In this M.C.C. match Ramadhin was not playing, and what his absence meant to the strength of their bowling was subsequently emphasized.

The West Indies selectors were evidently blessed with second sight, for in choosing Ramadhin and Valentine they brought into international cricket two very young bowlers who were scarcely known in their own islands. How wise their bold policy proved, for Ramadhin was a great bowler—slow to medium right, with flight, length, and spin—and Valentine, a left-hander, a little above slow in pace, who, if he did not flight the ball, kept a most accurate length, with plenty of spin. In the four Test Matches they took fifty-nine wickets between them—Valentine thirty-three and Ramadhin twenty-six. On previous tours the West Indies had relied chiefly on fast bowlers, but though there were three bowlers of this type in the team—Johnson, Jones, and Pierre—very little use was made of them. Pierre, indeed, did not play in a single Test Match. All of them suffered from strains at various times.

Ramadhin and Valentine were so accurate that they often bowled with two silly points and without a deep fieldsman, though mid-off stood very deep. They were clearly very hard to 'get at,' but, with a few exceptions, our batsmen seemed to lack quickness of foot. It is easy, however, to criticize from the pavilion, and the fact remains that Ramadhin and Valentine bowled more overs for fewer runs than any other pair of bowlers in cricket history, so far as Test Matches are concerned.

The West Indies had three very fine batsmen in Worrell, Weekes, and Walcott. Not one of them had been coached! They were natural players, and none of them used a bat more than 2 lb. 3 oz. in weight. They told me they could "waggle" it quicker. Worrell may claim to be as great a batsman as Hutton or Compton on his day, and Weekes is not far behind either of them. I do not place Walcott in quite the same class, but he is very good. Stollmeyer, a beautiful stylist, and Rae, a left-hander, were a fine opening pair, and the fielding was always keen and safe, and many a fine catch was made. Goddard worked his two principal bowlers hard, but his tactics were fully justified. He was a captain of ability, a great fielder, a bowler who got wickets at the right moment for his side, and an annoying batsman to the other side, for he made runs at critical moments.

Altogether this tour placed West Indies cricket on a high pinnacle, and their coming visit to Australia will be followed with intense interest, but they should endeavour to discover at least one fast bowler. Naturally I wanted England to win, but at the same time I did not grieve overmuch at their defeat! Off the field as well as on it, the West Indies won golden opinions, and in J. M. Kidney they had a manager who contributed largely to the success of the tour.

I had been a guest at Sir Stanley Holmes's dinners in the House of Commons to our Dominions teams, and always enjoyed them immensely. Members of all parties attended in large numbers, for, whatever political differences there may be, they do not extend to cricket. Mr Attlee is a great lover of cricket, and made a point of presiding. On Monday, July 3, 1950, I was honoured, as I believe no individual cricketer has ever before been so honoured, by being the guest of the evening, but I regarded it as a compliment not only to myself, but to cricket and to the M.C.C. Besides the Prime Minister, there were several Cabinet Ministers, ex-Ministers, and other well-known M.P.'s, and before such a critical, if very friendly, assembly I had to speak. It is not for me to say what sort of speech I made, and I therefore reproduce what was written in *The Spectator* of July 7:

> Sir Stanley Holmes' annual cricket dinner at the House of Commons is one of the most agreeable events of the Parliamentary year. This year—last Monday—the guest of the evening was Sir Pelham Warner, the new President of the M.C.C. The Prime Minister, as usual, proposed the principal toast, and his speech, Sir Pelham's in reply and Mr Eden's in honour of the Dominions were in their several and appropriate ways well comparable with the oratory provided in the Chamber along the corridor. Mr Attlee, who remarked aptly that he understood Sir Pelham Warner objected to the use of cricketers' Christian names (who would speak of Warner without the Pelham?), got little response from his Biblically untutored audience to his neat adaptation "Where shall Wisden be found?" Plum, as he became before the speeches had gone far, was everything that could be hoped for—reminiscent, but not too much so, studiously modest regarding his own achievements. J. M. Barrie, he recalled, had once written, "The first time I saw Mr Warner play he made one run; the second time he was not so successful." Sir Pelham proudly claimed to have made a duck in every British Dominion except India—which he had never visited. I doubt whether he is quite correct. Did he ever make a duck in Canada? It would be a historic culmination to a brilliant career to persuade the greatest Dominion to take up the greatest English game in earnest.

To be strictly accurate, I never made a duck in Canada, though I got pretty near to it with scores of 4 and 4 at Montreal. I would add that "the greatest Dominion" is taking up "the greatest English game" in earnest, and in the year in which I am writing (1951) the M.C.C. are sending, and not for the first time, a team to tour Canada.

Here is a list of the guests who attended this dinner:

H. Ashton, Esq., M.C., M.P.
The Right Hon. Clement R. Attlee, C.H., M.P.
J. E. Ball, Esq.
The Right Hon. Alfred J. Barnes, M.P.
A. Beverley Baxter, Esq., M.P.
Lieutenant-Commander J. Gurney Braithwaite, M.P.

Patrick Buchan-Hepburn, Esq., M.P.
Major-General John Buckley, C.B.E., D.S.O., M.C.
Herbert W. Butcher, Esq., M.P.
L. J. Callaghan, Esq., M.P.
J. Chaney, Esq., J.P.
S. W. Coleman, Esq.
D. Compton, Esq.

G. F. Congdon, Esq.

E. M. Cooper-Key, Esq., M.P.

Aidan M. Crawley, Esq., M.P.

The Right Hon. Sir Ronald Cross, Bart., M.P.

J. A. Culley, Esq.

The Right Hon. Clement Davies, K.C., M.P.

Rupert De la Bere, Esq., M.P.

The Right Hon. Anthony Eden, M.C., M.P.

W. J. Edrich, Esq., D.F.C.

C. O. Fensom, Esq., J.P.

A. T. Fletcher, Esq.

John Fowler, Esq.

Major E. E. Gates, M.P.

A. H. H. Gilligan, Esq.

W. E. Grant, Esq.

T. G. Grinter, Esq.

The Right Hon. W. Glenvil Hall, M.P.

The Hon. John Hare, O.B.E., M.P.

H. Wilson Harris, Esq.

The Hon. E. J. Harrison, M.P. (Resident Minister of Australia)

Air Commodore A. Vere Harvey, C.B.E., M.P.

C. B. Hearn, Esq.

The Right Hon. Arthur Henderson, K.C., M.P.

Dr Charles Hill, M.P.

Errol R. T. Holmes, Esq.

F. L. Horn, Esq., J.P.

D. J. Insole, Esq.

J. Selwyn B. Lloyd, Esq., C.B.E., K.C., M.P.

P. B. Lucas, Esq., D.S.O., D.F.C., M.P.

The Right Hon. Oliver Lyttelton, D.S.O., M.C., M.P.

The Right Hon. Harold Macmillan, M.P.

J. C. McTurk, Esq.

J. P. W. Mallalieu, Esq., M.P.

The Right Hon. W. S. Morrison, M.C., K.C., M.P.

Arthur Moyle, Esq., M.P.

F. H. Newnham, Esq.

Commander A. H. P. Noble, D.S.O., D.S.C., M.P.

The Right Hon. Philip Noel-Baker, M.P.

H. D. Pawsey, Esq.

T. N. Pearce, Esq.

A. B. Quick, Esq., J.P.

Lieutenant-Colonel R. S. Rait Kerr, C.B.E., D.S.O., M.C.

R. W. V. Robins, Esq.

Captain R. E. D. Ryder, R.N., V.C., M.P.

W. H. Sexton, Esq., J.P.

The Right Hon. Sir Hartley Shawcross, K.C., M.P.

Brigadier J. G. Smyth, V.C., M.C., M.P.

Sir Patrick Spens, K.B.E., K.C., M.P.

R. A. Ward, Esq.

The Right Hon. Charles Waterhouse, M.C., M.P.

The Right Hon. Maurice Webb, M.P.

John Webbe, Esq.

The Right Hon. J. Harold Wilson, O.B.E., M.P.

R. J. Woodford, Esq., J.P.

On August 2, the first day of Rugby *v.* Marlborough, another great compliment was paid me when I was the Guest of Honour at a dinner given at the Holborn Restaurant by the Old Boys of Robert Whitelaw's House. Lord Elton presided, and among some ninety Old Boys there were present Sir Maurice Peterson, Sir John Maude, the Dean of Westminster, the Bishop Suffragan of Hulme, Major-General L. D. Grand, Major-General G. N. Russell, Air Vice-Marshal F. P. Don, and three brothers Lloyd— the Rev. J. Hastings Lloyd, E. M. H. Lloyd, and A. W. Lloyd. A. W. Lloyd had arranged the dinner, and the Dean of Westminster paid a tribute to him for all the trouble he had taken.

I sat on the right of Lord Elton, and on my right was the Dean of Westminster, who was in the Rugby Eleven of 1902 and 1903. Lord Elton told me that Whitelaw made such tremendous demands on the XX that he and another boy in Whitelaw's used often to get up at half-past five in the morning in order to cope with him! He agreed with me that he was a bit of "a slave-driver," but a most amazing, if exacting, scholar, and a lovable man.

It was an evening of unforgettable memories for me, and I thought of the day when I arrived at Rugby a somewhat lonely small boy, but how from the 'first ball' I was very happy, and delighted in, and appreciated, the life and traditions of a great school, even if it meant being in chapel at seven o'clock—and I had never seen snow!

To the Lloyd family I would like to render my gratitude and thanks. I had played at Hartley Wintney for the Free Foresters as far back as 1894, when I was caught off Baldwin, the old Hampshire bowler, for 39, and by a curious coincidence a son of Baldwin was umpiring when I paid a visit to Hartley Wintney in 1948. I had chanced during my visit to refer to my age, and Mrs Lloyd, who is ninety-six, said, "You're a cockerel." A more delightful and amusing old lady than Mrs Lloyd it would be hard to imagine, with a spirit and an energy which defy the passing of time.

I have been a member of Our Society, the Crimes Club, for many years, and in October 1950 was honoured with Life Membership. The Club was formed in 1903, and Arthur Lambton was President and Secretary until his death in 1933.[1] There are only some seventy members, and we dine together three or four times a year, when a Paper is read on some famous case. Many distinguished men have spoken at these dinners, but

[1] Arthur Lambton founded the Crimes Club with S. Ingleby Oddie, the other four original members being H. B. Irving, Professor Churton Collins, J. B. Atlay, and H. Crosse.

one is in honour bound not to disclose what takes place on these occasions, and no mention of them has ever appeared in the newspapers. It is not necessary to have any criminal propensities to be elected a member, but merely an interest in crime! All I would, and can, say here is that these dinners are eagerly looked forward to, for one hears the very 'insides' of a trial.

I was not there in person, but in imagination I batted, bowled, and fielded every ball on the recent M.C.C. tour in Australia. We lost the rubber, but may in all fairness plead "extenuating circumstances," as the lawyers would put it, in the shape of an abnormal number of accidents and illnesses; and I do not think that it is extravagant to suggest that there was no great difference between the two sides.

The Australian bowling and fielding was as fine as ever, but in batting the loss of the great Bradman and Barnes was a tremendous handicap. Moreover, they had a long tail, owing to the falling-off of Lindwall, Tallon, and Johnson. They, like us, lacked concrete in the middle, and Barnes as a No. 1 was not replaced. Morris, a great player, made only one big score (202), and one fifty in nine innings, Bedser dismissing him over and over again; and not one of the other opening batsmen came off. Where they did have an advantage over us, however, was in the possession of Miller, the best all-rounder in the world to-day, who on more than one occasion changed the whole course of the game by a brilliant innings, a glorious catch, or a devastating spell of bowling. Hassett, the Australian Captain, batted with marked consistency; Harvey made several scores of between 40 and 50, but they had, generally speaking, to rely on two or three batsmen for runs.

Turning to the M.C.C. side, Brown was a great captain, both on and off the field. He set the highest standard of courage and determination, and I have it on the authority of the Prime Minister of Australia that no more popular team has ever visited Australia.

The greatest leaders do not always achieve victory. I will give one instance from history. Robert E. Lee, the famous Southern General in the American Civil War, was compelled to surrender to Ulysses S. Grant,[1] but as he passed through the lines of the

[1] The story is told that on a visit to England, some time after the Civil War, Grant was invited to Apsley House, and there saw the portrait of the Great Duke. After gazing

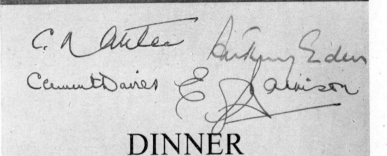

DINNER

IN HONOUR OF ·

SIR PELHAM WARNER
President of the M.C.C.

IN THE STRANGERS' DINING ROOM OF

THE HOUSE OF COMMONS

MONDAY, 3rd JULY, 1950

CHAIRMAN - - SIR J. STANLEY HOLMES, M.P.

AUTOGRAPHED COVER OF THE MENU CARD FOR
THE DINNER AT THE HOUSE OF COMMONS
IN 1950

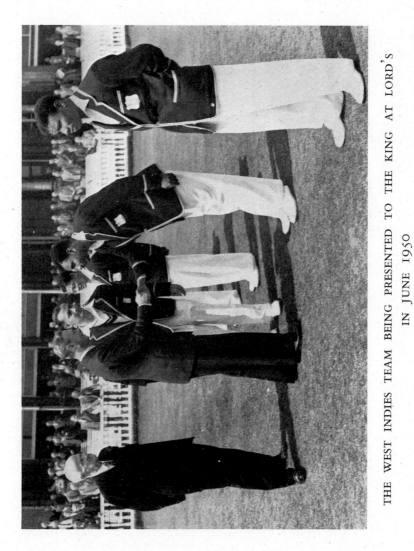

THE WEST INDIES TEAM BEING PRESENTED TO THE KING AT LORD'S
IN JUNE 1950

His Majesty is shaking hands with Walcott. The other players seen are Goddard, the West Indies
Captain, Christiani, and Weekes.

Northern soldiers he was cheered to the echo amid shouts of "Well done, Uncle Robert!" We may well say the same of Frederick Richard Brown.[1]

Our batting stood or fell by one man, Hutton, with occasional support from Brown and Simpson. His play was magnificent in every respect, and he may well claim a place among the greatest batsmen of all time. His record in Test Matches not only here in England, but in Australia, South Africa, the West Indies, and New Zealand is very impressive. I place him in Class I in any Honours School of cricket. And he has the courage which has always been the characteristic of Yorkshiremen. When one has done so splendidly as a captain as Brown I hesitate to make any sort of criticism, but was not a mistake made in putting Hutton in anywhere else but first, as was done in the first and second Test Matches? In the second Test, which we lost by only 28 runs, he was not out in both innings. Happily he was restored to his rightful place in the other matches, with the results we know. He is, and always has been, a born No. 1.

Simpson is naturally a fine batsman, but he seems on occasions to go into his shell, and not make the most of the many strokes he possesses. He reached his full stature, however, in the final Test, when he played a great innings; and this should give him the confidence to give full scope to his undoubted natural ability.

Brown played some fine and characteristically brave innings at critical times, but the great Compton failed completely in the Test Matches, though he made many runs against the same bowlers in the state games. I could give many instances of great players having a run of ill-success—Ranjitsinhji, Fry, Trumper, Bardsley, and Morris, for example—and here it is well to remember what was written in *Tom Brown*: "The goddess who presides over Cricket loves to bring down the most skilful players." Compton's knee may well have troubled him, and yet his fielding was splendid, and he made many catches of an acrobatic nature which demanded exceptional quickness of movement.

The younger generation were very disappointing. Dewes was

---

at it for some minutes he remarked, "And to think that I commanded more Army Corps than that man did Battalions." "Yes, yes, yes," replied the then Duke of Wellington, "but I believe he was quite a good man in his day." A masterly example of understatement, which is one of the characteristics of the English people!

[1] Brown's father, R. E. Brown, took five wickets for 50 runs against the M.C.C. team at Lima, Peru, in February 1927. I was one of his victims, 'yorked' for 2.

N

successful on many occasions, and J. H. Fingleton, in the *Sunday Times*, praised his batting. Dewes, like Sheppard, played in only two Test Matches, one of them on the difficult pitch at Brisbane, and the other at Melbourne, when he rose from a sick-bed. He has great power of stroke, and a strong defence, but was apt to give away his wicket by a careless stroke.

Sheppard's method appealed to the critics, and the experience of this tour should have taught him much. Close, a good judge tells me, "is full of cricket, and may yet make the grade," but at present he lacks that concentration and appreciation of a tactical situation for which his fellow-Yorkshiremen have for so long been noted. Parkhouse suffered from continual ill-health, but he too has it in him to make good.

The fielding, so castigated by some of the critics in the early part of the tour, was very good in the Test Matches, and Evans increased his already great reputation as a wicket-keeper, and stands forth as the best wicket-keeper of the day. His understudy, MacIntyre, played his part excellently.

When the team left England many lugubrious criticisms were passed on our bowling: "We shall never get the Australians out for under 500." But as it happened our bowlers did uncommonly well, and Bedser was compared to Tate. This strong and courageous cricketer bowled superbly on all occasions. In this country he sometimes gives the impression of being an ordinary fast-medium-paced bowler, but this, I am certain, is due to the fact that he is greatly overworked with continuous daily cricket from May to the middle of September. I would urge that he should be given occasional rests. You can break the back of the most willing and stout-hearted horse.

Bailey was a great success, and his accident in the third Test was a stunning blow, while Wright, if his figures are not impressive, was, in his best moments, a considerable force.

I have left the captain to the last. He bowled, for a time, in the style we know best in this country—leg-breaks—but his adaptability to circumstances and conditions was shown when he turned himself into an accurate medium-paced bowler. His splendid physique and determination were shown to the full in the third Test, at Sydney, when, deprived of both Bailey and Wright, he held an end throughout a day and more, and in the final Test, at Melbourne, he achieved a veritable triumph. He

so captured the hearts of the Australian public that his progress
from the pavilion to the wickets was invariably greeted by a
storm of cheering, seldom, if ever, known on Australian grounds.
His victory in the last Test Match has given a tonic to English
cricket, and if ever anyone disproved the theory of "too old at
forty" it is he.

It is pleasant to record that the matches were played in the best
manner and spirit, and for this we are much indebted to Hassett,
so well known and liked in this country.

The "Cricket Brains Trust" was the idea of C. H. Taylor, a
master at Eton. He had played for Westminster, Oxford, and
Leicestershire, and scored 114 (by "beautiful batting," says
Wisden) in the University Match of 1923, and thereby achieved
a record, for "never before had a Freshman made a hundred in his
first innings on the big occasion" (*Wisden*).

The first appearance of the "Brains"—a high-sounding title
indeed!—at Eton was in March 1946, so that this year's meeting
was the sixth in succession. On the first occasion prepared questions were allowed, but since then none of the questions are
known beforehand, which is far more fun for both sides. The
meetings take place in the Concert Room of the Music Schools,
and the "Brains" sit on a platform and undergo the most searching cross-examination. The Concert Room holds just over three
hundred, and there are many more applications for seats than can
be satisfied. Cricketing enthusiasts of all ages get a chance to
attend—not only the older boys.

There is a Question-master—the Hon. G. W. Lyttelton in 1946
and 1947, and since then B. G. Whitfield. I can confidently
recommend both of them to the B.B.C.!

The "Cricket Brains Trust" has been represented by, among
others, G. O. Allen, H. S. Altham, R. W. V. Robins, the Hon.
C. J. Lyttelton (now Viscount Cobham), R. E. S. Wyatt, C. B.
Fry, I. A. R. Peebles, R. H. Twining, E. R. T. Homes, Colonel
R. S. Rait Kerr, R. Aird, B. G. Castor, W. J. Edrich, J. Sims,
G. Geary, B. A. Barnett (the Australian wicket-keeper), and
myself. The 'team' usually numbers five or six at a time, not
counting the Question-master.

The Provost of Eton and the Headmaster honour us with their
presence, and it is an occasion to which I always look forward

with the greatest of pleasure. We begin to assemble at Mr Taylor's house just opposite Agar's Plough at tea-time, and then make our way to the platform in the Concert Room, where we receive a tremendous welcome. Then follows the cut and thrust of debate, always conducted in the most amiable and delightful manner. One has to have one's wits about one, for the most searching questions are put. It has become a great event, and if the boys enjoy it the "Brains Trust" most certainly do.

Later we dine, and dine very well, I may add, in one of the master's houses—I have been lucky enough to have as my hosts Mr and Mrs Whitfield—and we talk cricket—and many other things—until time is called, and we depart on our various ways "swearing by the best of schools."

24

PRESIDENT OF THE M.C.C.

1950–51

ON MAY 3, 1950, I was nominated President of the M.C.C. by H.R.H. the Duke of Edinburgh. His Royal Highness was unable to be present at the Annual General Meeting, as he was on service in the Mediterranean, and Lord Cornwallis, President in 1947, presided in his absence. It was the greatest moment in my life, and my nomination to the "Woolsack of Cricket," as Lord Cadogan, a President in the seventies, had described it, seemed to meet with the approval of the Members.

There is no cricketer, if he is honest (which all cricketers are!), who would not give his soul to be called to such a high position in the world of cricket, and it meant almost everything to me. The day after my nomination I went to Lord's, and as I passed along the St John's Wood Road I could not help recalling the day—May 20, 1887—when I first saw Lord's. As I made my way it occurred to me that I would try to put the pages of my life back sixty-three years. And so I did not go in at the Members' entrance, but went through the turnstile and paid my entrance, as I had done when Mr Bowen had first introduced me to Lord's. It was the same entrance, though the actual turnstile has naturally been succeeded by another more modern one. As I entered the ground I halted for a few seconds, and my mind worked like this. Could the small boy, in Eton jacket and top-hat, from an outpost of Empire, really have become President of Lord's? It seemed a dream far too good to be true.

I believe I am accurate in saying that I am the second oldest man to have been made President. Mr Stanley Christopherson, who was President in 1939, on the nomination of Earl Baldwin of Bewdley, was born on November 11, 1861, so that at the date of his nomination, in May 1939, he was seventy-seven and six months of age. He beat me by a year, for I was seventy-six and seven months old! It is a great age to occupy such a position, for one's energy is apt to fail, but it had the contrary effect on me, acting as a stimulus and a spur.

The "Woolsack of Cricket" is not so soft as many people might be inclined to think. There are many problems apart from cricket, and the membership, some 3700 odd when I was elected in 1892, has grown to over 7000. Lord's is now a huge organization, with its influence and interest extending the world over, and there are many problems of finance, building, and organization, apart from cricket itself. These are difficult times, and these difficulties by no means pass by Lord's. We are the trustees and the guardians of the game, and it is not only necessary to have cricketers on the Committee, but men, too, of standing, who are versed in finance and other walks of life, for matters other than cricket are constantly cropping up, though we are first and foremost a *cricket club*, and this must always be borne in mind. But above all the great traditions and prestige of the Club must be maintained. We stand for something—a great deal, in my opinion—in English life, and in the life of our Dominions and Colonies, for the game has spread the world over. No institution was ever harmed by a good tradition, as Mr Churchill has said, and it is most important that the great traditions of the Club should be maintained.

I ceased to be President on May 2, 1951, and I retired with feelings of gratitude and pride. Gratitude in that I had attained the highest honour cricket has to give, and pride in that I had been called to serve the Club in this great office. To the powers at Lord's, one and all, from the highest to the lowest ranks, I here tender my sincere thanks for their support and understanding at all times. And so my Long Innings is drawing to its end. The Arabs have a saying that "the fate of every man is hung around his neck," and that whatever happens to us in life is decreed from the day of one's birth. Whether that be true or not, I do not pretend to know, but I do know this, that cricket has been a tremendous factor in a very happy life.

APPENDIX I

SOME THOUGHTS ON CAPTAINCY

I HAVE been captaining elevens since I was fifteen years of age, and I was but twenty-three when I took a team to the United States. When I began, I "knew nothing at all," like the student at Magdalen Hall:

> There once lived at Magdalen Hall
> A man who knew nothing at all;
> He was fifty-three
> When he took his degree,
> Which is youngish for Magdalen Hall.[1]

However, captaincy always interested me intensely, and I took every opportunity to learn from others, to watch closely their methods, to read cricket history and the varying phases in great matches, and to *think*. I "read and re-read the works of the great Captains," as Napoleon urged, and tried to follow Von Moltke's advice—"First ponder, then dare." I was fortunate indeed in many ways, for I played under many admirable captains, and had opportunities, both here and in our Dominions and Colonies, of putting their precepts into practice. Especially were the tours abroad of great value, for one had to learn to captain not only on the field but off it; and there is a great deal to learn as to how to manage men away from the field of play.

One sometimes hears it said that a captain should 'crack the whip,' or 'put them on the carpet,' but I dissent from these views. You cannot drive men; you must lead them. Discipline is, of course, essential, but there are other ways of maintaining discipline than by 'cracking the whip' or 'carpeting' people. Gain the respect and liking of your team and their belief in your impartiality and fairness, instil into them zest and enthusiasm, impress them with the fact that they are representing England, and, therefore, theirs is a great responsibility, that good manners are a great asset, and they will do anything for you. Understanding, too, and sympathy are of great consequence. If you can do these things you will create a band of brothers and a happy

[1] *Lays of Modern Oxford.*

family. As I say, some, no doubt, will differ from me, but I have found in my own case that this policy paid, and produced an uncommon loyalty.

It is important to make your eleven believe in themselves. If a captain succeeds in doing this he can almost persuade them to bat, bowl, and field above their normal form. It will help to remind them of their former prowess, and especially so when they are 'down on their luck' after a run of ill-success, which comes occasionally to every cricketer, however great. The atmosphere of a dressing-room is most important—no strained feeling, no fussing, not too much 'jawing,' but happy and pleasant.

Cricket has become so scientific that a captain of to-day has to work hard. Gone are the days when a captain could change the bowling by the clock or set the field in the same position for every batsman. Different styles have to be studied, and the captain and the bowler between them must endeavour to set the field so that a batsman's favourite strokes are blocked.

One of the most difficult problems to solve is when a side has to bat for half an hour or so at the end of a day. Many things have to be taken into consideration—the state of the wicket, the light, and, above all, the temperament of the batsmen. A sound line to adopt is not to alter the order if half an hour remains, but if one of the opening batsmen should be dismissed with, say, only a quarter of an hour to go I should almost invariably keep back my No. 3 batsman and send in a steady, defensive player. J. W. H. T. Douglas and D. R. Jardine were masters in a situation of this kind.

And now as to the actual field of play. One should note the direction of the wind, watch the pitch carefully for any worn spots, any peculiarities in the ground, such as at Lord's, where the slope helps an off-break bowler at the Pavilion end, and, conversely, the Nursery end helps a left-hander and a leg-break bowler; but that is no reason why they should not be tried at the opposite ends. I have known J. T. Hearne take six wickets in an innings when bowling from the Nursery end, and he, with his deadly off-break, must have bowled more overs from the Pavilion end than any other man.

Googly bowlers can bowl at either end. J. W. Hearne invariably bowled from the Pavilion end at Lord's, and it was from this end that Balaskas, the South African googly bowler, accomplished his great feat in the England v. South Africa match in 1935. Verity, a left-hander, took every one of his fifteen wickets against Australia at

Lord's in 1934 from the Pavilion end, and to me, at any rate, Blythe was more difficult to play from this end, as I did not see him quite so well against the background of the crowded pavilion seats as when he was bowling at the Nursery end. I was the first to whose lot it fell to captain a googly bowler, B. J. T. Bosanquet, the pioneer of this then new type of bowling. We were great friends, and we worked together in perfect unison. The placing of the field to a bowler of this type is a special study, and in this respect I am a firm believer in a googly bowler always having third man back, rather square, and also a deep square leg, on a fast wicket. This saves many a four from the loose ball which nearly all bowlers of this type occasionally send down. I used sometimes to take Bosanquet off after he had sent down only two overs—as I have said, we worked in complete unison—and yet later he would hit a length, with happy results. I recall an incident at Sydney in 1904, when we were playing New South Wales. We set New South Wales over 400 runs to win. Four wickets fell for 41 runs, but the 100 went up without further loss. Then 22 runs came off three overs (six balls to the over) from Bosanquet without his taking a wicket, and between the overs I remarked to Lilley, "What about this Bosanquet of ours? Shall we give him another over?" He replied, "I think I should. You never know what he will do, and we have plenty of runs to play with." I took his advice, and Bosanquet finished with an analysis of six wickets for 45 runs in 9.4 overs. Lilley was a splendid judge of the game, and I owe much to him for his sound and considered judgment on that tour.

Another incident concerning Bosanquet occurred in the fourth Test, also at Sydney, immediately following this match. Australia had 329 runs to win, and Clem Hill, at lunch, said in his pleasant manner, "We're going to win, Plum." We had Trumper, Duff, and McAlister out for 59, but Noble and Hill were there. Arnold and Hirst were bowling very well, but something in the back of my head kept hammering, "Put on Bosanquet, put on Bosanquet," and at a quarter to four—the tea interval was at four o'clock—I said to Arnold, who had got rid of Trumper and Duff, "Let Mr Bosanquet have a bowl." He looked a bit surprised, but on went Bosanquet, and in his first over he had Hill stumped off a beautiful-length googly and Gregory out l.b.w. We went to tea with five Australian wickets down for 76 runs. Immediately after tea Bosanquet had Hopkins, and at one time his analysis was five for 12. He eventually finished with six for 51.

He won the match. Here is an example of being guided by one's instinct, but if it had not come off I admit that I should have been open to serious criticism. In the tactics I adopted I was strongly prompted by the idea I always had in my head—that a googly bowler should be put on a quarter of an hour or so before an interval, and for the following reason. The batsman's mind is set on being not out at the interval, and he is apt to play a bit 'pawky,' while the googly needs a strong approach. A captain should try to imagine what a batsman is thinking. Which bowler would he dislike most at this moment? Of course, you need the gods on your side, but I merely give my own experiences.

Here is the score of this match at Sydney:

AUSTRALIA *v.* ENGLAND

Played at Sydney, February 26, 27, and 28, and March 1, 2, and 3, 1904

Result: England won by 157 runs

ENGLAND

First Innings		Second Innings	
P. F. Warner (Capt.), b. Noble	0	not out	31
T. Hayward, c. McAlister, b. Trumble	18	l.b.w., b. Trumble	52
J. T. Tyldesley, c. Gregory, b. Noble	16	b. Cotter	5
R. E. Foster, c. McAlister, b. Noble	19	c. Noble, b. Hopkins	27
A. E. Knight, not out	70	c. McAlister, b. Cotter	9
L. C. Braund, c. Trumble, b. Noble	39	c. McLeod, b. Hopkins	19
G. H. Hirst, b. Noble	25	c. Kelly, b. McLeod	18
B. J. T. Bosanquet, b. Hopkins	12	c. Hill, b. McLeod	7
E. G. Arnold, l.b.w., b. Noble	0	st. Kelly, b. Noble	0
A. A. Lilley, c. Hopkins, b. Trumble	24	b. McLeod	6
W. Rhodes, st. Kelly, b. Noble	10	c. McAlister, b. Cotter	29
Byes 6, leg-byes 7, no-ball 1, wides 2	16	Leg-byes	7
Total	249	Total	210

AUSTRALIA

V. T. Trumper, b. Braund	7	l.b.w., b. Arnold	12
R. A. Duff, b. Arnold	47	b. Arnold	19
C. Hill, c. Braund, b. Arnold	33	st. Lilley, b. Bosanquet	26
P. A. McAlister, c. Arnold, b. Rhodes	2	b. Hirst	1
A. J. Hopkins, b. Braund	9	st. Lilley, b. Bosanquet	0
C. E. McLeod, b. Rhodes	18	c. Lilley, b. Bosanquet	6
J. J. Kelly, c. Foster, b. Arnold	5	c. Foster, b. Bosanquet	10
M. A. Noble (Capt.), not out	6	not out	53
S. E. Gregory, c. Foster, b. Rhodes	2	l.b.w., b. Bosanquet	0
H. Trumble, c. Lilley, b. Rhodes	0	st. Lilley, b. Bosanquet	0
A. Cotter, c. Tyldesley, b. Arnold	0	b. Hirst	34
Bye 1, wide 1	2	Byes	10
Total	131	Total	171

BOWLING ANALYSIS
AUSTRALIA

First Innings	O.	M.	R.	W.	Second Innings	O.	M.	R.	W.
Cotter	14	1	44	0	Cotter	18.3	3	41	3
Noble	41.1	10	100	7	Noble	19	8	40	1
Trumble	43	20	58	2	Trumble	28	10	49	1
Hopkins	8	3	22	1	Hopkins	14	5	31	2
McLeod	8	5	9	0	McLeod	20	5	42	3

ENGLAND

	O.	M.	R.	W.		O.	M.	R.	W.
Hirst	13	1	36	0	Hirst	12.5	2	32	2
Braund	11	2	27	2	Braund	16	3	24	0
Rhodes	11	3	33	4	Rhodes	11	7	12	0
Bosanquet	2	1	5	0	Bosanquet	15	1	51	6
Arnold	14.3	5	28	4	Arnold	12	3	42	2

Umpires: R. W. Crockett and P. Argall

As for the order of going in, I do not believe in altering the order except in the circumstances I have already mentioned. Batsmen like the places to which they are accustomed and at which they have been successful. Who could imagine W. G., Hobbs, Sutcliffe, or Hutton anything but No. 1, or Tyldesley anywhere but No. 3? Lord Hawke, who, of course, was fortunate in having the same side in match after match, for years never wrote out a batting order!

Coming to the placing of the field, great care should be taken that every man is on the right spot—short slip not too fine, especially if the wicket-keeper is standing back, and second slip not too near to first slip, but, most important of all, *every man should be in the position to which he is accustomed.* A Hobbs moved from cover-point to, say, short slip may easily lose you the match, as happened at Old Trafford in the famous match of 1902, when Australia won the match by 3 runs, and with it the rubber. There was *only one ball of the over to go,* and F. W. Tate, the father of M. W. Tate, who had never before fielded in the deep field, was placed at wide long-on. Braund, leg-break, was the bowler, and Darling, a left-hander, on a difficult wicket, was hitting at almost every ball. Up went a catch to Tate, and he missed it. This incident was remarkably well described by Braund himself in a broadcast some months ago.

An eleven is the reflex of its leader, as is a company or a battalion, and even higher formations. But loyalty and co-operation are essential, for without them a captain would be terribly handicapped. I have always been lucky enough to command both.

There have been many most able captains, but if my life depended on the result of an England *v.* Australia match I should select as captain of the England team D. R. Jardine, as I wrote in *Gentlemen v. Players, 1806–1949.*[1] Jardine was a master of both tactics and strategy, and was especially adept in managing fast bowlers and thereby preserving their energy. He possessed a great capacity for taking pains, which, it has been said, is the mark of genius. He left nothing to chance, and he never asked anyone to do anything which he would not have done himself. As a field tactician and a selector of teams he was, I consider, surpassed by no one and equalled by few, if any.

In these days there are many declarations, and a large majority result in what I would call 'false values,' often turning out unfair, for example, to a county which at the time is in the running for the Championship. I think these tactics are often overdone, but I should be cautious here, for I twice lost Middlesex matches by a declaration. The first occasion was against Essex at Lord's in 1905. We left Essex 254 runs to make in two hours and forty minutes, and they won by seven wickets, with twenty minutes to spare. The wicket was perfect, and the outfield very fast, but Perrin (103, not out) batted magnificently, and was well supported by Carpenter, Reeves, and Tosetti. Nothing we could do, in spite of such bowlers as J. T. Hearne, Tarrant, Trott, Bosanquet, and Mignon, could stop the scoring. I think the declaration was reasonable, but great batsmanship defeated us.

The second occasion was in 1908. I declared, against Kent, with two wickets in hand when the scores were equal on the first innings (207), hoping to obtain a wicket during the last quarter of an hour on the second day. On the following day Kent scored 204 for seven wickets and declared, leaving Middlesex two hours to win, or save, the game. At half-past five—stumps were to be drawn at six o'clock, for it was the end of August and Daylight Saving was not then in vogue—we had six wickets standing, but in twenty minutes Woolley took six wickets in four overs and three balls for 8 runs, the last seven batsmen making only 13 runs between them! It was not an easy wicket—there had been a good deal of rain—but the batting was poor in the extreme. On the evidence, I do not think, writing, I hope, impartially, that we should have lost. In criticizing others, however, it is always as well to remember one's own lapses.

Let us now consider a style of bowling that in its incidence and its management has, to some extent, revolutionized English cricket. Swing, or swerve, was always known in cricket, but only as a ball

[1] Harrap, 1950.

occasionally delivered, perhaps sometimes by accident, though a few bowlers delivered it of set purpose, such as W. Wright, of Kent, Rawlin, of Middlesex, W. E. W. Collins, like Wright a left-hander, and, on the evidence of a letter of C. E. de Trafford which I quoted in my book *Gentlemen v. Players*, Lohmann. In 1901 Hirst, when the ball was new, developed an immense swerve, so great that the ball seemed to be almost bowled from the region of extra-cover, to a field set with three short legs and, in place of a slip, a leg slip. Hirst had many seasons of great success, and gradually came imitators.

Incidentally, many left-hand bowlers, bowling round the wicket, have a natural curve from the off to the leg, and this curve was turned into a sudden swerve, the effect being produced, before, of course, the ball pitched, by a definite use of the seam; it was helped by the state of the atmosphere and the direction of the wind. The natural curve, or swerve, of a right-hand bowler should be from leg to off, which is an out-swinger, but it is a curious fact that the right-hand bowler seems to find it harder to bowl the out-swinger than the left-hander does the in-swinger.

The practice of swing bowling has become very prevalent, and has led to a new vocabulary of bowling, such as 'seam bowlers,' 'using the new ball,' 'making her move in the air,' and so on.

Swing bowling, being most effective when the ball is new and still has the shine on it, has led to a new conception of bowling management at the start of an innings. Generally speaking, a swerving bowler is used at each end, so as to conform to the new belief of 'using the new ball.' This has meant discarding the old method of a slow bowler at one end and a faster bowler at the other. Where has the new method led us? One thing is apparent: there are many 'seam' bowlers who, once the shine has disappeared, resume only when a new ball is available, after sixty-five overs. It is difficult to believe that any bowler is a great bowler whose method is confined to one type of delivery, and it is equally difficult to believe that any captain can become a master of tactics if his management of the bowling is governed by set custom and convention.

A year or two back C. B. Fry wrote an article in which he was good enough to put me among the best four captains he had met, and said that I always put on the bowler he disliked most. I noticed also, in a book written by a professional who played under me, that he said that when a new batsman came in I often at once changed the bowling, and seemed to know the bowler most likely to get out that particular batsman. I dare say he meant that I knew the bowler who could best attack a weakness in the batsman's defence, or, perhaps, feed a pet stroke which, if attempted early in an innings, often leads to a mishit, with the resulting catch. This was all very complimentary to me, but could such tactics be employed to-day? If a wicket fell early on, would a spin bowler be put on, or, later in the innings, a seam bowler, if the ball were old? Yet such bowlers might be the very ones required on the advent of a new batsman. In other words, are many modern captains too stereotyped in their methods?

In *Wisden* for 1901 Lohmann wrote a short article on the art of bowling. The first principles of bowling, he said, were deception in delivery, variety in method, and attack on the batsman at every point. Lohmann must be regarded as a great authority; anything he wrote on bowling demands attention. Can it be said that any of these principles are observed by bowlers who, over after over, rely solely on swing for their wickets?

In my time one nearly always began with a contrast in styles—J. T. Hearne and Tarrant, A. R. Litteljohn and Mignon, for example, for Middlesex, while Hirst and Rhodes opened for Yorkshire, Fielder and Blythe for Kent, and so on. To-day the 'seamer'—a horrid word!— is, to my mind, overdone, but I am glad to note that the practice is changing, and, I venture to think, for the benefit of the tactical side of the game. Yardley, the England and Yorkshire Captain, sometimes begins with Wardle, slow left, and there have been other instances.

If you have, for example, a Richardson and a Lockwood, or a Lindwall and a Miller, on your side, and the wicket is fast, you would, of course, begin with them, but what I am driving at is that there should be no rigid rule involving invariably opening with a swing bowler.

I am now seventy-seven, and I am still studying the art of captaining a cricket-team; and I learn every day. You cannot do something for sixty years and more without learning a good deal about it. I have, therefore, given my own ideas in the hope that they may be of use, at any rate, to some others.

CRICKET THEN AND NOW

I HAVE described elsewhere my first visits as a small boy to Lord's and the Oval. The two figures that most impressed themselves on my mind were those of W. G. Grace, at Lord's, and George Lohmann, at the Oval, one the greatest batsman and the other the greatest bowler of his time. Sitting on the grass at the Oval, little did I realize that I was witnessing the dawn of what has been called the Golden Age of Cricket; and that I was to be fortunate enough to play in that period. This era of cricket stretched more or less from 1893 to the outbreak of the First World War.

In the early eighties there was a continuous cry, as there is to-day, for fast bowlers. These bowlers had been almost driven out of cricket by the dominance W. G. had shown over their methods. It was said that he had 'murdered' them. Shacklock, of Nottinghamshire, and Christopherson, of Kent, were fine fast bowlers in 1883; and S. M. J. Woods began his career in 1888 in the Cambridge Eleven. From this trickle emerged a continuous stream of fast bowlers, right up to the First World War. Alongside it were two other streams, one of great amateur batsmen and one of great left-hand slow bowlers, and they all merged into one great flood of players who formed this Golden Age.

What was the reason for this sudden flow of great amateur batsmen? I think it is to be found in the batting of W. G. When I first saw him, at Lord's in 1887, he had been playing for twenty-two years in first-class cricket, and it was he who had led the way in a larger range of stroke-play. It is abundantly clear that the schools, which were the nurseries of University cricket, were the gateway to first-class cricket, and it was the Public Schools that supplied the nucleus of the batting strength of the amateurs in this great age of cricket, with players like Jackson, Maclaren, Fry, Palairet, R. E. Foster, and Spooner.

When I first played for Middlesex in 1894 the stream of fast bowlers was at flood-level, and batsmen who disliked extra pace had to face it on every county ground. If you could not play fast bowling you might just as well give up any claim to batsmanship. Surrey had that incomparable pair Richardson and Lockwood, followed later by Knox and Hitch; Essex had Kortright and Pickett, followed by Buckenham; Kent had Bradley, followed by Fielder; Lancashire had Mold, followed by Brearley; Yorkshire had the great left-hander Hirst; Leicestershire had Woodcock, followed by Jayes and Skelding; Derbyshire had Porter, Warren, and Bestwick; Warwickshire had Field; Sussex had Bland; Hampshire had Soar and Heseltine; Somerset had Woods; Gloucestershire had Jessop; Worcestershire had Burrows and Burns; Nottinghamshire had Mee and, later, Wass, who was almost fast. Only my own county had no regular fast bowler until Mignon in 1905, though Rawlin was medium-fast.

In the early nineties the three best slow left-handers were Briggs, of Lancashire, Peel, of Yorkshire, and Martin, of Kent. The first two had almost right of place for England, and Briggs, in Test Matches against Australia, took 97 wickets for an average of 20·54, and Peel 102 wickets for an average of 16·81. Yet Martin, in the only Test in which he played, at the Oval in 1890, took twelve wickets for 102 runs. Briggs was followed by Dean, Peel by Rhodes, and Martin by Blythe and Woolley. The bowling of Rhodes and Blythe in Test Matches became famous. Other slow left-handers were Dennett, of Gloucestershire, Cox, of Sussex, Tyler, of Somerset, Hargreave, of Warwickshire, Hulme, of Derbyshire, and Tarrant, an Australian, who came to live in England and played for Middlesex.

Of medium bowlers George Lohmann, until he broke down in 1896, was a master of his art, and excelled every bowler in England. In 1885 he took 152 wickets for Surrey at an average of 13·85. Five years later, in 1901, S. F. Barnes, a discovery of MacLaren's, was taken to Australia, and began his great career. He and Lohmann have never been equalled in their particular styles in any period of English cricket. Other good bowlers of this type were Relf, of Sussex, Thompson, of Northamptonshire, and Lees, of Surrey, while Attewell, of Nottinghamshire, and J. T. Hearne, of Middlesex, were great bowlers of impeccable length: the latter was the first bowler in English cricket to take 3000 wickets. Another fine medium-pace bowler was Pougher, of Leicestershire, whom Abel thought the most difficult bowler he ever played. On wet wickets Yorkshire had a fine bowler in Haigh. Of medium pace, he could 'cut through' with a devastating off-break: 58 per cent. of his wickets were bowled.

Of slow right-handers Townsend, of Gloucestershire, Mead, of

Essex, and Smith, of Surrey, the last two almost medium, were out-standing. Townsend lost his bowling after a few seasons, but in August 1895, when he was only eighteen years of age, in eight matches he took 94 wickets. Mead twice took seventeen wickets in a match, and I personally found Smith one of the best bowlers I ever played.

Three other great bowlers remain to be mentioned. The first, who, though an Australian, played for Middlesex for many years, was Albert Trott. It was said of Lohmann that he was "neither fast nor slow man," and the same might be said of Trott, for he mixed his bowling with every sort of delivery, and, if at times a rather wayward genius, he had some astonishing successes. The two others were J. W. H. T. Douglas and F. R. Foster. Douglas, fast-medium, was the most successful amateur bowler of his time, and took more wickets (1879) than any other amateur bowler except W. G. He was a man of splendid courage and pertinacity, who had a great record in Gentle-men v. Players matches, and who bowled very well in Australia. Foster was a left-handed fast-medium bowler, with an occasional very fast ball, who had an easy action and was very quick off the pitch, and whose bowling, with Barnes as an opening partner, won the rubber in Australia in 1911-12. No opening pair of bowlers ever proved so destructive in Australia.

To return to batsmen. To two players might be applied the term *sui generis*—Ranjitsinhji (afterwards the Jam of Nawanagar) and Jessop. The Jam Sahib had a wonderfully quick eye, and flicked balls to leg as if handling a walking-stick; he was also a great late-cutter, a magnificent driver, and could play back to the fastest bowling. His 154, not out, against Australia at Old Trafford in 1896 was a great classic in batsmanship, over which the Australians themselves enthused for many a day. It was in this match that Richardson performed probably the greatest of all fast-bowling feats in Test Matches. He took thirteen wickets in 110 overs (five balls to the over), and in the second innings his analysis was six wickets for 76 runs in forty-two overs, bowling unchanged for three hours. "Keep at it, Tom," W. G. urged him, and keep at it he certainly did.

Jessop was the fastest scorer cricket has ever known. There have been hitters who have achieved a 'longer carry' than he, but no batsman has scored at such a pace and kept up his form so consistently over so many years. His highest score, 286 against Sussex at Hove in 1903, was made in 175 minutes, and he reached 200 in two hours. In 1897 he scored 101 against Yorkshire at Harrogate in forty minutes.

o

Twice he scored 28 in an over—off Braund in 1904 and off Burrows in 1910. At one time it was said that "he had reduced rustic batting to a science." This was hardly accurate. Most of Jessop's strokes were in style and execution quite orthodox, and no one watched the ball more closely. It was only in their application that he was unorthodox, as when he cut fast bowlers off the middle stump and swept good-length balls round to leg, his quick footwork enabling him to make balls his own length. His incalculable asset to any side was his ability to dominate or eliminate the time factor in any game. Never was this more clearly shown than in the famous Test Match at the Oval in 1902, when he made the fastest century in Test Matches—104 in seventy-five minutes.

W. G. Grace played his last Test Match at Trent Bridge in 1899. In that season the greatest amateur batsmen were Ranjitsinhji, MacLaren, Fry, and Jackson. There was a majesty about MacLaren's batting, a sort of "imperial sway," as Neville Cardus put it, over bowlers that he exhibited directly he arrived at the wicket, yet Ranji thought that on all wickets there was no greater player than Fry, in that he was as good as W. G. on fiery wickets, equal to anyone on sticky wickets, and on any wicket as likely to make runs as anyone. Nevertheless in Test Matches Jackson has a finer record than any English amateur. On a big occasion no one seemed more secure or more in complete command of himself in any conditions that arose, and when he captained England in this country in 1905 he headed both batting and bowling averages. If not so brilliant as Ranji or MacLaren, or such a big scorer as Fry—he played on fewer occasions than these players—yet in Test Matches he was more consistent than any of these great batsmen. All were masters of off-side strokes, the cut, and the on-drive, though Fry cut less than his famous contemporaries. Jackson, like Palairet and Spooner, was never able to go to Australia, and their inability to do so was a great loss to English cricket. Palairet and Spooner were in grace and elegance unsurpassed, and both were beautiful stroke-players, whose drives, apparently effortless, reached the boundary almost in a flash, with perfect timing and faultless execution.

Another great player was R. E. Foster, who went with the M.C.C. side to Australia in 1903–4, and by scoring 287 at Sydney made what was then the highest individual score in Test cricket. As a stylist, he approached MacLaren, with great variety of stroke, and he excelled at the off-drive and the late cut. Business restricted his cricket, but in

1907 he captained England against the South African team, and led the side with marked ability.

Of amateur batsmen who never played for England H. K. Foster, brother of R. E., was a really fine player, and there was no better player of fast bowling than P. Perrin, of Essex, who had a commanding style, and, like Ranji, could play back to the fastest bowling. Another player who might well have played for England was C. J. Burnup; he was very successful in Gentlemen *v.* Players matches, and Jessop, in *A Cricketer's Log*, supports this view. J. R. Mason, though he went to Australia in 1897–98, was never chosen to play against Australia in England, yet he was, as batsman, change bowler, and slip, among the great players of his day, and a most able captain. Two young players who had short careers in English cricket were K. L. Hutchings and J. N. Crawford. Hutchings was a brilliant batsman and fieldsman, who in his brief career was idolized by Kent followers while Crawford came straight from Repton to be a prominent figure at the Oval. He was a powerful driver and a dangerous bowler, and his decision to settle in Australia was an immense loss to Surrey and English cricket.

Two great figures of the early years of the Golden Age were A. E. Stoddart and Sir T. C. O'Brien. Both were attacking batsmen, O'Brien excelling on soft wickets, while Stoddart, who led two teams to Australia and went with Lord Sheffield's team, captained by W. G., in 1891–92, scored a century in a Test Match for this side, and another for his own side in 1894–95. W. W. Read, during the eighties and early nineties, was another great batsman.

A. O. Jones, who was in the Cambridge Eleven with F. S. Jackson, and who captained the M.C.C. side to Australia in 1907–8, first made his name as a superb fieldsman, and was a powerful bat, with a terrific drive past cover-point. He frequently played both for the Gentlemen and England. In Australia his health broke down, and he handed over the captaincy for most of the tour to F. L. Fane. Fane was a prominent batsman in his day, and if, in an age of giants, not quite among the greatest, he played many fine innings.

Of professional batsmen Shrewsbury, William Gunn, and Abel were the stars in the eighties and the nineties, and were followed by Hayward, J. T. Brown, J. T. Tyldesley, W. G. Quaife, and Denton, and later by Hobbs, Woolley, Hendren, G. Gunn, and J. W. Hearne.

Of the earlier players Hayward had the greatest record, and was the first professional to score a hundred centuries. In 1906 he scored 3518 runs, a record only beaten by Compton and Edrich in 1947.

There was a soundness about Hayward that made him a great opening batsman, but on soft wickets he was not such a good player as J. T. Tyldesley, who was the only professional chosen for his batting in the great England side of 1902 at Birmingham and Lord's. At the Oval and Lord's Abel made a great many runs, but he had not the style of these two players, and it was said, though never proved, that he disliked fast bowling. On his figures against such bowling this seems an overstatement.

J. T. Brown was a beautiful cutter and hooker, and he played an historic innings of 140 in the Test Match at Melbourne in 1895 which decided the rubber.

W. G. Quaife, though very short in stature, was a model in style, and in an age when there was less competition would have played more frequently in Test Matches. Denton played only once for England, but he was a beautiful player, a fast scorer, and a great deep field, and hardly, perhaps, received due recognition.

There is no necessity to emphasize here the greatness of Hobbs, for, as I have said elsewhere, there has never been a greater batsman on all wickets.

George Gunn, nephew of William, was one of the most interesting players of his day. He went to Australia for his health in 1907, but when Jones broke down was pressed into the first Test Match, scored 119 and 74, and then played in every Test Match, scoring 462 runs, with an average of 51.33. He could be brilliant in an almost nonchalant manner, and also retire into his shell and stonewall all day. In 1929 against Yorkshire in scoring 58 runs he batted for five hours and twenty minutes, which certainly rivals Scotton's 90 in five hours and three-quarters for England v. Australia at the Oval in 1884. Gunn was something of a genius, who was overlooked by the selectors when Hobbs was unable to play for England in 1921.

J. W. Hearne had a beautiful style, but, not being blessed with good health, never quite realized expectations. He scored a century in a Test Match before he was twenty-one, and had he been stronger he might well have been as great an all-rounder as anyone. His strokeplay was almost faultless, but never quite developed into brilliance. Hendren became a great batsman. He bristled with strokes, was quick on his feet, and his play was full of enterprise and dash. Woolley was a glorious left-hander, who made batting look very easy, a fine slip fieldsman, and an effective bowler on sticky wickets.

When I think of all the great players with whom I played an almost bewildering galaxy of talent arises. I cannot help feeling that English cricket to-day has lost something of its glamour. The lustre has become dimmed, and we find that, though the batting is maintained at a high level by a few—Hutton and Compton, for example—bowling has generally declined.

But in attempting a comparison we must not forget that two great wars have left their mark. I am no *laudator temporis acti*, and though the Golden Age no doubt deserved its title, I am not sure that it did not arrive later. The 1902 England Eleven was a very fine side, but we lost the rubber here to the Australians, and in 1907-8 in Australia, and in England in 1909 the Australians won again; and I believe that the M.C.C. team in Australia in 1911-12, which won the rubber by four matches to one, and Chapman's and Jardine's M.C.C. sides in Australia in 1928-29 and 1932-33, both of which also won by four matches to one, were their equals. Anyhow, I should not be prepared to lay two to one on the 1902 eleven if conditions of weather and wicket were even. I give the sides in the batting order:

1902	1911-12[1]	1928-29	1932-33
MacLaren	Hobbs	Hobbs	Jardine
Fry	Rhodes	Sutcliffe	Sutcliffe
Ranjitsinhji	Gunn	Hammond	Hammond
Jackson	Warner	Jardine	Ames (w.k.)
Tyldesley	Hearne, J. W.	Hendren	Leyland
Lilley (w.k.)	Woolley	Chapman	Wyatt
Hirst	Douglas	Larwood	Paynter
Jessop	Foster	Geary	Allen
Braund	Smith (w.k.)	Tate	Verity
Lockwood	Barnes	Duckworth (w.k.)	Larwood
Rhodes	Hitch	White	Voce

Here is matter for discussion on rainy days in pavilions and during the winter of a cricketer's discontent. And, as Andrew Lang, I think, wrote, "There is no talk, none so witty and brilliant, that is so good as cricket talk, when memory sharpens memory . . . and the old happy days of burned-out Junes revive."

The England Eleven which played at Lord's in 1938 was another team of outstanding ability—Hutton, Barnett, Edrich, Hammond (Capt.), Paynter, Compton, Ames (w.k.), Verity, Wellard, Wright, and Farnes. They held the powerful Australian Eleven of that year to

[1] This was the side which defeated the Rest of England at Lord's, as already mentioned.

a draw, and but for a series of accidents would, I believe, have won the rubber. Not even W. G. was a greater all-round cricketer than Hammond; Hutton is the best batsman in the world to-day on all wickets, being especially so on false turf, and his technique cannot be faulted; Compton, on his day and in his hour, is a genius; Barnett, Edrich, Paynter, left-hand, and Ames represent a wealth of batting; Farnes was a great fast bowler, with his arm in the sky; Verity a left-hander of the Peel, Rhodes, Blythe class; Wright, on his day, a match-winner; Wellard a fine all-rounder and a prodigious driver of a cricket-ball; Edrich a useful fast 'tearaway' bowler; and I have seen Hammond bowl some overs which recalled Barnes. Finally there was Ames, a wicket-keeper of the first class, with an outstanding record. So not all the great English cricketers lived in the Golden Age! And in spite of many, and somewhat grievous, reverses in recent years, when, perhaps owing to the effects, both physical and mental, of the Second World War, illness and accidents have befallen many of our key cricketers, we shall surely come again.

There are many young cricketers of promise, University cricket being especially good, but what they need is encouragement. There is too much criticism, too much theory, and in one of his always most interesting articles in the *Sunday Times* (of January 7, 1951) J. H. Fingleton, their able cricket correspondent in Australia, is in agreement with me on this point. The critics should try to mellow; they are too harsh. They sometimes seem to forget that cricket is a difficult game, and that it is not always possible for either batsman or bowler to dictate to the other.

You cannot bat better than Hobbs, a master on all wickets and against every type of bowling, but may not Hutton be placed in almost the same class with him? His record is very fine indeed, and though he often meets rather moderate bowling in county matches, he has played many great innings against the Australians and other Dominion teams, who really do know how to bowl! As I have said, he is an outstanding batsman on false turf, and has Yorkshire steel in his heart.

Compton is an individualist, but a wonderfully fine natural player, with a veritable battery of strokes and a record of great achievement when things are at their worst, but an injured knee has recently handicapped him greatly.

And then there is Washbrook. He is, perhaps, not 'fashionable' with the critics, but his record is consistently good—until the 1950–51 tour in Australia. He has a cool head, and his courage beats full high.

A great man when things are going badly, I do not think that sufficient credit has been given him; anyway, I should like him on my side.

Simpson too is another not yet in the class of the great, but with his beautiful upstanding style he may well become so. It looks to me as if he does not always get his nose over the ball and 'smell' it, as Tom Emmett used to urge the Rugby boys. A point greatly in his favour is his splendid fielding.

There are others in embryo, but I have the impression that many of our batsmen are too correct, too stereotyped, and by that I mean that they do not give enough scope to natural ability and enterprise, and that they do not attack enough. We saw a good deal of this in the summer of 1950, when Ramadhin and Valentine, the West Indian slow bowlers, were allowed to bowl with a silly point—sometimes two!—and without a man in the deep field. No batsman of any repute should stand for that. It would be better to die in the attempt! Our bowlers have many critics, but I do not hold their discouraging and, I think, wrong views. Bailey is a good fast bowler, if wisely used; Bedser is a first-class fast-medium bowler, who is far from being an "up-and-downer," as I have heard him described; and Wright is Wright, unpredictable, but on his day he "bowls the best ball in England," as Lillywhite said of his own bowling, and he is highly thought of by the Australians, who ought to know.

What we most need is a fast bowler pure and simple, whose only business is to bowl, and an all-rounder like Hammond, Hirst, or Jackson. We have Bailey, of course, who is a batsman as well as a bowler, and, incidentally, a fine fieldsman.

As to wicket-keepers, we have the great Evans, a dynamo of energy and activity, and an inspiration to a side, but we are not so well off as we need to be in this respect, as we have no other wicket-keeper at present in his class.

So I end this short comment on our present-day players on a note of optimism, but I am, and always have been, an optimist, and, anyway, it is surely better than being a Jeremiah! You gain nothing, and lose much, by pessimism and disparagement.

In my time as an active cricketer there was no broadcasting, no television. I should like to pay a tribute to both, for they have done a great deal to bring the game to millions of people, and the increased gates are largely due to them. Some people thought that the contrary would be the result, but it has not proved so. And, quite apart from this, their commentaries are an immense boon and comfort to those who, because of ill-health or other reasons, are unable to visit a cricket-ground. As for television, it is only in its infancy, and I believe that the day is not far distant when we in England will see a cricket-match in Australia *during the actual moments of play*.

But may I be so bold as to plead for an elimination of Christian names and nicknames? Their use is surely unnecessary and undignified, and also their omission would save time. The power of the B.B.C. is terrifying: they speak to millions. I would, therefore, submit that the greatest game in the world deserves the most careful treatment from an organization which possesses world-wide influence.

And now I venture to ask a pertinent question. Is our present system of cricket well organized? Do we play too much county cricket? When I first came into cricket in 1894 there were only nine first-class counties, which each played sixteen matches. Six years later (1900) there were fifteen counties, Yorkshire, Lancashire, and Surrey playing twenty-eight matches, Nottinghamshire, Warwickshire, and Derbyshire eighteen, and Somerset as few as sixteen. To-day (1951) *every one of the seventeen counties plays twenty-eight matches*. The Findlay Commission, some few years ago, recommended a reduction of the programme, but this did not appeal to the majority. Indeed, only Middlesex and Kent were in favour of the proposal.

For many long years both by pen and word I have urged a smaller programme, for I am convinced that we sacrifice quality to quantity. A county match, except in the case of certain fixtures with a long tradition behind them, has become a habit, and not an event. We should have more representative games, such as England *v*. The Rest; North *v*. South, Players of England *v*. The Australians and other Dominions teams, Under Thirty *v*. Over Thirty, and these matches should be played at Lord's, the Oval, Old Trafford, Leeds, and Nottingham, and the gate-money divided among the counties. These games would bring together the leading cricketers, would give that extra touch of class which is lacking in many of the present-day county engagements, and would add interest and variety to a programme which as a whole is lacking in tone, vitality, and atmosphere. There are still some really good bowlers, but in county cricket, speaking generally, there are too many loose balls sent down, and when our men meet consistently accurate bowling in Test Matches, backed up by fine fielding, many of them are at a loss. They are too often pinned down.

I am aware that these ideas may well be heaping coals of fire on my head, but I feel that the general standard of cricket would be greatly improved thereby, and surely county cricket is only a means to an end —the improvement of our cricket? What is the purpose if we have this heavy programme and yet lose the rubber to our Dominions, who play far less cricket than we do, with excellent results to themselves? I believe that, with the world as it is to-day, what I am urging will eventually come about by the march of events. It is certainly a matter which deserves immediate and careful consideration. We must think again.

J. H. Fingleton, in an article in the *Sunday Times* of January 12, 1951, writes:

If the system is at fault, that system should be scrapped or amended. One detected in England in 1948 a rooted objection in influential quarters to tinkering with county cricket. It seemed to be accepted that a system so long established permitted no liberties in grafting or pruning.

After watching the products of the county system in action for the past four months Australian opinion is convinced that county cricket these days either attracts poor quality or dulls ability and initiative.

Let us have done with excuses and soft words. There might be a reason for thinking that manifold excuses over these post-War years have made the way easy for continued failures by these young Englishmen. But to give continued absolution to successive failures is to by-pass the good work of the few stalwarts and ignore the long run of English batting brilliance which has gone before. What, fundamentally, is wrong with English batting? I am inclined to think that there is far too much theory about it. One young M.C.C. gentleman told me he could not drive because he was pigeon-toed; when, trying to be helpful, I suggested to another newcomer that the Melbourne soil had more life than any other soils here I was not allowed to finish my sentence, but was deluged in a donnish treatise of involved batting theory which left me limp.

So much is revolving above the neck that no message ever gets down to the feet.

As regards the Press, I wish that some closer liaison could be established between the proprietors of the Press, and their editors, and the cricket authorities. I feel that a frank and confidential talk round a table would be of real benefit to the game. The present situation is one that, if allowed to continue, may well do irreparable harm. Cricket is a game which should be written about in a dignified manner.

I realize that in saying this I may well be open to criticism, but my only object in writing as I do is the interest and well-being of cricket. Great newspapers do not appoint as their Diplomatic, Naval, Military, Air, Economic, or Financial Correspondents men who are not thoroughly versed and experienced in these matters, and I would urge that the same attitude should be adopted in regard to all Cricket Correspondents. Some of them are very good and write with a due appreciation of what cricket means and stands for, and of the tradition surrounding it. Others, on the other hand, make, as it seems to me, a point of discouraging our players, instead of seeing the best in them and encouraging it. The newspapers have almost as great an influence as the B.B.C. They are read by millions day after day, both morning and evening. In all matters the greater the responsibility the greater the care that is essential.

APPENDIX III

NOTE ON THE WARNER FAMILY

THE FAMILY of Warner is not an illustrious one, though I think we may claim that Sir Thomas Warner, Joseph Warner,[1] the surgeon, and my father, Charles William Warner, were, in their day, great men. But we are of long descent, going back to the

JOHN LE WARNER

From the original pedigree. The inscription reads:
"John le Warner, the first of the familie that is
mentioned in the Records of the Tower of London,
flourished at Great Waltham, in Essex, under King
Edward III."

---

[1] Joseph Warner (1717–1801), F.R.S. There is a portrait of him in the Royal College of Surgeons.

SIR THOMAS WARNER'S COAT OF ARMS

The quarterings are (*first line*) Maldon, Packlesham, Dines; (*second line*) Helion, Swinborne, Gernon, Boutetort; (*third line*) Appleyard, Thornbury, Everard.

thirteenth century, and our quarterings include such names as Gernon and Botetourt.

The Gernons were of great note in the counties of Norfolk and Essex, being lineally descended from Robert de Gernon, a famous Norman, who assisted William the Conqueror. . . . Sir Ralph de

Gernon died in the second year of King Edw. I, and was succeeded by William. . . . This William was knighted, dy'd 20 Edw. II leaving issue John his son and heir, who departed this life 8 Edw. III, and was father of Sir John Gernon, of Lees, in Essex, who was Sheriff of Essex and Hertford in the 39th of Edw. III, and deceased on 13 Jan. in 7 R. II, leaving issue two daughters his co-heirs, Joan, wife of John de Botetourt; and Margaret, wife of Sir John Peyton.[1]

Quarterings subsequent to 1629 are those of Ashton, Shipley, Rudyerd, Harvey, Maddox, and Aucher.

[1] Collins, *Peerage of England* (1756 ed.), vol. i, Part I, pp. 289, 290.

APPENDIX IV

TOURS ABROAD

M.C.C. TOURS

To Australia

1903–4	1911–12
P. F. Warner (Capt.)	P. F. Warner (Capt.)[1]
R. E. Foster	J. W. H. T. Douglas
B. J. T. Bosanquet	F. R. Foster
T. Hayward	W. Rhodes
A. A. Lilley	S. F. Barnes
J. T. Tyldesley	J. B. Hobbs
G. H. Hirst	G. Gunn
W. Rhodes	H. Strudwick
E. Arnold	S. P. Kinneir
A. E. Relf	J. Iremonger
L. C. Braund	J. Vine
A. E. Knight	F. E. Woolley
H. Strudwick	C. P. Mead
A. Fielder	E. J. Smith
(Manager: J. A. Murdoch)	J. W. Hearne
	W. Hitch
	(Manager: T. Pawley)

[1] Douglas captained in the Test Matches. I was ill.

To Australia and New Zealand

1932–33

D. R. Jardine (Capt.)
R. E. S. Wyatt
G. O. Allen
The Nawab of Pataudi
F. R. Brown
W. R. Hammond
H. Sutcliffe
M. Leyland
H. Verity
W. E. Bowes
E. Paynter
G. Duckworth
L. Ames
T. B. Mitchell
H. Larwood
M. W. Tate
W. Voce

(Managers: P. F. Warner and R. C. N. Palairet)

To South Africa

1905–6

P. F. Warner (Capt.)
H. D. G. Leveson Gower
Captain E. G. Wynyard
F. L. Fane
J. N. Crawford
L. J. Moon
J. C. Hartley
D. Denton
S. Haigh
J. H. Board
A. E. Relf
E. G. Hayes
W. Lees
C. Blythe

To South America

1926–27

P. F. Warner (Capt.)
Captain T. O. Jameson
Captain R. T. Stanyforth
Captain L. C. R. Isherwood
M. F. S. Jewell
G. J. V. Weigall
G. O. Allen
G. R. Jackson
J. C. White
Lord Dunglass
H. P. Miles
T. A. Pilkington

(Hon. Manager: T. Carlton-Levick)

To Holland

1928

P. F. Warner (Capt.)
R. H. Twining
G. T. S. Stevens
E. R. T. Holmes
G. D. Kemp-Welch
N. G. Wykes
M. A. McCanlis
M. J. C. Allom
H. P. Hunloke
T. A. Pilkington
E. H. Tattersall
E. P. Warner

To Denmark

1939

G. C. Newman (Capt.)
R. Aird
N. M. Ford
C. G. Ford
G. E. B. Abell
P. M. Studd
J. G. W. Davies
J. H. Nevinson
E. Bromley-Davenport
J. C. Cornu
F. A. Instone

("Father": P. F. Warner)

WITH LORD HAWKE'S TEAMS

To West Indies	To South Africa
1907	1898–99
Lord Hawke (Capt.)	Lord Hawke (Capt.)
H. R. Bromley-Davenport	H. R. Bromley-Davenport
C. Heseltine	F. Mitchell
H. D. G. Leveson Gower	C. E. M. Wilson
G. R. Bardswell	F. W. Milligan
J. M. Dawson	A. G. Archer
R. W. Wickham	P. F. Warner
A. E. Leatham	J. T. Tyldesley
R. Berens	W. R. Cuttell
A. D. Whatman	A. E. Trott
W. H. Wakefield	S. Haigh
P. F. Warner	J. H. Board

P

To New Zealand and Australia

1902–3

P. F. Warner (Capt.)[1]
C. J. Burnup
F. L. Fane
T. L. Taylor
E. M. Dowson
B. J. T. Bosanquet
A. E. Leatham
P. R. Johnson
J. Stanning
A. D. Whatman
S. Hargreave
G. J. Thompson

For the tour in Australia A. E. Trott joined the side.

WITH T. WESTRAY'S TEAM

To Oporto

1898

T. Westray (Capt.)
F. W. Westray
H. R. Bromley-Davenport
R. N. Douglas
S. A. P. Kitcat
L. C. V. Bathurst
W. N. Fletcher
A. C. Taylor
H. G. Peachey
E. A. Field
P. F. Warner

---

[1] Lord Hawke was unable to go on the tour owing to the illness of his mother.

WITH MY OWN TEAMS

To America

1897

P. F. Warner (Capt.)
G. L. Jessop
H. D. G. Leveson Gower
H. B. Chinnery
H. H. Marriott
F. W. Stocks
J. N. Tonge
F. G. Bull
R. A. Bennett
J. R. Head
W. McG. Hemingway
A. D. Whatman

To America and Canada

1898

P. F. Warner (Capt.)
C. J. Burnup
F. Mitchell
C. O. H. Sewell
V. T. Hill
E. H. Bray
G. E. Winter
E. C. Lee
B. J. T. Bosanquet
R. S. A. Warner
R. Berens
E. F. Penn
J. L. Ainsworth

INDEX